Becoming a Teacher-Researcher

ALSO AVAILABLE FROM BLOOMSBURY

Writing a Watertight Thesis, Mike Bottery, Nigel Wright and Mark A. Fabrizi

Research Methods for Understanding Professional Learning, Elaine Hall and Kate Wall

Reflective Teaching in Higher Education, Paul Ashwin with David Boud, Susanna Calkins, Kelly Coate, Fiona Hallett, Gregory Light, Kathy Luckett, Jan McArthur, Iain McLaren, Monica McLean, Velda McCune, Katarina Mårtensson and Michelle Tooher

Using Questions to Think, Nathan Eric Dickman

Narrative Inquiry, Vera Caine, D. Jean Clandinin and Sean Lessard

Embodied Inquiry, Jennifer Leigh and Nicole Brown

Diary Method, Ruth Bartlett and Christine Milligan

Community Studies, Graham Crow

Inclusive Research, Melanie Nind

A GUIDE TO YOUR RESEARCH JOURNEY

Becoming a Teacher-Researcher

EDITED BY
MARIA CAMPBELL,
DEIRDRE HARVEY AND
MARY SHANAHAN

BLOOMSBURY ACADEMIC
LONDON • NEW YORK • OXFORD • NEW DELHI • SYDNEY

BLOOMSBURY ACADEMIC
Bloomsbury Publishing Plc
50 Bedford Square, London, WC1B 3DP, UK
1385 Broadway, New York, NY 10018, USA
29 Earlsfort Terrace, Dublin 2, Ireland

BLOOMSBURY, BLOOMSBURY ACADEMIC and the Diana logo are trademarks of Bloomsbury Publishing Plc

First published in Great Britain 2025

Copyright © Maria Campbell, Deirdre Harvey and Mary Shanahan, 2025

Maria Campbell, Deirdre Harvey and Mary Shanahan have asserted their right under the Copyright, Designs and Patents Act, 1988, to be identified as Editors of this work.

For legal purposes the Acknowledgements on p. xiii constitute an extension of this copyright page.

Cover image © wacomka /Adobe Stock

All rights reserved. No part of this publication may be reproduced or transmitted in any form or by any means, electronic or mechanical, including photocopying, recording, or any information storage or retrieval system, without prior permission in writing from the publishers.

Bloomsbury Publishing Plc does not have any control over, or responsibility for, any third-party websites referred to or in this book. All internet addresses given in this book were correct at the time of going to press. The author and publisher regret any inconvenience caused if addresses have changed or sites have ceased to exist, but can accept no responsibility for any such changes.

A catalogue record for this book is available from the British Library.

A catalog record for this book is available from the Library of Congress.

Library of Congress Control Number: 2024943064

ISBN: HB: 978-1-3504-0899-9
PB: 978-1-3504-0898-2
ePDF: 978-1-3504-0900-2
eBook: 978-1-3504-0901-9

Typeset by Deanta Global Publishing Services Chennai India
Printed and bound in Great Britain

To find out more about our authors and books visit www.bloomsbury.com and sign up for our newsletters.

CONTENTS

List of Figures and Tables vii
List of Contributors viii
Foreword xi
Acknowledgements xiii

Introduction: What key themes need to be addressed when navigating a research journey? *Maria Campbell, Deirdre Harvey and Mary Shanahan* 1

PART I Getting Started – Grappling with Ideas, Concepts, Frameworks and Ethics 25

1. How Do You Develop and Answer Research Questions? *James Kelly* 27
2. How Does Your Research Question Influence Your Methodology? *Laura Balcon* 41
3. What Are the Epistemological Challenges Faced When Studying Teachers' Beliefs, Judgements and Decision-making? *Beccy Thompson* 55
4. How to Navigate Ontology and Epistemology to Develop a Conceptual Framework? *Marc Turu Porcel* 69
5. How Can the Lens of Cultural-Historical Activity Theory (CHAT) Help Conceptualization? *Ciara Molloy* 83

6   Why Do I Need a Conceptual Framework Anyway? *Tanya Davies* 99
7   Is Objectivity the Aim? *Ceridwen Owen* 113

PART II Up and Running – Grappling with Methodology, Tools, Participants and Ethics 127

8   How Can We Design Data Collection to Explore Children's Learning? *Kirstin Mulholland* 129
9   What Research Tools Might be Appropriate to Use with Young School-Age Children? *Sinéad Gallagher* 145
10 How Do You Choose an Appropriate Data-Gathering Tool? *Christion Hutchinson* 159
11 How Do You Design and Use a Questionnaire to Answer Your Research Questions? *Caoimhe Donovan* 175
12 How Do You Use Semi-structured Interviews and Fortune Lines? *Kathryn McCrorie* 193
13 How Does Your Choice of Participants Influence Your Research Study? *Kathryn McClure* 207
14 How Can You Address the Power Imbalance between Researcher and Participants? *Alison Weatherston* 219
15 How Do You Address Ethical Issues When Engaged in Online Research? *Diana Tremayne* 237
16 What Does Ethical Inquiry within a Transformative, Critical Educational Framework Look Like? *Victoria Wasner* 251

Conclusion: What Can We Learn from the Insights of Other Teacher-Researchers? *Maria Campbell, Deirdre Harvey and Mary Shanahan* 267

Index 272

FIGURES AND TABLES

Figures

4.1	Basic conceptual framework	75
5.1	Cultural-Historical Activity Theory model (Engeström 1999)	94
8.1	An example of a completed pupil views template (PVT)	136
8.2	An example of the two-column analysis format used for the embedded case-studies in my thesis	141
12.1	School Placement Fortune Line (2021)	199
16.1	Mechanisms for generating data	261
16.2	Pyramid model for pedagogy of C.A.R.E. (Wasner 2019)	262

Table

14.1	Coaching Outcomes Proforma (self-designed)	232

CONTRIBUTORS

Laura Balcon was awarded a postgraduate certificate in Leading Effective Inclusive Practice in Special Education Needs, National SENCO Award from the University of Derby, UK. She is currently working as SENCO and Teacher at Fairmeadows Foundation Primary School, Derbyshire, England.

Tanya Davies was awarded a PhD in Education from Monash University, Boonwurrung Country, Australia, and is currently working as a lecturer in the School of Education at Charles Sturt University, Wiradjuri Country, Australia.

Caoimhe Donovan was awarded a Professional Master of Education (with Home Economics) from the National University of Ireland, Galway, Ireland, and is presently working as a post-primary Home Economics and Irish teacher in Coláiste Gleann Lí, Tralee, Co. Kerry, Ireland.

Sinéad Gallagher was awarded an EdD – Doctorate in Education – from Queens University, Belfast, Northern Ireland, and is currently Assistant Professor of Accounting at Juniata College, Huntingdon, PA, in the United States.

Christion Hutchinson was awarded an MA in Special Education from St Angela's College, Sligo, Ireland, and is working as a teacher for autistic learners in Ballyduff National School in Co. Waterford, Ireland.

James Kelly was awarded a Masters in Education and the Law from St. Angela's College, College of National University of Ireland, Galway, Ireland, and is currently a primary school teacher and assistant principal in Scoil Bhríde, Kill, Co. Kildare, Ireland.

Ian Menter is Emeritus Professor of Teacher Education at the University of Oxford, UK. He is Senior Research Associate at Kazan Federal University, Russia, Visiting Professor at Ulster University, Northern Ireland, Visiting Professor at Bath Spa University, UK, and Honorary Professor at the University of Exeter, UK.

Kathryn McClure was awarded an MSc in Psychology from the University of Glasgow, Scotland, and is presently teaching in an Additional Support Needs School within a Local Authority in Scotland.

Kathryn McCrorie completed her Master of Arts at the University of Aberdeen, Scotland. She is currently studying for her EdD at the University of Strathclyde where she is a teaching fellow.

Ciara Molloy was awarded a Masters in Education from Maynooth University, Ireland, and is currently studying for her doctorate at University College Dublin, Ireland. She is Deputy Principal in Mucklagh National school, Co. Offaly.

Kirstin Mulholland was awarded a doctorate in Education from Newcastle University, England, and is currently Associate Professor in Education at Northumbria University, England.

Ceridwen Owens was awarded a PhD in Education from Monash University, Boonwurrung Country (Clayton, Victoria), Australia, and is currently working in the School of Education at Deakin University, Wurundjeri Country (Burwood, Victoria), Australia.

Beccy Thompson was awarded Doctorate in Education (EdD) from King's College London, England, and is currently Senior Lecturer in Professional Studies in the School of Education at the University of Roehampton, England.

Marc Turu Porcel was awarded a PhD from Leeds Beckett University, England, and is currently subject leader on the MA Education at the School of Education, University of Huddersfield, England.

Diana Tremayne was awarded a PhD from Leeds Beckett University, England, and is currently working as a lecturer in the Carnegie School of Education at Leeds Beckett University, England.

Victoria Wasner was awarded a Doctorate in Education from Durham University, England, and currently works as a lecturer and researcher in the University of Teacher Education, Lucerne, Switzerland.

Alison Weatherston was awarded a B.Ed and PG Diploma from University of Strathclyde, Scotland, and is undertaking research as an EdD student, also at Strathclyde. She currently works as Lead Specialist in Professional Learning and Leadership for a national organization in Scotland.

FOREWORD

The importance of research literacy for teachers in schools and colleges has been widely recognized over recent years. The report published in 2014 by the British Educational Research Association, *Research and the Teaching Profession* (BERA-RSA 2014), offered convincing evidence that the quality of teaching depends to a great extent on teachers' workplaces being 'research-rich' environments. Furthermore, that report demonstrated that effective and self-improving school systems are characterized by being underpinned by strong commitments to the benefits that a research orientation brings to practice as well as to policy in education.

The present book offers an enormously rich collection of accounts by teacher-researchers, written in accessible language, outlining principles and practices, insights and challenges, opportunities and barriers, in the implementation of research-oriented approaches towards teaching. The contributors are based in many parts of the world but what unites them is a shared interest in offering cogent and considered advice, based on their own experiences of undertaking teacher research. The approach taken in all chapters is rigorous, theoretically informed as well as being pragmatic in recognizing the heavy workloads experienced by teachers in their classrooms.

In their introductory chapter, the three editors identify seven themes that can be identified throughout the book (and they return to these in the concluding chapter). These themes may be used as a checklist by teacher-researchers to make sure that they are addressing the important issues that all teacher research must be concerned with. Maria Campbell, Deirdre Harvey and Mary Shanahan are to be congratulated on drawing together such a superb set of accounts that should inspire readers and give the teachers the confidence to undertake their own research, leading to the improvement of educational experiences and outcomes for the learners in their classrooms.

Ian Menter
Emeritus Professor of Teacher Education
University of Oxford
United Kingdom

Reference

BERA-RSA. (2014), *Research and the Teaching Profession - Towards a Self-improving School System*. London: BERA.

ACKNOWLEDGEMENTS

The editors would like to thank each of our contributors for agreeing to be part of this publication. Their chapters are testament to their hard work, professionalism and willingness to be part of a supportive learning community. We have really enjoyed working with them and we have learnt so much in the process.

We would like to acknowledge the following for their encouragement when we first broached our idea and asked for their support to source contributors for the book: Professor Mhairi Beaton, Carnegie School of Education, Leeds Beckett University; Professor Viv Ellis, Dean of the Faculty of Education, Monash University, Australia; Associate Professor Scot Bulfin, School of Curriculum Teaching and Inclusive Education, Monash University, Australia; Prof. Kate Wall, School of Education, University of Strathclyde, Glasgow, Scotland; Dr Shona Hunter, Programme Director for Research Degrees, Carnegie School of Education, Leeds Beckett University; Dr Geraldene N. Codina, Associate Professor, University of Derby; Dr Sarah Steadman, School of Education, Communication and Society, Kings College London.

We would also like to thank the editorial team at Bloomsbury, led by Alison Baker, for their support throughout the process.

Finally, we would like to thank our families, friends and colleagues for their unwavering support. Your kind words, encouragement and confidence in our ability to complete this project have helped us in more ways than you will ever know.

Introduction

What key themes need to be addressed when navigating a research journey?

Maria Campbell, Deirdre Harvey and Mary Shanahan

For each individual, the motivational factors or reasons for becoming a teacher-researcher may vary considerably from a personal desire, to addressing issues relating to one's own practice, to an interest in exploring educational policy development and/or enactment at an institutional, national and/or global level, to achieving a qualification needed to progress a professional journey. Consequently, some teacher-researchers may have decided to engage in research for the very first time, while others, having completed some research with colleagues as part of a research team, or as part of their Bachelors, Masters or Doctoral studies, may find themselves in a position where they wish to engage in further research. Regardless of the motivation for, focus of or level of previous experience, the research journey can prove daunting and, at times, off-putting.

This book constitutes a supportive companion, a point of reference for the teacher-researcher. It differs from other research handbooks and guides in that it guides you through the various themes that inform and encapsulate the research journey using the authentic voice of other teacher-researchers. In turn, these teacher-researchers share their insights, experiences and learning, and offer suggestions to support you the teacher-researcher. Key themes central to the research journey are discussed and critiqued by each of the contributors through the lens of real-life exemplars and personal learning experiences. In this way, you are guided through the research journey incrementally, with indications of and possible solutions to many of the challenges and opportunities you can expect to experience, enabling you to navigate through your own research journey alongside and in the company of the contributors. It is important to note that while you get glimpses of and insights into the various research projects undertaken by the contributors, this book does not constitute a collection of research undertaken by teacher-researchers, but instead, consists of their experiences and learning from engaging in research at postgraduate certificate, Master's and Doctoral level. Consequently, the insights provided in the chapters vary in complexity from more fundamental aspects such as how best to design a questionnaire or survey to answer specific research questions (Chapter 11) and refining your research question (Chapter 1) for example, to grappling with one's ontological stance (Chapter 4) and aligning this with an appropriate conceptual framework (Chapter 6) to addressing complex ethical dilemmas (Chapters 7, 15 and 16). Therefore, this book constitutes a companion text, one which you can refer to at various stages along your research journey, providing insights to help direct, support and critique your thinking and decision making.

How the book is structured

This chapter provides an overview of seven themes which we have identified as being central to navigating the research journey, especially for the beginning researcher, and points to the chapters which illustrate these themes further. Each of the following chapters which outline the learning experiences of the contributors focus primarily on one key theme or element of the research process. However, it is important to note that research cannot always be subdivided into neat and distinct packages as one theme or element influences others (Akkerman et al. 2013). For example, the phrasing of a particular research question influences the appropriate tools needed to gather data in order to answer that question. Consequently, in each chapter the contributor invites you to join them and share their experience, including the lessons learned as they critique their navigation of a specific theme with insights into how it influenced other key themes or aspects of their research.

To help you navigate your way through their experiences, the chapters provided by the contributors are organized into two sections. Section 1, *Getting started: grappling with ideas, concepts, frameworks and ethics* contains the chapters which focus primarily on themes relating to the first stage of the research process, where you begin to think about what it is you wish to research and what aspects will inform how you go about structuring and carrying out your research. This includes the themes *refining your research focus* and/or *formulating research question/s*; second, selecting or aligning with a *paradigm* which involves identifying your worldviews and/or beliefs (or your *ontology*) and what you see as constituting knowledge (or your *epistemology*); third, deciding on a *conceptual and/or theoretical framework* to guide you through your research journey and inform your choices, while identifying key theorists and literature that you need to support your assertions and help answer questions you may have; and finally, coming to terms with addressing *ethical issues* that may influence how you go about designing your research project.

The second section, *Up and running; grappling with methodology, tools, participants and ethics*, contains chapters which focus on the themes, decisions and steps involved as you attempt to select an appropriate *methodology* aligned with your ontology and epistemology, identifying the most appropriate *data gathering and analysis tools*, deciding on how best to select and gain access to *participants* and dealing with *ethical issues* which arise during the research process (which you may not have anticipated at the onset). Throughout all the chapters, the extent to which actions and decisions taken during the research journey impacted on the ability to answer the research question is addressed. In the Conclusion, *What can we learn from the insights of other teacher-researchers?*, the three editors examine the learning highlighted throughout the chapters and indicate some key pointers, lessons learned, hints and tips to consider going forward.

The following sections explore each of the themes we have identified as being central to the research process for beginning researchers. This list of themes is not exhaustive and as a teacher-researcher you may have other considerations in relation to your research such as reliability and validity, to name but a few. We have identified and selected what we maintain are the key themes for consideration for the teacher-researcher and, in particular, the beginning or early-stage researcher as they undertake their research journey.

Theme 1: Refining a research topic and/ or formulating research question/s

As you begin your research journey, you may have identified an area you would like to research further. For example, you may wish to explore how best to offer language support in your school to children who have recently arrived in the country with a different mother tongue to that operating in your school and/or national context. Having established a broad area or the starting point for your research, the next step is to continue to narrow and refine your focus. One approach to help support this process is to clearly state your rationale, that is, why you wish to carry out this research. From our experience in supervising research students, understanding why you wish to focus on this area and doing this at the outset, often helps you arrive at a decision as to what exactly you wish to examine, that is, is it how teachers' views, values and beliefs impact on pedagogical practices? If this is the case, then your research will focus on teachers' opinions and viewpoints and the research question you will develop will reflect this.

On the other hand, you may wish to examine the role of the school leader/head or principal in supporting staff to address some of the challenges and opportunities posed by supporting newly arrived learners with a different mother tongue. In this case you will need to ask yourself if you wish to do an in-depth examination or case study (Yin 2018; Merriam 1998; Stake 1995) of what occurs in one school or a comparative study, comparing and contrasting the role and approaches taken by a number of school leaders/heads/principals which will influence how you phrase your research question.

Alternatively, your gaze may be more outwards; you may wish to explore the impact of one or more policies on practices and/or identify the policy drivers and/or examine the role of parents in various forms of policy enactment. Continuous reflection and self-interrogation of what it is you want to focus on in your research and your rationale for doing so, will help refine your focus and, ultimately, your research question/s. In Chapter 16, Victoria Wasner clearly outlines how the drafting and re-drafting of her research question enabled her to identify the focus of her research as service learning and a select a methodology which encapsulated a collaborative learning process while reflecting the ethical principles of her topic, service learning. In Chapter 1, James Kelly indicates the steps he took to ensure he addressed the vagueness and ambiguity which his original research question embodied. Meanwhile in Chapter 2, Laura Balcon indicates that the use of reflective journals helped organize her thoughts and refine her focus. Of course, we are not suggesting you do this reflection and interrogation of your topic in isolation. Capitalizing on the support of your tutors, supervisors and peers provides additional insights, varying perspectives and probing questions, all of which help you refine your focus and research question (Carton 2014).

Another essential approach is to search for varying perspectives on your topic and read extensively and continuously (Williams 2020). The rationale for and important role reading played in narrowing the focus and identifying a gap in research carried out on young children and maths anxiety is clearly outlined by Sinéad Gallagher in Chapter 9 and explicitly by James Kelly, in Chapter 1, when he details exploring the relationship between the Catholic Church, Irish schools and the legislature. Indeed, Laura Balcon (Chapter 2) indicates how initial extensive reading to explore why her school had higher than national average numbers of children diagnosed with autism spectrum disorder (ASD) revealed that some children may be misdiagnosed as having similar traits to ASD which are evident in other conditions. This sent Laura's research down a different path than the one she had initially anticipated. Ensuring you have the skills to search the various databases and sources of policy documentation is key in enabling you to sift through varied contexts, approaches, stances and perspectives on your topic. In Chapter 6, Tanya Davies outlines how reading extensively around issues pertaining to race relations in Australia, played a key role in helping her to narrow her focus. Indeed, all the contributors indicate the importance of initially reading and sourcing a wide range of literature before narrowing this down to a more specifically focused range as you progress through your research journey. In Chapter 1, for example, James Kelly clearly outlines an approach to take and the hurdles which you may encounter.

Finally, trying to understand what constitutes research can be a little overwhelming. In other words, identifying what rules, protocols and steps are needed to ensure the work you do constitutes research can prove daunting, especially if this is your first attempt at carrying out research. For example, you may notice advertisements on various media claiming that 'research indicates' that the best toothpaste or shampoo is this or that. However, the small print, if evident, may indicate that only eight people were surveyed or, alternatively, the number of participants or means of gathering data are not indicated at all, making it challenging to check the validity of the claims made. Consequently, you may wonder what would happen if you were to approach three colleagues in your staffroom and ask them a variety of questions in an effort to determine their opinions on whether the school should do away with uniforms. Would you be able to present your 'findings' to the principal or governing body as evidence of the need to change practice or maintain the *status quo*? The answer is no, and as you make your way through your research journey it will become evident that for research to be deemed legitimate, to enable you to make claims based on your findings, certain guidelines and principles must be adhered to. There is considerable scope within the guidelines and principles to allow for individual contexts, but the overarching principles remain consistent and are explored and critiqued in this book. Having explored the first theme, it is our intention to guide you through and help you explore another key theme involved in undertaking educational research as a teacher-researcher.

Theme 2: Paradigms, ontology and epistemology

One of the most daunting aspects for beginning researchers can be unpacking terminology and coming to terms with concepts and their relevance for individual research journeys. Possibly top of this list is research paradigms and associated 'ologies', namely ontology and epistemology. We will look at methodology (Cohen et al. 2018), later in this chapter and at axiology (Lincoln and Guba 1985) under the heading of ethics. Having a fundamental grasp of these concepts is important for beginning researchers in order to understand their influence on the direction your research takes and, indeed, it is also essential for developing a more in-depth and nuanced understanding of them as you undertake more complex research projects.

To begin, what is a paradigm? According to Kivunja and Kuyini (2017, p. 26) 'the educational research term paradigm is used to describe a researcher's "worldview"' (citied in Mackenzie and Knipe 2006). This means that one's worldview can be interpreted as a set of beliefs or how the researcher sees the world, how she/he rationalizes how events occur and the drivers behind them. For example, some may see the world in terms of right and wrong being clearly defined, where taking a life is always wrong regardless of the context or circumstances. For another, the world may constitute a much greyer entity, where the taking of a life may be justified based on particular circumstances or contextual factors. These views or beliefs constitute one's worldview and shape how individuals act, what questions they may ask and ultimately, in relation to their research journey, determine their research question, what they believe should be investigated and how they will go about designing their research project and interpreting results (Salvador 2016; Bryman 2012).

You may ask: if research paradigms fall under specific categories, how will alignment with one or more of these categories impacts one's research journey? According to Adom et al. (2016) while many philosophical paradigms exist, all have roots in or can be associated with one of 'the two paramount theories, positivism and interpretivism' (Adom et al. 2016, p. 1). However, Candy (1989) indicates that paradigms fall under three categories, namely Positivist, Interpretivist and Critical paradigms. Indeed, more recently, a fourth, known as the Pragmatic paradigm, has been identified (Tashakkori and Teddlie 2003). In Chapter 5, Ciara Molloy indicates how she came to align with the Pragmatic paradigm and how this decision shaped her research design and journey. It is also important to note that there is a lack of agreement about what constitutes a paradigm within some disciplines and/or fields, with Morgan (2007) indicating that social scientists' interpretation of the term varies from that in science studies. Consequently, it is not surprising that the teacher-researcher may be daunted when grappling with which paradigm their research most closely aligns to. In Chapter 1, James Kelly indicates how and why he aligned with the constructivist paradigm and the impact that had on the design of his research going forward. We recommend reading extensively about the various paradigms with a view to finding the one that most closely aligns with your own set of beliefs. In order to help you attempt this task, we examine below the impact of aligning with a particular paradigm and, for the purpose of this, we have selected the positivist paradigm. In Chapter 4, Marc Turu Porcel indicates that when submitting his PhD proposal, he initially aligned with a Positivist stance. On further exploration of his ontological and epistemological beliefs, he traces how he eventually aligned with the Interpretivist paradigm, and the factors which influenced this decision.

It is important to note that the concept of Positivism was first proposed by Auguste Comte, a French philosopher (1798–1857). He proposed the use of experimentation, observation, and subsequent reasoning as the means to 'explain cause and effect relationships in nature' (Kivunja and Kuyini 2017, p. 30). Researchers aligning with the Positivist paradigm will rely on

> deductive logic, formulation of hypotheses, testing those hypotheses, offering operational definitions and mathematical equations, calculations, extrapolations, and expressions, to derive conclusions. (ibid, p. 30)

This means that the results obtained from research carried out in accordance with the Positivist paradigm tend to be or claim to be generalizable, namely they should be applicable to other contexts. Aligning with the Positivist paradigm will also influence the methodology chosen by the researcher and leans towards quantitative methods. Consequently, it is important to ask yourself if your beliefs align with the characteristics associated with the Positive paradigm (to include, but not be limited to, the belief that context is not important, and that the truth is attainable or waiting to be discovered). A comprehensive list of beliefs associated with Positivism is illustrated by Kivunja and Kuyini (2017, p. 31). It is important to note that there are various interpretations, iterations and versions of and within paradigms, each foregrounding particular points of significance and/or considerations. One such example is Constructivism and Constructivist Grounded Theory (Charmaz 2014); as your confidence grows, you may consider selecting one of the more nuanced options. In Chapter 3, Rebecca Thompson indicates she is a Social Constructivist for example, and how she came to that decision.

As stated previously, within a particular paradigm, and depending on which article/text you read and whose perspective you align with, there can be up to four components (ontology, epistemology, methodology and axiology) associated with a paradigm. We will discuss ontology and epistemology in this section, methodology under the methodology theme and axiology under the theme of ethics.

What is ontology and what significance does it have for the researcher? Ontology is concerned with the nature of existence or reality, what exists in the world and what can be understood as a truth (Moon and Blackman 2014). Your ontology or ontological perspective as a Pragmatist may infer that truth exists and is waiting to be discovered. However, as a Constructivist, the truth may be dependent on the context and the nature of the relationship between the researcher and participant, at the time and/or place where the research is undertaking, meaning there is no definitive truth waiting to be discovered. Similarly, your research question/s will reflect your association with a particular paradigm and your ontological stance. In Chapter 6, Tanya Davies indicates how identifying her ontological and epistemological positioning directly influenced how she approached data generation and the overall design of her research project. Similarly, in Chapter 9, Sinéad Gallagher maintains that from her ontological perspective, children have multiple realities, created and construed in their minds which are formed from their previous life experiences, which was reflected in her choice of data-gathering tools.

Epistemology, on the other hand, is concerned with knowledge, what constitutes knowledge, if knowledge is derived from experiences and, as such, can it differ from person to person, or is it based on reasoning and/or both (Sosa 2017)? Your epistemological stance is aligned with your chosen paradigm, which will influence your perception of what constitutes knowledge in your research and consequently, how knowledge should be gathered and analysed. For many Pragmatists, knowledge may come in the form of empirical evidence such as in statistics, while for constructivists (Lee 2012; Guba and Lincoln 1994) for example, it may be discovered in the narratives, accounts and perspectives of research participants. In Chapter 3, Rebecca Thompson indicates how questioning her interpretation of what constitutes knowledge and in particular, teacher knowledge, presented epistemological challenges due to the varying interpretations of Special Educational Needs and/or Disability (SEND) over the last century.

Theme 3: Conceptual and theoretical frameworks

A key challenge for many researchers is to locate their work or research project within a wider context or framework. This means that while your immediate concern may relate to addressing the needs of specific learners in your class, or institution, the theoretical or conceptual underpinnings of your work may be 'located' within a wider concept. For example, such concepts may include 'Rights' or 'Rights of the child/adolescent/adult', which may cause you to question theories associated with issues of 'Power' and/or 'Accountability'. Grappling with what constitutes a theory and a concept can prove challenging, as can aligning these theories and concepts with a chosen paradigm. To begin, your first question may relate to what can be considered as a concept. According to Sartori (1984, p. 17), 'words that signify meaning, constitute units of thinking' can be considered as concepts. However, the purpose and meaning of concepts may 'vary among and between disciplines' (Wald and Daniel 2020, p. 498). According to Cohen et al. (2000) conceptual frameworks can be viewed as an inter-related chain of concrete and related concepts which relate to a topic or phenomenon under exploration.

The task for the researcher is to find a concept/concepts and/or theory/theories that explore(s) the relationship between the issues under investigation and in a way that aligns with their paradigm and research beliefs. In Chapter 11, Caoimhe Donovan provides insights into the struggle to find a conceptual or theoretical framework which addressed her three themes of motivation, self-efficacy and academic performance, indicating theories she considered and how she finally arrived at a decision. Meanwhile, in Chapter 5, Ciara Molloy details how and why Cultural Historical Activity Theory formed the cornerstone of her research process and identity as a researcher, causing her to question her worldviews, eventually aligning with the Pragmatist paradigm. To help elicit how to go about selecting a suitable framework, a practical example may be helpful. For example, O'Toole et al. (2021) utilize the conceptualization of children to examine developments in primary school curricula in both the Republic of Ireland and Northern Ireland following partition in the 1920s. They utilize Sorin and Galloway's (2006) constructions of childhood as a conceptual tool or lens to analyse curricular and policy documents. In doing so, O'Toole et al. (2021) explore five of the ten constructions of childhood put forward by Sorin and Galloway (2006) to 'capture the rich and varied ways in which children and childhood have been understood and represented over time' (O'Toole et al. 2021, p.1025), including the child as innocent, the child as evil and so on. Such a concept could potentially be used as a lens to explore how the needs and/or rights of the child are addressed through curricular provision and/or pedagogical approaches based on teachers' beliefs. In Chapter 6, Tanya Davies indicates some of the struggles she faced, and options considered when selecting a conceptual framework. These options included feminist theory, before eventually selecting the concepts of culture and difference to constitute a lens to enable her examine teachers' attitudes towards intercultural education and their subsequent pedagogical approaches and choices. In other words, a conceptual framework can function 'as a powerful reference point for the researcher ensuring targeted work and evidence of alignment between epistemology, ontology and methodology' (Wald and Daniel 2020, p. 498 in Berman and Smyth 2015, p. 127).

However, the term conceptual framework and theoretical framework are often used interchangeably (Rocco and Plakhotnik 2009, p. 120), which can add to confusion for the beginning researcher. In Chapter 4, Marc Turu Porcel, indicates how he considered several theories in order to establish a conceptual framework or lens with which to see what one is researching in a particular light or way. Furthermore, when referring to a theoretical framework, Creswell (2003) indicates the role of theory specifically as being essential, in particular in quantitative studies, where the design of the study involves testing the theory or theories chosen. In other words, claims associated with certain theories may be tested within an empirical study to determine the accuracy of the theoretical claims, thus using a theoretical framework. However, Wald and Daniel (2020) maintain that not all theories can be tested as theories range from empirical to more abstract theories which are untestable. They state that utilising theories as opposed to concepts means the researcher 'needs to state the theory's key assumptions and clearly identify any possible shortcomings' (2020, p. 499), claiming that 'theories always have an explanatory purpose that is at a higher cognitive level than the more basic and descriptive nature of concepts' (2020, p. 502). While concepts on the other hand, or conceptual frameworks can also be used to test theories, they are often used in more exploratory research, and with a view for discovering emergent theory (Creswell 2003). In exploratory research, theories may be combined to create a conceptual framework as evidenced by Gonzalez (2015).

For the beginning researcher, coming to terms with the selection of one or more concepts and/or theories to use as a lens to critique, design and organize their research can prove exciting and challenging at the same time. In Chapter 12, Kathryn McCrorie explains how after extensive reading and reflection, she selected an accessible option, namely an 'Inquiry and Professional Knowledge model', as her conceptual framework. Again, certain concepts and theories will align more easily with various paradigms and so the toing and froing, the extensive reading, the moving forward and back between your own views and beliefs and those encapsulated in conceptual (and/or theoretical) frameworks can take time and considerable effort, as outlined by Tanya Davies in Chapter 6.

Theme 4: Ethical issues

According to Creswell (2012), a researcher needs to engage in ethical practices which embody duty of care principles, at all stages of the research process or journey. He stresses that ethics are much more than 'following a set of static guidelines such as those from professional associations or conforming to guidelines from campus institutional boards' (2012, p. 23). From this perspective, while research students will be required to adhere to prescribed ethical guidelines – many of which refer to methodology decision and practices relating to accessing participants, data gathering, publication and so on – ethical decisions and considerations stretch beyond guidelines contained in bounded texts and are linked to their philosophical values (Given 2008).

The researcher may be aware of and have concerns regarding issues of power dynamics or dimensions, conflict of interest, as outlined in Chapter 3 by Rebecca Thompson, who details her initial concerns in undertaking research as an insider or within her own institution. Other concerns may relate to objectivity, openness, non-discrimination based on the context of a research project. For example, a head teacher or principal wishing to carry out research in their own school and with their staff could be perceived as abusing their position of power, either knowingly or unknowingly, if they attempt to ensure participation by all staff in their research. While their motivation may be admirable, founded on a desire to improve their own leadership practices, it is essential that they are aware that their role as researcher is distinct from and may be in conflict with that of school leader. Such considerations gain particular relevance, based on the researcher's worldview or the paradigm the researcher has aligned with. Diana Tremayne in Chapter 15 clearly outlines how from the onset, ethical considerations regarding her positionality as an insider researcher were prevalent. Furthermore, conducting online research which encapsulated formal and informal talk, impacted on the design of her research. Consequently, other ethical or axiological issues (Given 2008; Biesta 2015) may emerge at the onset or planning stage of the research journey which are not specifically addressed in guidelines, as in Diana's situation, and arise from axiological assumptions and associations related to various paradigm and associated beliefs. Such beliefs are referred to in Chapter 9, by Sinéad Gallagher, in citing the influences of values such as dignity, celebrating differences, perseverance, among others in her entire research journey. Similarly, Victoria Wasner in Chapter 16 outlines the pivotal role that ethical concerns relating to critical service learning played in directing and designing her research. The following themes and associated chapters may be found in the second section of the book.

Theme 5: Methodology

According to Mackenzie and Knipe (2006) research methodology encapsulates the overarching approach taken to any research project which is clearly aligned with the paradigm, conceptual and/or theoretical framework identified by the researcher. In other words, the philosophical assumptions and assertions are linked with the research design and action plan (Creswell 2003). This means that the methodology could be viewed as the master plan, offering theoretical justifications and conceptual underpinnings, outlining the steps involved and tools to be used in order to address the research in question. This distinguishes it from what are often referred to as methods, which refer to the tools and procedures which can be used to gather and analyse data (Igwenagu 2016). A number of methodologies are available for selection (Cohen et al. 2018) and include case study (Yin 2018; Stake 1995) – which describes human relationships – action research (Cohen et al. 2018a; McNiff 2013; MacDonald 2012; Somekh 2005) – which has both a practical dimension and generates theoretical knowledge – and experimental research (Lavrakas et al. 2019; Ross and Morrison 2013; Guthrie 2010) – which enables one to test hypotheses. In Chapter 12, for example, Kathryn McCrorie provides insights into how an ethnographic case study was selected as the methodology of choice as the research intended to challenge existing assumptions about mentoring in initial teacher education. Similarly, in Chapter 15, Diana Tremayne details how she ultimately selected a version of ethnography entitled netnography for her methodology, in order to address the online dimension of her research. Ultimately, the paradigm you select, your research focus and ethical concerns all help direct you towards the most suitable or applicable methodology, as will guidance from tutors and supervisors.

Another consideration when selecting a methodology relates to your understanding of the terms quantitative and qualitative methodologies. In simple terms quantitative methodologies focus on 'determining the 'what', 'how many' or 'how much'' (McCusker and Gunaydin 2015, p. 538) associated with any given context. Quantitative methodologies are concerned with objectivity, 'utilising structured procedures and formal instruments for data collection' (Queirós et al. 2017, p. 370) or in other words, the statistical facts and/or accurate and reliable measurements and so are often associated with the Positivist or Pragmatist paradigms (Kaplan 2004). On the other hand, qualitative methodologies are 'not concerned with numerical representativity, but with the deepening of understanding of a given problem' (Queirós et al. 2017, p. 370). Consequently, qualitative methodologies focus on the 'why' and 'how', exploring complex realities and the more nuanced perspectives. In Chapter 16, Victoria Wasner justifies her conviction to adopt a qualitative methodology, with clear linkages to her ethical, ontological and epistemological stances. These may not be measurable, but which provide insights into individual and/or specific cases and contexts and as such are associated with the Interpretivist and associated paradigms (Berg 2016). Queirós et al. (2017, see p. 371) provide a table which clearly outlines the differences between both methodologies in a concise manner. Some research projects may adopt a mixed methodologies approach, including utilising and selecting elements from both quantitative and qualitative methodologies. Sinéad Gallagher in Chapter 9, outlines why she adopted a mixed methodology approach in her research on math anxiety and young children, providing optimum scope to capture the childrens' perceptions, thoughts and feelings. Similarly, Christion Hutchinson, in Chapter 10, traces the chain of decisions which lead him to select the approach he took in his research with teaching colleagues. This then paved the way for the selection of his data collection tool and adaptation of same.

Theme 6: Data gathering and analysing tools: often referred to as research 'methods'

Having decided on your methodology, considerations regarding which tool/s to select to gather and analyse data are important. In some instances, such tools are referred to as research methods as distinct from methodology. Many texts are available which offer detailed accounts of the various tools, ways they can be used and considerations when deciding on which one to select (Hennink et al. 2020; Hall and Wall 2019; Connolly 2016). It may be helpful to consider selecting your research tools in the same way as you would select an appropriate tool for gardening tasks. For example, if you decide to prune a delicate rose bush, small hand-held secateurs could be deemed the most suitable tool. On the other hand, if cutting back a lengthy hedge, you may consider sheers or even a powered cutting device to be most appropriate as opposed to the small hand-held secateurs. In the same way, a large shovel would be the optimal tool for moving large piles of stones or earth while a small hand-held trowel would prove most effective when clearing weeds away from a fragile plant. In essence you select the tool most appropriate for the task in hand, the one you consider or believe most likely to achieve your desired outcome and in a way that fits with your 'world view' of how your garden should look and be cared for.

Once you have familiarised yourself with the various tools available to you, the next step is to consider which tool/s are best placed to gather data to answer your research question/s, to analyse that data and which are aligned with your chosen paradigm and conceptual and/or theoretical framework. It may be helpful to consider the following scenarios. If you believe yourself to be a Pragmatist, and you consequently believe there is a definitive answer to your research question waiting to be discovered, you may consider tools often associated with quantitative methodologies, such as a tightly structured survey/questionnaire conducted before and after an intervention, as the best tool to ascertain the impact of the intervention. On the other hand, if your world view is more nuanced, believing that people construct their understanding and knowledge through experience and reflection, you may consider tools usually associated with qualitative methodology and, which align with Constructivism (Denicolo et al. 2016) for example. From this perspective, reality is deemed subjective, meanings are constructed through the experiences of the researcher and participant/s (Guba and Lincoln 1994) and consequently tools such as semi-structured interviews and/or observation may be deemed the most appropriate choice. In Chapter 12, Kathryn McCrorie indicates how she came to choose semi-structured interviews and concludes that this was the optimal choice on reflection. She also selected fortune lines to gather data, and explores the dilemmas, advantages, and pitfalls of using fortune lines to enable student teachers to record their feelings about the mentor-mentee relationship while on school placement. It is important to ensure that both the design and use of your tools align with your paradigm, such as including all open-ended questions or a mixture of question styles in a questionnaire. This point is clearly illustrated by Caoimhe Donovan in Chapter 11 where both closed and open-ended questions were used, thus repositioning it from a tool associated primarily with quantitative methodologies. Indeed, many of the contributors, including Caoimhe, stress the importance of piloting a tool, to provide insights into changes that may be needed from the participants' perspective.

In Chapter 8, Kirstin Mulholland discusses the process of selecting the most appropriate tool for her participants (9- and 10-year-old pupils) which allowed them to express their experiences, in their own words, consequently, enablingtheir authentic voice. Kirstin recounts the many tools deliberated on and rejected at the design stage, eventually arriving at pupil views template (PVTs). Importantly, this chapter also points to the nature of the data collected and how it can be analysed, reminding researchers to consider if it will answer their research question/s. Other considerations such as selecting the most appropriate tool or modifying it for a particular cohort, such as young children for example, is detailed by Sinéad Gallagher in Chapter 9, where modified questionnaires, drawings, vignettes/stories and small group interviews were utilised. While aligning with the Pragmatist paradigm, Sinéad in choosing a mixed methods approach, utilised a number of tools as the best way to answer her research questions with a cohort of young children, which she justifies in detail.

In the same way you have a selection of data-gathering tools to choose from, you also have a range of data analysis tools at your disposal, many of which align with quantitative or qualitative methodologies (Lester et al. 2020; Freeman 2017: validatedMiles and Huberman 1994; Jopling 2019; Stockemer 2018; Bors 2018; Bryman and Cramer 2005). Deciding on which tool is the most appropriate to analyse the data you have gathered and is aligned to your chosen paradigm is a key consideration. You may select thematic analysis (Braun and Clarke 2021), one of the most popular qualitative data analytical techniques or tools, which in itself has variations within (Braun and Clarke 2016). Alternatively, if your methodology is quantitative in nature, you may decide upon descriptive and/or inferential statistics as your optimal data analysis tool or technique, to calculate, describe, summarize, or compare data sets and generalize about the larger population of subjects (Abu-Bader 2021). The decision to select discourse analysis (DA), implications of same and lessons learned are detailed in Chapter 4 by Marc Turu Porcel.

Theme 7: Participants or sample

Although presented as Theme 7, you may have decided who the participants or your sample population are at an earlier stage in your research journey. Once you are clear on the specific focus of your research, deciding who is best placed to provide insights into your question or questions becomes apparent. For example, in Chapter 13, Kathryn McClure provides clear insights into how reading and refining her research question, focusing on the use of restrictive repetitive behaviours as coping strategies by autistic children, enabled her to define inclusion and exclusion criteria for her participants. This finally led her to select a specific cohort of participants, namely teachers and staff working within complex special schools.

Some considerations which fall under participants/sample include, how many participants you need, how best to select them, how to gain access to them, whether your positionality or your perceived status and/or relationship to the participants will impact the data you gather? In Chapter 14, Alison Weatherston, reflects on the potential power imbalance that can exist between the researcher and participants. Alison emphasizes the importance of addressing researcher positionality and having critical self-awareness and transparency in this role, particularly when conducting research in one's area of work, in this case with newly appointed headteachers in Scotland. Against this backdrop, the decisions and processes undertaken in her study are considered.

Identifying and reading texts which provide detailed insights and directions regarding the selection of your participants supports decision making in relation to participant selection (Clark et al. 2021; Hennink et al. 2020). Aligned with your paradigm, you may opt for probability sampling techniques meaning 'you can specify the probability that a participant will be from a population you are targeting' (Rooney and Evans 2019, p. 126). This may be essential to answer your research questions/s if you need to gather data from a particular group of parents or cohort of learners for example as indicated in Chapter 13 by Kathryn McClure. On the other hand, if you wish to test a theory as opposed to describing the perspectives of a given population, then 'nonprobability sampling techniques' (Rooney and Evans 2019, p. 131) would be a logical choice for you.

Theme 4 revisited: Ethics

Finally, ethical issues may arise at various stages of your research journey, which you may not have anticipated at the onset. As a beginning researcher, it may be difficult to predict or anticipate issues relating to power dynamics, the unintended disclosure of sensitive information or issues emerging due to forced changes in your methodology as experienced by many researchers due to Covid-19 restrictions. Yet, the importance of continually revisiting and addressing ethical challenges is paramount and never ending. Ceridwen Owen, in Chapter 7, recounts the continual nature of considering ethics, tracing it from the project's aims, research questions, methodology and analysis framework and back again. In doing so she highlights the prescribed, regulatory measures assumed by all researchers, as well as more specific considerations relating to the individual project and its time and place. Examples of ethics in action are also presented, including reflexivity and answerability.

Similarly, in Chapter 15, Diana Tremayne indicates how continuous reflection on her role as she engaged online with her participants in gathering data, caused her to continuously consider the ethical implications of her actions. Laura Balcon, in Chapter 2, also discusses some of the challenges associated with ethical issues in relation to her research. In particular, Laura draws attention to some of the sensitivities associated with her research, particularly the ethical issues which emerged for her when working with parents and their children.

Conclusion

In the same way that we all align with various paradigms, have varying world views and beliefs, your research journey will be individual to you. The details and sequencing in this book are not deemed to be prescriptive but are offered as a supportive device, a way to help you address various themes, issues and questions you may have about research in a manageable way. You may have access to tutors, guidelines from various institutions or funding bodies and supportive peers, all of which provide essential support when undertaking research. Ultimately, as you navigate your own way through your research journey, as your companion this book will enable you to capitalize on and learn from the experiences of other teacher-researchers, some of whom engaged in initial small-scale research and others who undertook large-scale research projects. Our hope is that you are inspired and encouraged by the accounts and insights provided by the contributors to continue your research journey, with additional confidence and competence.

References

Abu-Bader, S. H. (2021). *Using statistical methods in social science research: With a complete SPSS guide*. USA: New York: Oxford University Press.

Adom, D., Yeboah, A., and Ankrah, A. K. (2016). Constructivism philosophical paradigm: Implication for research, teaching and learning. *Global Journal of Arts Humanities and Social Sciences*, 4(10), pp. 1–9.

Akkerman, S. F., Bronkhorst, L. H., and Zitter, I. (2013). The complexity of educational design research. *Quality & Quantity*, 47, pp. 421–39.

Berg, B. L. (2016). *Qualitative research methods for the social sciences, Book 1*. 9th ed. London: Pearson.

Berman, J., & Smyth, R.(2015). Conceptual frameworks in the doctoral research process: A pedagogical model. *Innovations in Education and Teaching International*, 52(2), 125-136.

Biesta, G. (2015). On the two cultures of educational research, and how we might move ahead: Reconsidering the ontology, axiology and praxeology of education. *European Educational Research Journal*, 14(1), pp. 11–22.

Bors, D. (2018). *Data analysis for the social sciences: Integrating theory and practice*. London: SAGE Publications.

Braun V. and Clarke, V. (2016). (Mis)conceptualising themes, thematic analysis, and other problems with Fugard and Potts' (2015) sample-size tool for thematic analysis. *International Journal of Social Research Methodology*, 19(6), pp. 739–43.

Braun, V. and Clarke, V. (2021). *Thematic analysis: A practical guide*. London: SAGE Publications.

Bryman, A. (2012). *Social research methods*. 4th ed. New York: Oxford University Press.
Bryman, A. and Cramer, D. (2005). *Quantitative data analysis with SPSS 12 and 13: A guide for social scientists*. London: Routledge.
Candy. P.C. (1989). Constructivism and the study of self-direction in adult learning. *Studies in the Education of Adults*, 21(2), pp. 95–116.
Carton, J. (2014). *Research supervisors support and development: Review of Policy, Practices and Procedures in five U21 Partner Universities* [online]. Universities 21 and UCD International. Available: Research Supervisor Support Development Report - U21 Project.pdf https://www.ucd.ie/t4cms/Research%20Supervisor%20Support%20%20Development%20Report%20-%20U21%20Project%20.pdf [accessed 28 November 2023].
Charmaz, K. (2014). *Constructing Grounded Theory*. 2nd ed. London: SAGE Publications.
Clark, T., Foster, L., Bryman, A., and Sloan, L. (2021). *Bryman's social research methods*. New York: Oxford University Press.
Cohen, L., Manion, L., and Morrison, K. (2000). *Research methods in education*. London: Routledge.
Cohen, L., Manion, L., and Morrison, K. (2018). *Research methods in education*. 8th ed. London: Routledge.
Cohen, L., Manion, L., and Morrison, K. (2018a). Action research. In: Cohen, L., Manion, L., and Morrison, K. (eds), *Research methods in education*. London: Routledge, pp. 440–56.
Connolly, M. (2016). Selecting appropriate research methods for an educational context. In: Palaiologou,I., Needham,D., and Male, T. (eds), *Doing research in education: Theory and practice*. London: SAGE Publications, pp. 136–55.
Creswell, J. W. (2003). *Research design: Qualitative, quantitative, and mixed methods approaches*. 2nd ed. Thousand Oaks, CA: SAGE Publications.
Creswell, J. W. (2012). *Educational research*. Boston: Pearson.
Denicolo, P., Long, T., and Bradley-Cole, K. (2016). *Constructivist approaches and research methods: A practical guide to exploring personal meanings*. Thousand Oaks, CA: SAGE Publications.
Dumay, J. C. (2008). *Research methods and research sites employed*. Sydney: SeS Library, USYD.
Freeman, M. (2017). *Modes of thinking for qualitative data analysis*. New York: Routledge.
Gage, N. L. (1989). The paradigm wars and their aftermath: A historical sketch of research on teaching since 1989. *Educational Researcher*, 18(7), pp. 4–10.
Given, L. M. (2008). Axiology. In: Given, L. M., ed. *The SAGE encyclopedia of qualitative research methods*. Thousand Oaks, CA: SAGE Publications, pp. 53-56.

Goldschmidt, G. and Matthews, B. (2022). Formulating design research questions: A framework. *Design studies*, 78, 101062.

Gonzalez, L. M. (2015). Barriers to college access for Latino/a adolescents: A comparison of theoretical frameworks. *Journal of Latinos and Ēducation*, 14(4), 320–35.

Guba, E. G. and Lincoln, Y. S. (1994). Competing paradigms in qualitative research. In: Denzin, N. and Lincoln, Y. S. (eds), *The SAGE handbook of qualitative research*. Thousand Oaks, CA: SAGE Publications, pp. 105–17.

Guba, E. G. and Lincoln, Y. S. (2005). Paradigmatic controversies, contradictions & emerging confluences. In: Denzin, N. and Lincoln, Y. S. (eds), *The SAGE handbook of qualitative research*. 3rd ed. Thousand Oaks, CA: SAGE Publications.

Guthrie, G. (2010). Experimental method. In: Guthrie, G. (ed.), *Basic research methods: An entry to social science research*. Thousand Oaks, CA: SAGE Publications, pp. 86–98.

Hall, E. and Wall, K. (2019). *Research methods for understanding professional learning*. London: Bloomsbury Publishing.

Hennink, M., Hutter, I., and Bailey, A. (2020). *Qualitative research methods*. Thousand Oaks, CA: SAGE Publications.

Igwenagu, C. (2016). *Fundamentals of research methodology and data collection*. Saarbrücken: LAP Lambert Academic Publishing.

Jensen, K. B. (ed.) (2020). *A handbook of media and communication research: Qualitative and quantitative methodologies*. New York: Routledge.

Jopling, M. (2019). Using quantitative data. In: Lambert, M. (ed.), *Practical research methods in education*. London: Routledge, pp. 55–66.

Kaplan, D. (2004). *The SAGE handbook of quantitative methodology for the social sciences*. Thousand Oaks, CA: SAGE Publications.

Kivunja, C. and Kuyini, A. B. (2017). Understanding and applying research paradigms in educational contexts. *International Journal of Higher Education*, 6(5), 26–41.

Kuhn, T. (1970). Postscript 1969. In: Kuhn, T. (ed.), *The structure of scientific revolutions*. 2nd ed. Chicago: University of Chicago Press, pp. 174–21.

Lavrakas, P. J., Traugott, M. W., Kennedy, C., Holbrook, A. L., de Leeuw, E. D., and West, B. T. (eds.) (2019). *Experimental methods in survey research: Techniques that combine random sampling with random assignment*. New Jersey: John Wiley & Sons.

Lee, C. J. G. (2012). Reconsidering constructivism in qualitative research. *Educational Philosophy and Theory*, 44(4), pp. 403–12.

Lester, J. N., Cho, Y., and Lochmiller, C. R. (2020). Learning to do qualitative data analysis: A starting point. *Human Resource Development Review*, 19(1), pp. 94–106.

Lincoln, Y. S., & Guba, E. G. (1985). *Naturalistic inquiry.* sage.
MacDonald, C. (2012). Understanding participatory action research: A qualitative research methodology option. *The Canadian Journal of Action Research,* 13(2), pp. 34–50.
Mackenzie, N. and Knipe, S. (2006). Research dilemmas: Paradigms, methods and methodology. *Issues in Educational Research,* 16(2), pp. 193–205.
McCusker, K. and Gunaydin, S. (2015). Research using qualitative, quantitative, or mixed methods and choice based on the research. *Perfusion,* 30(7), pp. 537–42.
McNiff, J. (2013). *Action research: Principles and practice.* New York: Routledge.
Merriam, S. B. (1998). *Qualitative research and case study applications in education.* San Francisco, CA: Jossey-Bass.
Miles M. B. and Huberman A. M. (1994). *An expanded sourcebook: Qualitative data analysis.* 2nd ed. Thousand Oaks, CA: SAGE Publications.
Moon, K., & Blackman, D.(2014). A guide to understanding social science research for natural scientists. *Conservation biology,* 28(5), 1167-1177.
Morgan, D. L. (2007).Paradigms lost and pragmatism regained: Methodological implications of combining qualitative and quantitative methods. *Journal of mixed methods research,* 1(1), 48-76.
O'Toole, L., McClelland, D., Forde, D., O'Keeffe, S., Purdy, N., Säfström, C. A., and Walsh, T. (2021). Contested childhoods across borders and boundaries: Insights from curriculum provisions in Northern Ireland and the Irish Free State in the 1920s. *British Educational Research Journal,* 47(4), pp. 1021–38.
Queirós, A., Faria, D., and Almeida, F. (2017). Strengths and limitations of qualitative and quantitative research methods. *European Journal of Education Studies,* 3(7), pp. 369–87.
Rocco, T. S. and Plakhotnik, M. S. (2009). Literature reviews, conceptual frameworks, and theoretical frameworks: Terms, functions, and distinctions. *Human Resource Development Review,* 8(1), pp. 120–30.
Rooney, B. and Evans, A. (2019). *Methods in psychological research.* Thousand Oaks, CA: SAGE Publications.
Ross, S. M. and Morrison, G. R. (2013). Experimental research methods. In: Spector, J. M., Merrill, M. D., Elen, J., and Bishop, M.J. (eds), *Handbook of research on educational communications and technology.* New York: Routledge, pp. 1007–1029.
Salvador, J. T. (2016). Revisiting the philosophical underpinnings of qualitative research. *International Education and Research Journal,* 2(6), pp. 4–6.

Sartori, G. (1984). Guidelines for concept analysis. In: G. Sartori, G. (ed.), *Social science concepts: A systematic analysis*. Thousand Oaks, CA: SAGE Publications, pp. 15–85.

Somekh, B. (2005). *Action research*. New York: McGraw-Hill Education (UK).

Sorin, R., & Galloway, G. (2006). Constructs of childhood: Constructs of self. *Children Australia, 31*(2), 12-21.

Sosa, E. (2017). *Epistemology*. New Jersey: Princeton University Press.

Stake, R. E. (1995). *The art of case study research*. Thousand Oaks, CA: SAGE Publications.

Stockemer, D. (2018). *Quantitative methods for the social sciences: A practical introduction with examples in SPSS and Stata*. Germany: Springer International Publishing.

Tashakkori, A. and Teddlie, C. (2003). Major issues and controversies in the use of mixed methods in the social and behavioral sciences. In: Tashakorri, A. and Teddlie, C. (eds), *Handbook of mixed methods in social & behavioral research*. Thousand Oaks, CA: SAGE Publications, pp. 3–50.

Wald, N. and Daniel, B. K. (2020). Enhancing students' engagement with abstract ideas through conceptual and theoretical frameworks. *Innovations in Education and Teaching International, 57*(4), pp. 496–505.

Williams, J. (2020). *How to read and understand educational research*. Thousand Oaks, CA: SAGE Publications.

Yin, R. K. (2018). *Case study research and applications (Vol. 6)*. Thousand Oaks, CA: SAGE Publications.

PART I

Getting Started – Grappling with Ideas, Concepts, Frameworks and Ethics

CHAPTER 1

How Do You Develop and Answer Research Questions?

James Kelly

What follows is the sequence employed during the initial stages of research which adopted a systematic approach to developing a definitive research title accompanied by a research question with a set of sub-questions. With a broad area of interest established prior to starting the thesis, as illustrated in Section 2, Section 3 reviews how relevant material was discovered in the field to both inform and narrow the focus of the study. Section 4 then examines the application of material collected into a research title and the thought process involved. Having established the clearly defined nature of the study with an explicit research title, Section 5 details the development of sub-questions which underpinned the study, providing for a more prescribed and detailed focus. Finally, Section 6 provides some pointers that helped support my study and would have been useful starting out as a novice researcher. It is by no means an exhaustive list but will hopefully provide a platform from which you can begin your research journey.

As you embark upon your research, try to think of the research title and questions as the foundation to your house. With a good foundation, the house will last for many, many years. With a poor foundation, the house may be rendered futile within a matter of time. So imperative is the time spent on such a small number of words that I think it worthy of taking some time to read about the planned process, pitfalls experienced, and eventual approach chosen within my own thesis that ultimately helped yield clear findings with definitive conclusions.

Context and rationale

Given my role as a primary school teacher in the Republic of Ireland I was, and am, continuously intrigued with the relationship between, and factors impacting upon, national policy and its implementation at a local (school) level. My intention was to supplement this as a student of Education and the Law via a Master's programme in 2019.

So, to start at the beginning, nearly 200 years ago, 1831, saw the establishment of the Irish national school system, the equivalent of modern primary or elementary school systems catering for four to twelve-year-olds. These were established on foot of ideals set out by Lord Stanley, then Chief Secretary for Ireland, in a letter to the ruling British government detailing the tenets of a multi-denominational education system for the island of Ireland. However, these ideals were short-lived, and, by 1890, a system heavily monopolized by the Catholic Church emerged (Mawhinney 2012). Catholic influence continued through the infancy of the Irish State in 1922, with a recognition that the newly formed Irish Constitution of 1937 'stopped short of making the Catholic Church the established church of the State' (Simmie and Edling 2016). Today, the 'former hegemony' of the Catholic Church is in national decline with succeeding censuses showing Ireland's increasing diversity of religions and cultures (CSO 2016). Yet the large volume of Catholic schools does not reflect this as Census 2016 indicates that 88.9 per cent of schools within the state are under Catholic patronage, an even greater proportion of children are attending these schools nationally, standing at 90.2 per cent (CSO 2020). Indeed, the Forum on Patronage and Pluralism 2012 supported this, reporting that 96 per cent of all schools were under denominational patronage categorizing it as a mismatch 'between the inherited pattern of denominational school patronage and the rights of citizens in the much more culturally and religiously diverse contemporary Irish society' (Coolahan et al. 2012). Following increasing pressures from various representative bodies in response to reported oversubscription for Catholic primary school places, the Irish government introduced the Education (Admission to Schools) Act 2018 stipulating that no school admission policy could use religion as a prerequisite to enrolment.

One year later, a student of education and the law in the west of Ireland, namely yours truly, was experiencing the prospect of a Master's thesis hurtling towards him. Within the first year of study (pre-thesis), the subconscious was already preoccupied with potential topics. However, my mind was well and truly 'inside the box'; a notion which changed on advice to review recent theses in the field of educational law. This process immediately ignited a thirst within me to explore something unexplored, something contemporaneous. Focus turned to myself as the researcher and to the context within which I work and live – in essence, what I know best. In the end, given my career in Catholic schools coupled with the context provided above I chose a broad topic of education and religion – two areas which dominate the Irish social landscape to varying degrees and intertwine at the juncture of school patronage.

Finding literature: The preliminary stage

The next step involved sourcing a broad array of relevant literature, considering the objectivity of the texts as well as if they were timely or out-of-date. Out-of-date content would not have acknowledged newer or emerging trends, or in my case, new legislation, which may potentially have already provided answers to my research questions. That said, I did use some more 'aged' documents which proved useful as comparatives to newer studies all-the-while being careful to acknowledge their date of origin so as to continuously strengthen the reliability of my study.

The objective of obtaining literature within the field was twofold:

1. To acquire a broader understanding of the Irish education system.
2. To identify any dearth in the existing information which may act as a platform to begin research.

First stop was a crash-course on the Irish education system using core educational and legal textbooks. Professor John Coolahan (1981) quoted Dr Paul Cullen (Archbishop of Dublin in 1850) who stated that 'the separate education of Catholic youth is, in every way, to be preferred'. This correlated with Glendenning's (1989) assertion that 'the rights of religious minorities became less precise' throughout the twentieth century with 'no provision' or allowance made for the rights of those who didn't belong to the majority religions (Hyland 2006).

Subsequent statistical investigations of the Department of Education's 2019 database revealed a 90 per cent Catholic monopoly of primary schools. Yet Census 2016 identified only 78.3 per cent of the Irish population as Roman Catholic while *The Irish Times* Behaviour and Attitudespoll (2018) detailed 84 per cent of those interviewed believed the school system needed reform (O'Mahony 2016). It was deduced from the results of this poll that there may have been a strong desire amongst the parent body for a more multi-denominational approach in Irish primary schools so as to cater for the needs of all children and families equally.

On foot of these intriguing results, access to journal article databases, including JSTOR, Taylor & Francis, Westlaw, Sage Journals Online, and University of Galway database, returned some interesting reasonings as to the current situation. Mawhinney (2012) believed the State empowered school patrons (mainly religious bodies) as the twentieth century progressed with Daly (2016) believing that the State was merely carrying out its constitutional duties. Databases proved to be highly informative but expansive creatures. They returned a huge wealth of information providing both answers and new knowledge whilst also providing opportunities to digress and stray from the original premise. Therefore, in order to avoid such distractions, it is important that your chosen topic is constantly to the forefront of your mind. To aid you in this, try the following pointers:

1. Write a one-line broad description of your topic, for example,

    The admissions process in Catholic primary schools in the context of modern-day Church–State relations in Ireland.

Attempting to explain the topic to someone outside of the field in question will allow for objectivity and refining, where necessary.
2. Consider key words that are most associated with this topic, for example,

'Catholic schools', 'Ireland' and 'school admissions'.

These should be your beginning point for your database journey. Remember words such as 'in' and 'the' should not be included in a database search as they are too generic and could return thousands of articles, many of which may not relate to your topic, but may increase your workload.

Refining your search will help retrieve the most pertinent documents. You can carry this out using Boolean operators (e.g. AND, OR, NOT). For instance:

1. Searching 'Catholic schools' AND 'admissions' will provide a broader international scope to provide comparisons to the Irish perspective.
2. Whilst 'Catholic schools' AND 'Ireland' AND 'admissions' will give a more refined and national viewpoint.

New phrases and words will begin to trend as you analyse what you retrieve, and you can use these in new combinations with the Boolean operators to delve even deeper into the databases. Don't forget to save or bookmark the articles you prefer as you go along to save you from the agony of a second, or even third, full-scale database search.

Within my own research the search for literature continued and whilst the potential causes for a climate of denominational schools were well-versed, remedies and responses to the issue were visibly less defined. The gap in knowledge was beginning to appear thus providing a platform to build upon.

Meanwhile, media articles, which can provide factual evidence along with personal and third-party narrative, quoted parliamentarians, including previous Minister for Education Richard Bruton who believed that parents 'feel pressure to baptise their children in order to gain admission to the local school' due to the right of schools to select children using religion should they need to (*The*

Irish Times 2018). Catholic representative bodies repudiated this, emphasizing their strong commitment to social inclusion (The Council for Education of the Irish Episcopal Conference 2017). This rebuttal demonstrates the importance in exploring a broad array of media so as to explore and represent all possible angles in order to remain as impartial and unbiased as possible.

To remedy the colloquially named 'Baptism barrier', the Irish government proposed a bill and legislation (Government of Ireland 2018) which upon reading demonstrated an immediate disadvantage to Catholic schools with exemptions granted to minority-faith schools only. Whilst Catholic press releases consistently referred to the act as 'the wrong answer to the wrong question' a dearth of reaction existed from 'on-the-ground' Catholic school management (McGarry 2018). This was the gap in the research which I was looking for. Now came the time to harness this idea into a research question.

A research title

Why did the Chicken cross the Road? (Specht 2019)

Although a beloved childhood joke for many, I did not realize the overly generalized questions I was imposing upon people from the age of five until my first college lecture on Advanced Research wherein we dissected the ambiguity of the above question. Which chicken? And what is the location of the road spoken of? Despite being robbed of some of the greatest one-line conversation openers, specificity was fast revealing itself as the pathway to success. However, a suggested title by Specht (2019) questioning 'What are some of the environmental factors that occurred in Oxford, England during April 2019 that changed the likelihood of chickens crossing London Road during that time?' lends definition to any potential research. And whilst it isn't advised to use this as a joke to the next five-year-old you meet; it will prove useful as a comparative when designing your own research title.

Similarly, my original research title echoed vagueness and ambiguity stating,

'The effect of the Admissions Act 2018 on primary schools'.

Familiarity with the topic had shadowed any acknowledgement of the topic from the stance of a reader who may never have encountered the legislation or indeed the Irish education system. For instance, what section of the fifty-page legislation did the title refer to? Which types of primary school were to be addressed? Giving a greater degree of consideration to the topic it eventually filtered down to:

> 'The effect of s.9 (new section 61(e)) of the Education (Admissions to Schools) Act 2018 on Catholic primary schools'.

Whilst analytical skills continued to progress, the title was still ambiguous. For instance, the words 'The effect' created the illusion that this thesis would present the full impact of the legislation in Catholic primary schools. Moreover, considering the layers of people that exist within primary schools (pupils, parents, staff and management) and the fact that over 3,200 Catholic primary schools exist across the Republic of Ireland the title concluded as:

> An exploration of perceptions of management in Catholic primary schools, in a region of Leinster, towards the prospective import of s.9 (new section 61 (e)) of the Education (Admissions to Schools) Act 2018.

Although the above title may look polished and descriptive, its development was an iterative process that involved continuous updates and refining at all stages to reflect the current state of play (Maxwell 2013). In essence it was a process of 'trial and error', that is, create a title, review it and modify it. The working title will begin to become your mantra and, in a way, you will subconsciously analyse, edit and rebuild it, whether that be whilst on a run, making dinner or even whilst singing some Sinatra in the shower. Your nights may even begin to be filled with sweet dreams of potential research titles and, if so, embrace this as a positive and not a nightmare – let the mind do its work!

The subconscious does not work alone, however. It is only one tool to help with this back-and-forth process. It is imperative that one records all ideas as they arise, insofar as is possible, either by paper or even voice recording. Nothing became more infuriating than experiencing an intellectual epiphany one week only to be followed by failure to recollect these insights a week later, which, for me, became increasingly common with an ever-increasing volume of data and ideas coming on stream during the data collection phase.

Moreover, do not try to write a research title or its questions in isolation. Be careful to match any potential changes in a title or question to your original rationale so that your study remains within scope. Equally read your title aloud to yourself and others so to ascertain their level of understanding of the intended study. If after reading it, you are greeted by bafflement and bemusement it may be time to go back to the drawing board.

All in all, designing a research title is a gradual process of restructuring. Gradual! A quality which can be difficult to grasp in today's society which is often pillared by the notion of 'instant gratification'. Designing a research title and its questions is like Aesop's fable of 'the Hare and the Tortoise' – slow and steady wins the race! Do not rush this process! Take your time! Release your inner tortoise!

The research question

The title was a statement of intent and, despite its precision, it was likely that it could not be answered all at once. A set of sub-questions were needed to refine the focus and underpin the study. This allowed answering of the main title in a step-by-step manner. Any question can have a domino effect on the development of the project whether that be the research methodology, sample size, data collection and data analysis (Lipowski 2008). Thus, determining the type of research (qualitative or quantitative, or both) one wants to do can help in developing the best type of research question.

Quantitative research questions are precise (Berger 2015), usually seeking to understand particular social, familial or educational experiences or processes that occur in a particular context and/or location (Marshall and Rossman 2014). On the other hand, qualitative research questions are adaptable, non-directional and more flexible (Creswell 2013). Some strong counsel I received during the initial stages of the research process was to compose a research question that would invite a concrete answer – a Yes/No answer per se so as to provide a structure to address the research title.

In the practice of my own research, the literature revealed that a dearth of reaction existed from the management partners (principals, chairpersons, school patrons) of Catholic schools towards the

Admissions Act mentioned in Section 2 and their beliefs towards the rationale behind this Act. Furthermore, a potential constitutional anomaly against Catholic schools had been noticed where it was proffered that the act discriminated between schools under the management of different religious denominations contrary to the protections of Article 44.2.4° of the Irish Constitution (Bunreacht na hÉireann 1937), indicating that aid for schools shall not discriminate between schools under the management of different religious denominations.

My initial naivety believing that a methodology simply involved deciding between either a questionnaire or an interview was disbanded upon recommended reading of Cohen et al. (2017) Research Methods in Education. My evenings became consumed with questions surrounding research paradigms, ontology and epistemology. Yet, despite my literature filled afternoons attempting to pigeonhole myself into a research category, I was being left with more questions than answers, resulting in what I can only characterize as some type of academic identity crisis! The expanse of literature pertaining to paradigms is extensive and if you are not careful, then it can become a little like 'going down the rabbit hole', so giving yourself time to absorb the plethora of information out there allows it to settle in without you realizing. Having eventually established myself as a constructivist, I felt my study was best accommodated by examination of the situation 'through the multiple lens of the individuals involved' (Cohen et al. 2017). This warranted a system of 'co-constructing' knowledge with the study's participants, complementing Burr's views that knowledge is sustained by social processes and that knowledge and social action go together.

It was evident that a qualitative approach would best cater for a successful exploration of the topic chosen to study. On determining such an approach to establish answers regarding the necessity of and motivations for such legislation and whether it provides equality for all or is unsympathetic to the rights of Catholic schools, the study was underpinned by the following research questions:

1. What are the implications of s. 9(61) (e) of the Education (Admissions to Schools) Act 2018 for the management partners of Catholic primary schools in guiding the moral and spiritual education of Catholic children in its catchment area?

2. Do management partners believe that the legislation has created a constitutional anomaly, and therefore a level of inequality, by placing the rights of those with no faith above those of the Catholic faith?
3. Do Catholic primary school management partners perceive that there is an agenda or drive to advance a more secular primary education system and, if so, who do they perceive is driving this agenda and to what end?

A broad study of literature had now led to a provisional title and was further underpinned by conclusive research questions. Now it was time to execute the plan. Remember, as already stated, that the definition of precision will change throughout your study. What you think is a defined question at the beginning of your research may in fact open up a plethora of information that is not possible to address in a full and succinct manner in your study. Furthermore, don't work on the methodology of the research in isolation. Rather, continuously examine it considering the full picture by consistently 'injecting' the research question and key research terms into your narrative and writing – this acts as a reminder for the reader of your work but also for you the researcher.

Now it's your turn . . .

It is now time for you to begin the journey that is research. It is both daunting and exciting. But it is an adventure and a learning experience. Given the research illustrated in this chapter and the rationale behind the decisions taken, below are some ideas you might consider before starting.

The pillars of precision

1. Remember that research is a method of informing: it will ideally improve understanding, but it does not always have to provide a definitive answer.
2. Consistently remember your audience. Anyone should be able to pick up a thesis and carry out your research due to

its precision and clarity. Your thesis should be a step-by-step set of directions.
3. Explore a wide array of literature and material in order to get a broad picture of your topic so you can make an informed choice on what to explore.
4. Once a topic is chosen, you will turn to the research title. This is a work in progress and will be subject to change. In fact, it is not only the first thing you'll think about in your research, but it more than likely will be the very last thing you'll change before final submission.
5. Research should attempt to augment contemporaneous debate or reflect broader societal issues that can be further built on at a later date by yourself or other researchers. It could:

   i. Have a degree of originality by focusing on a specific location/region or looking at something from a new angle.

   ii. Address a dearth in research that you may have noted within your initial reading on the topic chosen.

   Essentially, ask yourself what your research's 'unique selling point' is!

6. A set of sub-questions will refine the study (two to three questions is more than enough) and these should all tie back to the main aim/title. This will help scaffold a succinct response to your initial idea.
7. Start with broad questions and narrow them down gradually, not being afraid to go back and forth during the research process.

References

Berger, R. (2015). Now I see it, now I don't: Researcher's position and reflexivity in qualitative research. *Qualitative Research*, 15(2), pp. 219–34.

Bunreacht na hÉireann- The Irish Constitution (1937). [online]. Available: https://www.irishstatutebook.ie/eli/cons/en/html [accessed 30 November 2023].

Cohen, L., Manion, L. and, Morrison, K. (2017). *Research methods in education*. 8th ed. London: Routledge.

Coolahan, J. (1981). *'18', in Irish education: History and structure*. Dublin: Institute of Public Administration.

Coolahan, J., Hussey, C., and Kilfeather, F. (2012). *The forum on patronage and pluralism in the primary sector report of the forum's advisory group*. Dublin: Stationary Office.

Creswell, J. W. (2013). *Qualitative inquiry and research design: Choosing among five approaches*. London: SAGE Publications.

Central Statistics Office [CSO]. (2016). *Profile 8 - Irish Travellers, Ethnicity and Religion*[online]. Available: https://www.cso.ie/en/release sandpublications/ep/p-cp8iter/p8iter/p8rrc/ [accessed 25 October 2019].

Central Statistics Office [CSO]. (2020). *Religion - religious change* [online]. Available: https://www.cso.ie/en/releasesandpublications/ep/p-cp8iter/p8iter/p8rrc/ [accessed 8 August 2023].

Central Statistics Office [CSO]. (2021). *Statistical standards and quality* [online]. Available: https://www.cso.ie/en/methods/quality/statistical standardsandquality/ [accessed 8 August 2023].

Daly, E. (2016). Religion as public good and private choice in Irish constitutional doctrine. *Irish Jurist*, 56(103), pp. 103-122.

Government of Ireland (GOI). (2018). Education (Admission to Scools) Act 2018. Available: https://www.irishstatutebook.ie/eli/2018/act/14/encted/en/html [accessed 3 December 2023].

Hyland, A. (2006). *Challenges for the Irish education system for the next generation and beyond: the issue of school patronage*. Cork: UCC.

Hyland, A. and Glendenning, D. (1989). The multi-denominational experience in the National School System in Ireland. *Irish Educational Studies*, 8(1), pp. 89–114.

Lipowski, E. E. (2008). Developing great research questions. *American Journal of Health-System Pharmacy,* 65(17), pp. 1667–70.

Marshall, C. and Rossman, G. B. (2014). *Designing qualitative research*. Thousand Oaks, CA: SAGE Publications.

Mawhinney, A. (2012). A discriminating education system: Religious admission policies in Irish schools and international human rights law. *The International Journal of Children's Rights*, 20(4), pp. 603–23.

Maxwell, J. A. (2013). *Qualitative research design: An interactive approach*. Thousand Oaks, CA: SAGE Publications.

McGarry, P. (2018). The faith of Ireland's Catholics continues, despite all.*The Irish Times* [online], 11 August 2018. Available: https://www.irishtimes.com/news/social-affairs/religion-and-beliefs/the-faith-of-ireland-s-catholics-continues-despite-all-1.3592019#:~:text=Despite%20the%20betrayals%20mentioned%20above,still%20identified%20as%20Roman%20Catholic [accessed 17 March 2020].

O' Mahony, C. (2016). New minister must act quickly on denominational schools issue. *The Irish Independent* [online], 11 May 2016. Available: https://www.independent.ie/irish-news/education/going-to-college/new-minister-must-act-quickly-on-denominational-schools-issue-34703322.html [accessed 6 August 2023].

Simmie, G. M. and Edling, S. (2016). Ideological governing forms in education and teacher education: A comparative study between highly secular Sweden and highly non-secular republic of Ireland. *Nordic Journal of Studies in Educational Policy*, 2016(1), p. 32041.

Specht, D. (2019). *Media and communications study skills student guide*. London: University of Westminster Press.

The Council for Education of the Irish Episcopal Conference. (2017). *The role of denominational religion in the school admissions process and possible approaches for making changes*. Dublin.

The Irish Times. (2018). 'Baptism barrier': A step in the right direction. *The Irish Times* [online]. Available: https://www.irishtimes.com/opinion/editorial/baptism-barrier-a-step-in-the-right-direction-1.3345197 [accessed 8 August 2023].

CHAPTER 2

How Does Your Research Question Influence Your Methodology?

Laura Balcon

Context

After working as a Special Educational Needs Co-ordinator (SENCO) in an English primary school for several years, I decided it was time that I studied for my National Award for SEN Co-ordination. As part of this Postgraduate Certificate, we were asked to conduct a small-scale enquiry in our school to help improve and challenge existing practice.

To begin, I was asked to identify an area of practice or policy in my school which needed to be challenged. Within my role of SENCO, we are tasked with many different responsibilities such as overseeing the planning, assessment and progress of children with Special Educational Needs and Disabilities (SEND). This can often involve liaising with staff, parents, carers and external professionals to ensure the correct support for these children is co-ordinated and targeted effectively. A significant feature of undertaking this role is that it allows you to learn a lot about the lives of the children and their lived experiences. Over time, I noticed patterns emerging. These involved many parents in my setting asking for their child to be referred for an Autism Spectrum Disorder (ASD) assessment. As a result of this, each year our SEND register was increasing, and the number of children being diagnosed was significantly above the national average statistics. Consequently, this was an area that I wanted to investigate more as it raised many questions, such as: 'Why are so many children in our school being diagnosed with ASD?' 'What about the Nature versus Nurture debate in this context? Is ASD biological or can it be influenced by their home environment?'

I began reading widely in order to try to find answers to these questions and in doing so, came across information about some children being misdiagnosed with the condition. For example, Moran (2015) found that Autism has very similar traits to Attachment Disorder. These are both social communication difficulties and often present with the same behaviours. I had now begun to hypothesize that the reason for our large amount of ASD pupils could be because some may have Attachment Disorder instead and wondered if this was linked in any way to their upbringing and home life. I thought it would be interesting to find out if this was the case, but the cause and effect around this correlation was too difficult for me as a teacher-researcher to prove. We have no real proof of a child's lived experiences, so we cannot categorically say that this is what has caused their attachment needs. There is also a stigma involved with diagnosing attachment disorder, as this is perceived as blaming the parents and can result in shame (Wittkowski and Crompton 2023). I knew this was too difficult for me to research, due to having very limited time whilst still working full-time. There would also be many ethical considerations around sensitivity to consider. Based on all of these considerations, I knew I had to narrow down my interest and focus on something more specific in terms of my research question. However, this was not easy and later I discuss using reflective journals as a helpful way to record what I had learnt and how it helped me to identify a focus area for my school-based research.

The steps taken to refine my research focus and decide on my research question

Reflective journals: Non-linear approach

In order to gain my qualification, I had to conduct a small-scale enquiry in my school with a view to improving practice. It was recommended that I consider action research as my research approach. Parsons and Brown (2002) define action research as an investigation used by teachers to solve problems and improve practice in their school. Action research is a deliberate reflection that is documented and analysed to improve teaching and learning (Clark et al. 2020). Ros and Meyer (2002) maintain that when teachers design and implement their research this improves the performance of their students. This appeared to be a good fit for my intended research project. However, as a methodology it is not without its barriers, limitations and considerations.

Bryman and Bell (2011) highlight one such limitation, indicating that as the research undertaken is usually specific to one school or practitioner, it lacks repeatability and rigour. In comparison, other scientific research approaches help to advance knowledge and draw conclusions using the data collected (Discover PhDs 2020). What's more, the findings can also be generalized to wider populations. Some large-scale research projects take a large amount of time, money and resources, all of which I did not have available. So, by selecting the 'best fit' I decided action research was the most appropriate for my setting and job role, offering a practical approach that can inform change and enhance understanding.

Often action research is identified as a cycle or spiral of reflection. According to Parsons and Brown (2002), it is said to have five stages: 1) selecting a focus, 2) collecting data, 3) organizing data, 4) analysing data and 5) taking action. Following evaluation and reflection, the whole cycle is then often repeated to assess effectiveness and further refine the focus of the research. At this early stage of the research process, I was still trying to select an area of focus for my specific research question. I found reading beyond the confines of what I thought relevant was most helpful as it enabled me to develop my ideas further and consider other related options.

As a starting point, I began reading around the topic of autism and attachment needs which led me down a 'rabbit hole of information', as these topics were so broad. My next task was to sift through all this information and draw the key points together. I then integrated it further, to help decide where my research focus would be, in the first cycle of my action research project. What enabled me to do this effectively was writing 'Reflective Journal' entries.

What are reflective journals?

Reflective journals are first-person narratives of personal reflections (Ezezika and Johnston 2023). They contain multiple entries that help to track and monitor the research development over time (The University of Edinburgh 2018). I used these to evidence my learning and helped me to develop my ideas in a chronological way. They also helped me to change my initial enquiry into a more critical one. To begin with I wrote down everything that I found out, then as the findings started to slow down, I restructured and organized them into themes under three headings.

You may find it helpful to label or name your journals. In relation to my research, journal one, was named 'Problem and rationale', as this identified the issue in my current school and the links between autism and attachment needs. Journal two was called 'seeking expert advice and theory'. Rather than conducting formal interviews with an educational professional, with the advice of tutors on the programme, I contacted educational professionals and asked their opinion on an informal basis and this helped to verify my initial hypothesis. As I was working within a tight timeframe, this did save time and provided essential information for my project. If I had used an interview technique to gather data, then this would have required long transcripts and in-depth analysis. However, having an informal conversation with the local educational psychologist, helped to confirm the correlation and similarity between autism and attachment needs. If you have local contacts that you can seek advice from when pursuing a theory, I would definitely recommend asking a variety of different professionals. Swain and King (2022) maintain that informal conversations are underused in research and often produce more naturalistic data. They further stress that they can be used as the main method or to supplement more formal data created through interview. The educational psychologist explained that attachment needs can impact a child's development, but so can Adverse Childhood Experiences (ACEs), and both conditions are said to affect the child's developing brain.

I will admit that having been a SENCO for many years, I had never heard the term ACEs before. ACEs are defined as stressful and traumatic events that occur during childhood (Bush 2018). These can include abuse, neglect, mental ill health, substance misuse, criminality, violence and separation (Allen and Donkin 2015). On further reflection, I felt that if I was not aware of the term ACEs or the impact that could have on children's development, then surely the staff in my school were not aware either. It may be difficult to follow my 'train of thought' here, as my initial idea was to investigate Autism misdiagnosis, however the more I investigated and researched, the more information I found about ACEs and their links to attachment disorder. Kemmis and McTaggart (2000) explain that this is a natural part of the research process where your thinking is challenged, expanded and refined, and is particularly reflective of the action research cycle. I had my initial plan, but then following my discussion with the educational psychologist (informal data collection), I reflected on this new information and my research plan and focus were revised. This cyclical process helped me to refine my focus and turn what was initially a broad topic into a more sharply focused research project. The next step was to devise a research question that reflected this new focus. Pine (2009) explains that identifying a good research question requires reflection, conversation and observation (which I had carried out). He suggests, as I also found, that the first question in action research may change and become refined as new information surfaces.

As my initial idea around Autism had now changed to a consideration of attachment and ACEs, I needed to remember that my action research had to help bring about change. I wanted to find out how staff in my school could support pupils with ACEs. If adversity impacts on development, then how can we as practitioners help to overcome this? Further reading indicated that staff training and knowledge of attachment and adversity is crucial when supporting pupils (Attachment Research Community 2021). If the staff awareness in my school was developed, then this could help the pupils who have experienced adversities and those with attachment needs. I realized that this was definitely something I needed to put into action and so I was getting closer to my final research question.

Having a reflective entry that focuses specifically on methodology is an important consideration for you as a beginner researcher. In my context, journal entry three was about designing and using the tools I had chosen to collect the data. I had to undergo data collection as part of this project. My first tool was the informal conversation (Swain and King 2022) to help refine my research question and then in order to answer my research question, I chose to investigate staff members' prior or existing knowledge relating to ACEs. This required me to read about and consider tools for data collection. Simultaneously I continued to refine my research question. In comparison to traditional research, this may seem like an unorthodox way of working. However, as Mertler (2017) points out, action research is said to have a clear beginning but not necessarily a clear ending. I found that not having finalized the research question, but knowing what I wanted to find out and who from as well as using the data gathered helped me to better shape the question that I ended up with at the end of the research process.

Data collection method: Unpublished questionnaire data

The next step in my journey was to decide on a tool which would enable me to gather data which would further shape and inform my research question. In order to arrive at a decision, I needed to consider many options and restraints pertinent to my working environment. I ultimately decided on and designed a short online questionnaire consisting of ten questions. I chose a questionnaire because it would encourage more participants to engage with it and provide me with concise data which was within my remit to analyse. In comparison, if I had chosen interviews, this would have taken a substantial amount of time to analyse and transcribe (Mertler 2017) and I felt would extend me beyond where the programme intended me to go in the completion of a postgraduate certificate.

A consideration for you if using a questionnaire is whether to go for a paper version or an online version. I opted for an online version and the questionnaire was completed on a website where participants responded via a URL link. I found this was the quickest way to send out the questions to all staff members and collect their responses. The website helped to organize and present the findings in an accessible format. This left me free to analyse the data and draw inferences from it. I knew using an online system was best for me as I have conducted paper-based questionnaires in the past and found a poor response rate.

If using an online questionnaire, consider using simple, closed questions which make for easier data to analyse when beginning on the research journey. The questionnaire asked staff members to rate their understanding of ACEs and confidence in using attachment-focused strategies. The data gathered from the questionnaires was not published, it was used to inform journal entry three. Not publishing the data, keeps ethical implications to a minimum. Also publishing the data would have no benefit to people outside of my school, as the findings were specific to the staff in my setting and was key to informing me of staff knowledge and awareness. The sample was not reflective of the wider population as it was twenty-six people from one English primary school. This is common with action research and is a consideration for you when deciding if action research is a method you would choose. Although, the information was not published, the study itself did adhere to research ethical standards. I ensured that informed consent was gained; risk of harm was minimal; protected participant's anonymity and confidentiality; avoided deceit; and gave them the right to withdraw from the research afterwards (British Educational Research Association 2018). The data was used to inform the reflections in my journal entries and led the next steps within my action research cycle.

Conceptual framework

The term conceptual framework was completely new to me. It basically outlines the researcher's perception on the research problem and all issues pertaining to it. I knew that my postgraduate certificate was on inclusion, so it was clear that my research was going to be based around this. My research brought up lots of different topics, such as Autism, attachment, ACEs and even parental stigma. However, the overarching theme within inclusion was that of 'social inclusion'; which links to the social model of disability

(Oliver 1990). Broadly this involves individuals being accepted beyond their disability and environmental changes occurring.

Once you have selected a theme it is essential to read extensively as various authors may have different perspectives. For example, in relation to John Bowlby's (1969, 1973, 1980) research on attachment, he suggests that the quality of an attachment creates an 'internal working model', which later impacts on how the child develops future relationships. Many researchers believe once a working model is created this is permanent (Rutter et al. 2007). Whereas those who follow a more social model paradigm believe that the working model can be rewritten, with the right support and relationships (Schofield and Beek 2018; Fonagy and Allison 2014). With this opinion in mind, I would like to believe that this is true and that attachment difficulties do have the capability to be rewritten. This use of paradigm helped to shape my action research cycle, because I believe that we too can rewrite the working models for children. For practitioners working in a school, we build trusting relationships with our pupils daily; so, with the right intervention and support, this can bring about change. This viewpoint explains my stance as a researcher, and how it is the school that needs to change, not the pupil. I will admit that identifying my stance or what some term my conceptual framework was not easy, so I sought advice from the lecturers at university to help me identify this further. I found this support helpful, and you might find discussing it or reading about conceptual frameworks helpful too.

The focus becomes clearer

Inquiry cycles are messy and are not necessarily discrete or linear. They can move much more fluidly, double back on themselves, and take unpredictable routes. Moving from fog to clarity, and back to fog can be part of the process. Just because the inquiry is making less sense does not necessarily mean you are going in the wrong direction. (Ladkin 2004 et al cited in Pine 2009, p. 255)

Be assured that if you continue to read and edit your work, your focus will become clearer, but you may struggle deciding on a number of themes which all to some degree, underpin your research focus. After writing my reflective journals and looking at the data from the questionnaire, I was still toying with so many different potential topics to discuss and continually refining my research question. I had identified Autism, attachment needs, ACEs and parental stigma all as areas of interest. However, I wanted to ensure that I focused on the depth, not breadth of my enquiry. Thus, I steered away from the initial issue of Autism and chose to focus more on the effects that attachment and ACEs had on children's learning and development instead. The reason I did this is because if some children had been misdiagnosed or some have experienced ACEs, there was no current support in place for these pupils. There were so many different Autism friendly strategies already in place at my school, but nothing for attachment or ACEs. So, I wanted to introduce strategies to help them to overcome some of their potential barriers. Even though I moved away from my initial idea, this time spent was not lost and it was all a valuable part of my action research cycle, which was all tracked in my reflective journals.

Having now identified that I wanted to focus on attachment needs and ACEs for the next cycle in the action research, I needed to make this more specific too. I had read about many different strategies that could be introduced in my setting, I decided to split them into two areas: whole-school strategies to support pupils, and strategies that support parents and families.

To get to this point in my research, it took hours of further reading which is key in being able to organize your own writing into different sections. Knowledge around the topic is so important in filtering out what is needed and what is not. Then I was able to work backwards and finally I decided on a research question. Pine (2009) suggests identifying and stating the research question is one of the hardest most critical steps in action research.

Refining my research question within the action research cycles

Now I knew how my research was going to be structured, I needed to put these sections into a research question. This took several attempts at re-writing too. Initially for the purpose of my postgraduate assignment I kept the title short 'Attachment and Adversity: A whole-school approach'. It explained the two topics I had chosen and the discussion about strategies that schools can adopt. It worked for the small audience who would be reading it. The title was free of jargon. However, when this title is shared with a wider audience who were not familiar with my course, I needed to make it more specific to offer clarity to those reading. This is a key consideration as it is easy to presume others are familiar with the terminology that you use on an everyday basis.

Similarly, identifying the research location, sample size and methodology used helps the readers to know if it is a small-scale or a larger research project. As action research is often focused on a specific community (my school) outlining this makes it clear to the reader that the findings may be unique to this location. I settled on the research question 'What impact does attachment and adversity have on pupil outcomes, using an action research enquiry and what strategies can help support these pupils in an English Primary School?' This explains the methodology used, what is being investigated and the locality context. Pine (2009) recommends your question begins with a 'what', 'why' and 'how'.

For my postgraduate research I was happy with this research title. However, this can still be fine-tuned further if necessary. I think that writing your title or research question is often one of the last things you will do in your research as it can be changed and re-directed in some many ways. Zeichner (2013) agrees indicating that with action research you often begin in the middle of an issue, and keeping an account of what you are doing helps you to ultimately discover what the focus of your research is.

Seeking support from your tutors and lecturers is also key in the research journey. I asked for guidance from my university lecturer to help me to structure my research question. Having this discussion helped to really draw together my ideas and refine my ideas. However, some do not wish to seek this advice or do not have this available; if this is the case, there are a number of different support guidelines and diagrams that you can access to help you to refine your research question. Imagine an inverted pyramid, starting with your broad general topic, the next step is to refine this into a narrower topic, followed by a research focus, and this finally develops a research question (Golden Gate University 2022).

What I have learnt: Helpful tips for your research

Research is more purposeful and worthwhile when you are able to bring about change. As a teacher-researcher, consider things you would like to improve or develop as part of your current job role and focus your research in this area. Using your prior knowledge can also help steer your research. I worked in my school for six years before undertaking research. In some areas of SEND I identified myself as an expert, as I was the only person in the school doing this role. No one else had the information or experience that I had – so use this to your advantage. Be the expert in your own setting. You may already have background knowledge, opinions and views that will help you to identify your own research stance and ideas.

The order in which you research can also help. I worked backwards, initially with an idea, then did my further reading, and then the data collection. I used my reflective journals to identify my focus and then I finally decided on the research question. You don't have to work in this order, just find a way that works for you. Chronological isn't always the easiest.

Ask for help! This is the best tip I can give. Using your network of contacts can be the most helpful resource in your research. Sometimes search engines don't give us the answers we need, and we need to ask a real-life human to help guide us.

My final tip is to enjoy your research. Unless you're a researcher for a living, there won't be many chances to undertake projects like this. So chose an area that you are particularly interested in and that you want to learn more about, this makes the reading more enjoyable and less of a chore.

References

Allen, M. and Donkin, A. (2015). *The impact of adverse experiences in the home on the health of children and young people, and inequalities in prevalence and effects* [online]. Available: https://e5ed3774-d9e6-4c6d-87df-48a25ea021a4.filesusr.com/ugd/2d9f51_f2399d899943401b80666bcf7b808476.pdf [accessed 6 May 2021].

Attachment Research Community. (2021). *Call to action: Attachment and trauma awareness-teaching, learning and emotional wellbeing in schools* [online]. Available: https://the-arc.org.uk/Media/campaign/CTA%20Document%20Brochure.pdf [accessed 1 June 2021].

Bowlby, J. (1969). *Attachment and loss: Vol. 1: Attachment*. London: Howgarth Press.

Bowlby, J. (1973). *Attachment and loss: Vol. 2: Separation: Anger and anxiety*. London: Howgarth Press.

Bowlby, J. (1980). *Attachment and loss: Vol. 3: Loss: Sadness and depression*. London: Howgarth Press.

British Educational Research Association [BERA]. (2018). *Ethical guidelines for educational research*. 4th ed. [online]. London: British Educational Research Association. Available: https://www.bera.ac.uk/researchers-resources/publications/ethicalguidelines-for-educational-research-2018 [accessed 6 March 2021].

Bryman, A. and Bell, E. (2011). *Business research methods*. 3rd ed. Oxford: Oxford University Press.

Bush, M. (2018). *Addressing adversity: Prioritising adversity and trauma-informed care for children and young people in England*. London: The Young Minds Trust.

Clark, J. S., Porath, S., Thiele, J., and Jobe, M. (2020). *Action research* [online]. Available: https://kstatelibraries.pressbooks.pub/gradactionresearch/chapter/chapt1/ [accessed 15 October 2023].

Discover PhDs. (2020). *What is research? Purpose of research* [online]. Available: https://www.discoverphds.com/blog/what-is-research-purpose-of-research [accessed 15 October 2023].

Ezezika, O. and Johnston, N. (2023). Development and implementation of a reflective writing assignment for undergraduate students in a large public health biology course. *Pedagogy in Health Promotion*, 9(2), pp. 101–15.

Fonagy, P. and Allison, E. (2014). The role of mentalizing and epistemic trust in the therapeutic relationship. *Psychotherapy*, 51(3), pp. 372–80.

Golden Gate University. (2022). *Research process: An overview: Refining your topic* [online]. Available: https://ggu.libguides.com/c.php?g=106905&p=694002 [accessed 14 December 2022].

Kemmis, S. and McTaggart, R. (2000). *Participatory action research, handbook of qualitative research*. London: SAGE Publications.

Ladkin, D. et al. (2004). Back to the workplace. How organisations can improve their support for management learning and development. Journal of management development, 23 (3), pp. 234-255. Cited in G. J. Pine, 2009. Conducting teacher action research. London: SAGE Publications.

Mertler, C. (2017). *Action research: Improving schools and empowering educators*. 5th ed. Thousand Oaks, CA: SAGE Publications.

Moran, H. (2015). *The Coventry ASD vs Attachment problems grid* [online]. Available: https://www2.oxfordshire.gov.uk/cms/sites/default/files/folders/documents/virtualschool/processesandforms/resourcesandpublications/CoventryGrid.pdf [accessed 6 March 2021].

Oliver, M. (1990). *The individual and social models of disability* [online]. Available: https://disability-studies.leeds.ac.uk/wp-content/uploads/sites/40/library/Oliver-in-soc-dis.pdf [accessed 24 April 2022].

Parsons, R. and Brown, K. (2002). *Teacher as reflective practitioner and action researcher.* Belmont, CA: Wadsworth/ Thomas.

Pine, G. J. (2009). *Conducting teacher action research.* London: SAGE Publications.

Ros, H. and Meyer, A. (2002). *Teaching every student in the digital age: Universal design for learning.* Alexandria, VA: The Association for Supervision and Curriculum Development.

Rutter, M., Beckett, C., Castle, J., Colvert, E., Kreppner, J., Mehta, M., and Sonuga-Barke, E. (2007). Effects of profound early institutional deprivation: An overview of findings from a UK longitudinal study of Romanian adoptees. *European Journal of Developmental Psychology*, 4(3), pp. 332–50.

Schofield, G. and Beek, M. (2018). *Attachment handbook for foster care and adoption.* 2nd ed. London: Coram BAAF.

Swain, J. and King, B. (2022). Using informal conversations in qualitative research. *International Journal of Qualitative Methods*, 21, pp. 1–10.

The University of Edinburgh. (2018). *Reflective blogs/journals/diaries* [online]. Available: https://www.ed.ac.uk/reflection/facilitators-toolkit/components-tasks/reflective-blogs-journals-diaries [accessed 31 August 2023].

Wittkowski, A. and Crompton, C. (2023). *The journey from shame to awareness for parents of children with attachment related difficulties* [online]. Available: https://www.gmmh.nhs.uk/research-innovation-news/the-journey-from-shame-to-awareness-for-parents-of-children-with-attachment-related-difficulties-6046 [accessed 15 October 2023].

Zeichner, K. (2013). *Inclusion and behaviour management in schools.* London: David Fulton Publishers.

CHAPTER 3

What Are the Epistemological Challenges Faced When Studying Teachers' Beliefs, Judgements and Decision Making?

Beccy Thompson

2:15pm. Monday. Y8 Art.
Pupils sit in groups of 5 making papier-mâché people sculptures.

BT (teacher-researcher) wanders round the room.

Leigh:	Miss er, I don't mean to be rude, but what are you doing here?
BT:	As Sir explained last week, I'm doing a project at university and I'm observing all the arts teachers.
Pause	
Frank:	So, Miss you are *still* at Uni?' *shaking his head* that's dead.
Leigh:	*Smiling.* Miss yeah, you could have been something like an actor or something and earn lots of money, why do you still want to study?

I begin this chapter (using pseudonyms) with a note I took for my Doctorate in Education (EdD) thesis (Thompson 2021). I examined arts teachers' beliefs, judgements and decisions concerning pupils with Special Educational Needs and or Disability (SEND) in my then workplace, a large secondary school in London where I taught Drama. As a teacher-researcher, I conducted observations and interviews in my faculty. I was, as Adler and Adler (1987) classify, a 'complete member' or an insider in the sample group. Yet, I was also a student part of an outside institution. I was both an inside and outside researcher.

This chapter examines the epistemological positioning of being a teacher-researcher. I follow Rushton and King's (2020) proposal that having insider knowledge enables observation of contextual intricacies. I concentrate on the challenges of the role, particularly related to scepticism that might arise concerning the knowledge that is generated by such work. I hope that this will be useful if you are considering undertaking research in your own institution, or if you are sceptical, will be persuaded about the validity of my research.

Strangely enough, Frank and Leigh's queries regarding my presence did not make the final thesis. This said, their question of why (I wanted to study)is important. Before moving to discuss the challenges of being a teacher-researcher in more detail, I begin by explaining my rationale for the project.

Rationale

When I undertook my EdD I had been a secondary school drama teacher for several years and was frustrated by the quality of professional development offered. Specifically, I was angered by theories that suggest teaching is mere 'common sense' (Winch et al. 2015, p. 203). I also wanted to examine arts subjects, because these are under researched and have endured a 'downgrading' (Tambling and Bacon 2023, p. 13) in English schools.

Coinciding with my desire spotlight the arts, as an insider, a teacher, I had concerns that this blanket label of 'SEND' was problematic, not least because I viewed the children I worked with not just pupils with SEND, but learners with a range of multidimensional characteristics that intersect. Nonetheless, in

England, children with identified SEND are likely to be excluded, struggle with building friendships and their mental health, more than their peers with no registered SEND (House of Commons Education Committee 2019). The current broad definition of a young person with SEND is if they have 'a significantly greater difficulty in learning than the majority of others of the same age' (DfE/DHSC 2015, p. 15). Teachers in England have little influence over who *is* or *is not* formally classified with SEND, but they do make judgements about those they believe face barriers to learning in school. I wanted to give teachers a critical voice on the topic, and it is worth considering what your research project means to you, to understand your epistemological stance.

Early challenges

Somewhere in your research journey, you have probably been told (as I was) getting your research questions right is of upmost importance. To get to these though, I faced many challenges because I was seeking to bring together two fields which have their own epistemological traditions: SEND and teacher knowledge. This is a common issue for researchers; identifying not only your research field(s), but gaps in knowledge about it, is crucial to forming your questions. For me, experientially I *knew* teachers' snap judgements (Korthagen 2014) and microadaptations (Corno 2008) were considered a form of expertise and knowledge (Cochran-Smith and Lytle 1993). A microadaptation, as Corno (2008) indicates, is where teachers respond to their pupils in the moment. These occur 'on the fly' (p. 161) where a teacher diagnoses what a student needs, often from reading subtle behaviours. For example, in one of the Design and Technology (D&T) lessons I observed, pupils learnt how to saw. The teacher, James, explained that pupils showed him two bits of badly sawed wood and he reported saying to them: 'well you weren't standing with your shoulder behind the saw there'. By helping the pupils change body position, they were able to improve their work.

Defining concepts as knowledge, such as microadaptions, is necessary to demonstrate the validity of your work. In my research, decisions made by the teacher, like James helping students adjust their body position when sawing, might occur with little conscious thought (Corno 2008). As is probably a familiar experience to you, I read a lot, in this instance to try and make sense of such implicit decisions. I looked to discussions of knowledge, which are often characterized as 'practical' or 'procedural' knowledge; knowing-how as Ryle (1949/2009) defined it, to 'do something' (Gingell and Winch 1999, p. 126). Connected but distinct from practical knowledge is propositional knowledge or knowing-that (Ryle 1949/2009), and this is concerned with facts. Nonetheless, knowing-that a saw is used to cut wood does not automatically mean we possess the know-how to do it. Yet, I had doubts about how far any would resonate with teachers' experiences because, as Toom (2006) surmises, they rarely value theoretical distinctions. A chance encounter with Shavelson and Stern's (1981) paper about teachers' pedagogical thought processes gave me a suitable starting point to answer scepticism about the validity of teacher knowledge. The authors argue that teachers, as professionals, make judgements and decisions in a multifaceted evolving environment and alongside their beliefs these influence their classroom behaviour. As a result, teacher beliefs, judgements and decisions became how I framed teachers' knowledge. A gap I identified was what these were in relation to SEND, so my first two research questions were:

1) What beliefs and judgements do arts teachers hold or make about students with SEND?

and

2) How are arts teachers' beliefs and judgements manifested in the decisions they make for students with SEND?

In addition to teacher knowledge, I was interested in the school experiences of students with SEND, through teachers' lens and therefore I needed a third question. This presented an epistemological challenge as SEND in England has been conceptualized in various ways. For the first half of the twentieth century, SEND was medicalized, viewed as deficits and differences located in an individual (Harpur 2012). This was disputed by the disability rights movement in the 1970s and notably by Oliver (2013) who defined the social model in direct response. The social model refutes notions of impairment, instead locating the problem in the environment and disability as a concept constructed by society. At a superficial level the social model echoed ideas about inclusion in the classroom, resonating with findings that show arts teachers believe in creating spaces that enable all to participate (Thomson et al. 2012). I predicted teachers' beliefs about SEND might share sentiments of the social model, but this it is not without limitations. A common critique is that by viewing problems in the environment disabling, differences between people are potentially ignored. Teachers also have a statutory duty to make learning accessible to all (DfE 2011) and make adaptations for individuals. Further, research indicates teachers often conflate SEND and low ability (Mazenod et al. 2019) meaning deficit thinking was likely to pervade their beliefs. Clearly, some needs do require medical intervention and therefore I looked to interactionist models (Harwood and McHahon 2013) that attempt to combine either end of the model spectrum in their approach. Applying a theoretical framework which identifies the dynamism of disability and learning needs, such as the Human Development model defined by Mitra (2018), helped me understand there were not only societal assumptions that might permeate teachers' beliefs and judgements about SEND but that a variety of personal, structural, economic and environmental factors overlap to determine a person's capabilities. This framework also supported my suspicion that teachers' decision making could serve to include or exclude individuals and that this too would be multifaceted. Therefore, my final research question was:

3) In what ways do arts teachers' beliefs, judgements and decisions reinforce or undermine the inclusion of students with SEND?

I was enthusiastic about the prospect of working beside my colleagues in what I felt would be a valuable project. However, the purpose of this chapter is not to discuss my findings, rather the epistemological challenges I faced. This began by defining my position and then, as you may well be in the process of thinking about, I had to demonstrate the research was epistemologically fit for purpose, justifying being an inside schoolteacher and an outside doctoral student.

What challenges might you face as a teacher-researcher?

As a teacher-researcher you might, like me, have queried your researcher identity. The questions you ask about practice might 'emerge from discrepancies' (Cochran-Smith and Lytle 1993, p. 14) which is different from researchers querying existing theoretical assumptions and empirical evidence. However, as an 'outsider' researcher and an 'insider' teacher, you occupy the curious position of having a dual role. While these two positions appear disparate, Cochran-Smith and Lytle (1993) usefully outline that a teacher-researcher has a distinct relationship with their 'own knowledge, to one's students as knowers and to knowledge generation in the field' (p. 52). As a teacher researching your own setting, you are permitted reflexivity of insider perspectives, which an outsider striving for objectivity could not achieve. Furthermore, as Corbin-Dwyer and Buckle (2009) advocate, having insider membership does not mean the researcher is completely the same as the group, or as an outsider completely different. I accept that any researcher might share similarities *and* differences to others, which according to Corbin-Dwyer and Buckle (2009) is the basis of a space between, which reassuringly, enabled me (and could you) to pivot (McNess et al. 2016) across the positions.

Epistemological challenges of methodology

Once you have clarified your position as an insider-outsider and articulated the research questions, the next logical challenge is deciding how to investigate these. For me I anticipated there would not be straightforward answers. So far, I have explained that I chose to examine teachers' beliefs, judgements and decisions concerning students with SEND. Before explaining *how*, I should explain that methodologically this project had a phenomenological underpinning because this shaped how I view knowledge. I contend, following Heideggerian philosophy, we are always engaged in the world, making meaning from it. If, I took a Hursselian view, that phenomena can be boiled down, my approach would have been different, as the suggestion is that the researcher 'brackets' or separates themself from the work (Brinkmann and Kvale 2015). Rather, applying Van Manen's (1997/2016) Heideggerian phenomenology, I accept that a researcher cannot abandon their experiences or beliefs about the phenomena at hand, rather they have to keep them 'deliberately at bay' (p. 47). This aligned with my decision to conduct research my institution, not least because I am a social constructivist, meaning I recognize knowledge is formed between people and within the environment (Pfadenhauer and Knoblauch, 2018). This reconciled any confusion I felt about being an inside/outside researcher, because as McNess et al. (2016) state, such an epistemological stance renders identity as always in a state of flux.

Additionally, (which may be helpful to know) I found looking at some philosophy of science useful for justifying the validity of my position. Kuhn's (1962/2012) concept of paradigms or a group theories and methodologies that underpin a scientific topic (Okasha 2002) was a useful starting point. Kuhn asserts the paradigm which solves the most significant problem should be researchers' chosen approach because 'no paradigm ever solves all the problems it defines' (Kuhn 1962/2012, p. 109). Although social constructivists are not concerned with notions of objective truths, sceptics bound to fact-value distinctions (Hollis 1994) are troubled by this, as the former (facts) are considered knowledge, but values are dismissed as Hume wrote, 'perceptions in the mind' (Hume 1985, p. 21). Taught sessions on my EdD had helped me to understand that all research depends on subjective judgements being made somewhere in the process. The contribution a social constructivist lens makes to qualitative inquiry, that made it a particularly suitable fit for classroom research, is that it encapsulates 'multiple perspectives rather than seeking a singular truth' (Patton 2002, p. 267). Although unpicking epistemological traditions can be arduous, it can sharpen the theoretical lens through which you view the project and helps with later analysis.

Participants and data collection

Before discussing some of the epistemological challenges of data collection, I will briefly explain my workplace context and methods used. At the time of the study, the number of students with registered SEND in my school was in line with the national average (Gov. uk 2019) and therefore deemed a suitable setting. I recruited six participants across Art, Drama, Design and Technology (D&T), and Music departments. Broadly, phenomenological studies aim to uncover invariants experience (Dukes 1984) and if you choose this methodology then the number of participants will alter depending on the need of your study. I wanted to expose threads of understanding between participants, which would not be possible with a solo account for instance. However, my own lived experience (which again might resonate with yours) was that schools are unpredictable, students and teachers' views of them alter and so I decided to collect data over the course of one academic year, in two phases.

Phase 1 of my data collection involved an informal class observation and a semi-structured interview, asking the teachers about students in their class and their beliefs about SEND. Later in the year I returned to the same class and this time filmed a lesson, using this to form the basis of a Stimulated Recall Interview (SRI). SRIs employ video or audio clips of an event to help a participant recollect their thinking and decision making at the time (Calderhead 1981). Watching clips from the filmed lesson, teachers revealed their thinking aloud. One of the D&T teachers noted the 'difficulties with labels' when discussing children formally classified with SEND. In this instance, their thinking aloud related to their lived experience but also resonated with philosophical questions about 'what counts?' (Terzi 2005) as SEND. If you are thinking of using video as a tool to gather data, it did support me to gain insight into teachers' practice. Nonetheless, (in addition to ethical considerations) epistemologically it presents challenges as participants might 'sanitise' (Lyle 2003) their accounts. Therefore, conducting interviews on the same day as the observation and reading others' research on this method is super helpful; Peterson and Clark's (1978) paper is a great place to start.

What epistemological challenges might you face when collecting data?

As a teacher-researcher, it goes without saying that I had a close relationship with the participants. Potentially, this could have skewed what I reported as knowledge generated in the study and may well be something you are looking to mitigate for. Being aware of my possible biases or preferences I learnt did not need to be determined by a rigid framework and I aimed to apply practical wisdom accumulated over time (Brinkmann and Kvale 2015) in school, during the interviews. Using semi-structured interviews can permit you the flexibility to probe participants and as a teacher-researcher your working knowledge of the school means you have an awareness of sensitive issues in your context. I realized this is made possible by being close to the group. This was ratified by my colleagues; the drama teacher, Sarah said watching with me, she could 'pinpoint why exactly I was doing what I was doing'.

If you are concerned though about balancing interest with maintaining distance, Hitchcock and Hughes (1995) provide a really interesting discussion of simultaneous nature of the teacher-researcher role. Wickins and Crossley (2016) explain that distancing might mean taking a physical break from the research or, as Drake (2010) suggests, collaborating with researchers on the outside. I found that having regular meetings with my supervisors (who are Modern Foreign Languages and Mathematics specialists) exposed me to outsiders' perspectives and proved useful in keeping my biases about the value of arts education 'at bay'. For example, the applied and practical nature of the Arts subjects was cited by all teachers as making them inclusive and a way of gaining skills 'you don't get sitting' as the music teacher said about other subjects. As a drama teacher, this did not seem particularly controversial to me; being 'hands on' (Jaquiss and Paterson 2005, p. 14) was suggested as a reason for children facing barriers in learning as an attractive 'alternative'. Yet, in talking with my supervisors we unpicked how this well-intentioned sentiment could be carelessly excluding of children who need to sit down, or who cannot use their hands (see Thompson et al. 2023).

Implications and conclusion

I realized over the years of completing the project that the knowledge I possessed as a researcher meant I had a specialist theoretical knowledge base to focus the SRI. I was able to contextualize the epistemological focus of the data and used this to develop understanding about the chosen topic. Yet being a teacher at the research site afforded me contextual understanding of the students and school culture. As Rushton and King (2020) note about personal experience being akin to the subject studied, I was well positioned to 'draw meaning' (p. 381) from the data and observations.

One outcome of completing the study that surprised me, was how much the teachers gained from taking part. It gave them a chance to speak about their practice in depth and contribute to research; an opportunity rarely afforded to them. Sarah highlighted that watching herself teach 'was not something we get to do, we're too busy' and Alex, one of the Art teachers, said it was a conversation he probably 'wouldn't have been able to have otherwise'. In this way the video acted as an 'artefact' (Hollingsworth and Clarke 2017, p. 462) for the teachers to reflect on their processes in practice. My colleagues were, as Mason (2020) writes, 'sensitised' (p. 1) to knowledge about their practice they had not noticed before. As Alex, said: 'There's a lot of, after eighteen years of teaching, practice that is fully embedded, to the point where I've even forgotten that I do it'. As a small study of six participants, I could not make generalizations about teachers' beliefs, judgements and decisions regarding students with SEND. Nonetheless, findings in my study underlined important ambiguities such as teacher microadaptions in their decision making. As Cochran-Smith and Lytle (1993) reflect, research often makes the role teachers have 'invisible' (p. 7) in the generation of knowledge; research by inside-outside teacher-researchers has the potential to make teachers' voices visible, if, as hopefully this chapter has unpicked, epistemological challenges are fully considered.

Hints and tips

1. Consider and clarify your epistemological position before deciding on your methods as it should underpin your choices.
2. Discuss your work with other scholars who can view your work through a contrasting or alternative lens; their critique and questions will be invaluable!

For getting writing going (these really helped me)

3. If you procrastinate writing, give yourself permission to a 'bad version' which can easily be edited.
4. Set a timer for a short period of time and just keep pen to paper – like you are sitting an exam. Having a tangible text to work with is satisfying as opposed to feeling despair staring at a blank screen.

References

Adler, P. A. and Adler, P. (1987). *Membership roles in field research: Qualitative research methods (Vol. 6)*. Thousand Oaks, CA: SAGE Publications.

Brinkmann, S. and Kvale, S. (2015). *Interviews: Learning the craft of qualitative research interviewing*. 3rd ed. Thousand Oaks, CA: SAGE Publications.

Calderhead, J. (1981). Stimulated recall: A method for research on teaching. *British Journal of Educational Psychology*, 51(2), pp. 211–17.

Cochran-Smith, M. and Lytle, S. L. (1993). *Inside/outside: Teacher research and knowledge*. New York: Teachers College Press.

Corbin-Dwyer, S. and Buckle, J. L. (2009). The space between: On being an insider-outsider in qualitative research. *International Journal of Qualitative Methods*, 8(1), pp. 54–63.

Corno, L. (2008). On teaching adaptively. *Educational Psychologist*, 43(3), pp. 161–73.

Department for Education [DfE]. (2011). *Teachers' standards*. London: Department for Education [online]. Available: https://assets.publishing.service.gov.uk/government/uploads/system/uploads/attachment_data/file/665520/Teachers__Standards.pdf [accessed 13 July 2023].

DfE/DHSC. (2015). *SEND code of practice*. London: Department for Education [online]. Available: https://assets.publishing.service.gov.uk/government/uploads/system/uploads/attachment_data/file/398815/SEND_Code_of_Practice_January_2015.pdf [accessed 13 July 2023].

Drake, P. (2010). Grasping at methodological understanding: A cautionary tale from insider research. *International Journal of Research & Method in Education*, 33(1), pp. 85–99.

Dukes, S. (1984). Phenomenological methodology in the human sciences. *Journal of Religion and Health*, 23(3), pp. 197–203.

Gingell, J. and Winch, C. (1999). *Philosophy of education: The key concepts.* Oxon: Routledge.

Gov.uk. (2019). *Find and compare schools* [online]. Available: https://www.gov.uk/school-performance-tables [accessed 13 July 2023].

Harpur, P. (2012). Embracing the new disability rights paradigm: The importance of the convention on the rights of persons with disabilities. *Disability and Society*, 27(1), pp. 1–14.

Harwood, V. and McHahon, S. (2013). Medicalization schools. In: Florian, L. (ed.), *The SAGE handbook of special education: Volume 1.* 2nd ed. Thousand Oaks, CA: SAGE Publications, pp. 915–30.

Hitchcock, G. and Hughes, D. (1995). *Research and the teacher: A qualitative introduction to school-based research.* London: Routledge.

Hollingsworth, H. and Clarke, D. (2017). Video as a tool for focusing teacher self-reflection: Supporting and provoking teacher learning. *Journal of Mathematics Teacher Education,* 20(5), pp. 457–75.

Hollis, M. (1994). *The philosophy of social science: An introduction.* Cambridge: Cambridge University Press.

House of Commons Education Committee. (2019).*Special educational needs and disability: First report of session 2019*[online]. Available: https://publications.parliament.uk/pa/cm201919/cmselect/cmeduc/20/20.pdf [accessed 13 July 2023].

Hume, D. (1985). *A treatise of human nature.* London: Penguin Books.

Jaquiss, V. and Paterson, D. (2005). *Meeting SEN in the curriculum: Music.* London: David Fulton Publishers.

Korthagen, F. A. J. (2014). Promoting core reflection in teacher education: Deepening professional growth. In: Orland-Barak, L. and Craig, C. J. (eds), *International teacher education: Promising pedagogies (Part A).* Bingley: Emerald Group Publishing Limited, pp. 73–89.

Kuhn T. S. (2012). *The structure of scientific revolutions.* Chicago: Chicago University Press.

Lyle, J. (2003). Stimulated recall: A report on its use in naturalistic research.*British Educational Research Journal*, 29(6), pp. 861–78.

Mason, J. (2020). Learning about noticing, by, and through noticing. *Mathematics Education*, 53, pp. 231–43.

Mazenod, A., Francis, B., Archer, L., Hodgen, J., Taylor, B., Tereshchenko, A., and Pepper, D. (2019). Nurturing learning or encouraging dependency? Teacher constructions of students in lower attainment groups in English secondary schools. *Cambridge Journal of Education*, 49(1), pp. 53–68.

McNess, E., Arthur, L., and Crossley, M. (2016). 'Ethnographic dazzle' and the construction of the 'other': Shifting boundaries between the insider and the outsider. In: Crossley, M., Arthur, L., and McNess,

E. (eds), *Revisiting insider-outsider research in comparative and international education*. Oxford: Symposium Books Ltd, pp. 21–38.

Mitra, S. (2018). *Disability, health, and human development*. New York: Palgrave Macmillan.

Oliver, M. (2013). The social model of disability: Thirty years on. *Disability and society*, 28(7), pp. 1024–6.

Okasha, S. (2002). *Philosophy of science: A very short introduction (Vol. 67)*. Oxford: Oxford Paperbacks.

Patton, M. Q. (2002). Two decades of developments in qualitative inquiry: A personal, experiential perspective. *Qualitative Social Work*, 1(3), pp. 261–83.

Peterson, P. L. and Clark, C. M. (1978). Teachers' reports of their cognitive processes during teaching. *American Educational Research Journal*, 15(4), pp. 555–65.

Pfadenhauer, M. and Knoblauch, H. (eds.) (2018). *Social constructivism as paradigm?: The legacy of the social construction of reality*. Oxon: Routledge.

Rushton, E. A. and King, H. (2020). Play as a pedagogical vehicle for supporting gender inclusive engagement in informal STEM education.*International Journal of Science Education*, 10(4), pp. 376–89.

Ryle, G. (2009). *The concept of mind*. Oxon: Routledge.

Shavelson, R. J. and Stern, P. (1981). Research on teachers' pedagogical thoughts, judgments, decisions, and behavior. *Review of Educational Research*, 51(4), pp. 455–98.

Tambling, P. and Bacon, S. (2023). *The arts in schools: Foundations for the future* [online]. Calouste Gulbenkian Foundation. Available: https://www.anewdirection.org.uk/the-arts-in-schools [accessed 13 July 2023].

Terzi, L. (2005). Beyond the dilemma of difference: The capability approach to disability and special educational needs. *Journal of Philosophy of Education*, 39(3), pp. 443–59.

Thomson, P., Hall, C., Jones, K., and Green, J. S. (2012). *The signature pedagogies project* [online]. The University of Nottingham. Available: https://www.creativitycultureeducation.org/wp-content/uploads/2018/10/Signature_Pedagogies_Final_Report_April_2012.pdf [accessed 13 July 2023].

Thompson, B. (2021). *Towards a view of Inclusion: Arts teachers' beliefs, judgements and decisions concerning students with SEND*. (EdD) Thesis [online]. King's College London. Available: https://ethos.bl.uk/OrderDetails.do?uin=uk.bl.ethos.853762 [accessed 13 July 2023].

Thompson, B., Finesilver, C., and Jones, J. (2023). An exploration of arts teachers' beliefs and judgements concerning students with SEND. *Support for Learning*, 38(12), pp. 83–97.

Toom, A. (2006). *Tacit pedagogical knowing: At the core of teacher's professionality*. Doctoral dissertation [online]. University of Helsinki. Available: https://helda.helsinki.fi/handle/10138/19996 [accessed 13 July 2023].

Van Manen, M. (2016). *Researching lived experience*. Oxon: Routledge.

Wickins, E. and Crossley, M. (2016). Coming alongside in the co-construction of professional knowledge: A fluid approach to researcher positioning on the insider-outsider continuum. In: Crossley, M., Arthur, L., and McNess, L. E. (eds), *Revisiting insider-outsider research in comparative and international education*. Oxford: Symposium Books Ltd, pp. 225–40.

Winch, C., Oancea, A., and Orchard, J. (2015). The contribution of educational research to teachers' professional learning: Philosophical understandings. *Oxford Review of Education,* 41(2), pp. 202–16.

CHAPTER 4

How to Navigate Ontology and Epistemology to Develop a Conceptual Framework?

Marc Turu Porcel

Research philosophy seems to be one of the main challenges for new researchers, especially issues relating to ontology, epistemology and conceptual frameworks. Using my PhD thesis as a case study, this chapter explores ontological and epistemological dimensions and their links to the development of a conceptual framework. First, the context of the case study is presented, including the rationale behind the research. Second, the lessons learnt on ontology and epistemology and how the philosophical underpinnings of my research were established are discussed. Third, the steps I took in the development of the conceptual framework and its links to ontology and epistemology are examined. Then the rationale behind the choice of research methods and analysis is reviewed. Last, the links between ontology and epistemology and research findings are considered.

Getting into teaching: Early career teachers in England

As a Catalan primary school teacher, I found initial teacher training (ITT) in England baffling. England has a fragmented teacher training system with several diverse and contrasting routes to get into teaching: Bachelor's degrees, Postgraduate Certificates in Education, School Direct, School-Centered Initial Teacher Training, Teach first, Now Teach, Straight to teaching and Assessment only. I could not comprehend how some teachers only needed to complete a few weeks of training in a school whilst others had to complete four years at university. Since the 1990s, successive English governments have pushed towards a shift in ITT whereby schools would have more control over teacher training because it was claimed that teachers needed to train in the classroom instead of lecture theatres.

As former Secretary of State for Education, Michael Gove (2013) said 'the best teacher training is led by teachers [. . .] the classroom is the best place for teachers to learn as well as to teach'. Since I had always been interested in teacher education and professional development, I was curious about the legitimacy of Gove's claim and my first plan was to look into the impact of the different routes on teacher preparedness. Early on in my research, I engaged with the work of Winch et al. (2015) on teachers' professional knowledge, Biesta (2013) on the moral dimension of teaching, Evans (2011) on teachers' professionalism and Turner-Bisset (2001) on knowledge bases for teaching to conceptualize teacher preparedness. However, I quickly faced challenges that would reshape my research.

Ontological and epistemological dilemmas

Considering the ontology and epistemology of the research is a critical step as it sets the field for choosing the research design, data collection methods and data analysis. As Guba (1990, p. 17) highlighted, they are the 'basic set of beliefs that guide action'. In simple terms, ontology is the set of ideas about the nature of reality, and what we can know about the world (Mayan 2023). In other words, ontology is concerned about the kinds of things that exist and the nature of the things being investigated. Within this understanding of ontology, one finds a spectrum of possibilities, ranging from considering the world as an external objective reality independent of people's awareness (realism) to considering the world as a social construct built upon the people's perceptions and subjectivity (relativism). Whilst ontology is concerned about the nature of reality and knowledge, epistemology is the set of ideas about knowledge and how to acquire it (Mayan 2023). One extreme of the epistemological spectrum views knowledge as objective (positivism) whilst the other extreme's perspective is that knowledge is constructed by people and therefore mediated by human subjectivity (constructivism).

When I submitted the proposal for my PhD research, I embraced a positivistic stance. At first, I wanted to explore the effectiveness the different routes into teaching had on teacher preparedness. I believed I would be able to observe and measure teacher preparedness independently of human subjectivity and find causal relationships. However, this was a problematic position because not only had I assumed there was a grand narrative on teacher preparedness independent of people's perceptions but also that it was possible to capture teacher's quality objectively. But how can a student-teacher assess the quality of their training if they have only experienced one? How can we compare mentors' judgement on teachers' preparedness when their understanding of teaching differs?

Student teachers can report about their own preparedness; however, the validity of self-reported data remains contentious. There is research that suggests that perceptions and practice can be correlated (Klassen and Tze 2014). Others suggest that what teachers perceive they can do and what they actually do does not always match (Debnam et al. 2015). Student- teachers only experience one teacher training programme and therefore the data would only capture their perceptions of preparedness and not the impact on preparedness. Another way of assessing teacher preparedness is by capturing the judgement of a more experienced teacher or mentor. However, professional judgement is highly subjective and since different experienced teachers would assess different student teachers, there would also be issues with the validity and reliability of the data.

Reflecting on the underpinning ideas of my research, I came to the realization that teacher preparedness was ontologically subjective and mediated by human understanding, which can be captured by accessing the observers' perceptions (epistemology). This means that any measure of teacher preparedness will always be constructed upon a particular perspective and any attempt to objectively compare the effectiveness of different training routes would be conceptually flawed. Given my new more refined ontological and epistemological understanding of teacher preparedness, I decided to shift the focus on my study from the impact on preparedness to how new teachers are being judged and the different conceptualizations of what preparedness is. Independent of the teacher training route, all early career teachers (ECTs) must complete and pass their first two years of teaching to be fully qualified. During this time, ECTs are mentored by an experienced teacher who also assesses their preparedness. Although all new teachers are meant to be assessed against the English Teacher Standards (DfE 2011), it is the mentors' interpretation of the standards that is used to judge new teachers. Therefore, mentors are in a privileged and powerful position to decide who qualifies as a teacher and what new teachers need to know and do. For this reason, it seems increasingly important to understand how mentors conceptualize preparedness and to explore how they understand teaching and the teachers' role. Although there is a considerable body of research on teachers' perspectives on teaching, why mentors had those perspectives was an underexplored field. For this reason, I decided to focus on how mentors constructed their understanding of teaching and preparedness to teach, in particular, the ideas, assumptions and biases they use. The findings of this research could inform and develop more robust mentoring approaches in schools, identifying not only what ideas and practices are shared and encouraged among ECTs, but also recognizing those ideas and practices that are ignored.

From deciding on a worldview to developing a conceptual framework

Once the underpinning ontological and epistemological ideas about the nature of what I wanted to research (teacher preparedness) were developed, next in turn was refining the conceptual framework. For the purposes of this chapter, a conceptual framework is understood as presenting a theory of the phenomenon under investigation (Maxwell 2013). In other words, based on the set ontology and epistemology, what concepts and theories will be used to explore the object of the research? Sometimes, it is useful to imagine the conceptual framework as a *pair of lenses* that the researcher puts on and allows them to *see* what they are researching in a particular light. Is there a right conceptual framework? Yes and no. It all depends on the research aims and questions. Different *lenses*, conceptual frameworks, will allow researchers to see different things and therefore reaching different findings. However, different concepts and theories embrace different assumptions about the nature of reality and the way of accessing it, and therefore, it is critically important that they are aligned with your ontology and epistemology. Since you might explore and consider several theories and concepts during your study, it is important to think about the research questions as a living organism that can be refined and developed depending on the theories and concepts that are considered more interesting and useful. Although, the overall aim of the research might remain the same, the precise wording of the research questions is likely to evolve over time.

As mentioned previously, my overall research aim was to understand how mentors conceptualized teacher preparedness. Different concepts and theories were explored such as social judgement theory (e.g. O'Keefe 2015), organizational theory (e.g. Mullins 2008) and ecological systems (e.g. Chandler et al. 2011). However, the concept of discourse seemed to be a more interesting and useful lens to frame my study and it seemed to be coherent with the ontology and epistemology of the research. Teacher-mentors are subject to discourse(s) about teaching and learning that shape what they can think of and what is unthinkable (Burr 2015). In other words, discourse(s) acts as a lens, a system of representation, which mentors use to understand teaching and learning, and allows them to see and judge what they see. At the most basic level, discourse(s) is language in use. However, as Gee (2011, p. 28) explains, discourse also incorporates 'other stuff that is not language', such as assumptions, metaphors and conventions. For example, words such as accountability, performativity and free market are part of neoliberal discourse (Ambrosio 2013) and become a specific way of seeing the world. People draw from the discourse(s) available to talk about, comprehend and give meaning to their contexts. According to this particular understanding of discourse, at any given period in time and context, people can think, talk or write about objects and social events only in limited and specific ways and not others, using pre-existing linguistic resources. Within this conceptualization, discourse becomes a framework for thinking. Some discourse(s) become dominant and establish what is socially acceptable and common sense whilst other discourse(s) are marginalized and not even considered a reasonable option (Pitsoe and Letseka 2013).

At this point, the research questions for my research were refined to the following:

- How do mentors construct teacher preparedness?
- How does discourse shape mentors understanding of teacher preparedness?
- What do mentors value and ignore when constructing teacher preparedness?

Once I decided to use discourse analysis (DA) as the overarching framework for my research, I faced the challenge that there are different conceptual understandings, or branches, of DA including conversation analysis, critical discourse analysis (CDA) (e.g. Fairclough 2013) and discursive psychology to name a few. So, how do we choose? Recently, CDA has gained popularity and more and more research has been conducted through this critical lens. I briefly considered CDA for my research but its focus on power and the reproduction of social dominance made me reject it because I was more interested in exploring mentors' discourse(s) than their causes and consequences. My conceptual framework developed in a different direction and it was heavily influenced by the work of Foucault (2002) and Gee (2011) who both share the starting point that our ways of talking do not neutrally reflect our world, identities and social relations but, rather, play an active role in creating and changing them (see that this understanding is aligned with my ontology and epistemology). In particular, I drew from discursive psychology (Potter and Wetherell 2001) because it allows us to investigate how people use the available discourses in producing and negotiating understandings of their realities and identities through language. This would allow me to map the discourse(s) mentors' draw from when talking about teaching and

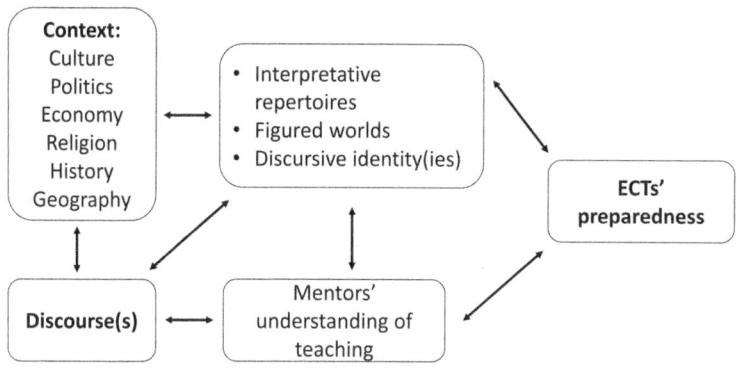

FIGURE 4.1 *Basic conceptual framework.*

teacher preparedness. For example, one of the concepts I used in my research was *interpretative repertoires*:

> Repertoires can be seen as the building blocks speakers use for constructing versions of actions, cognitive processes and other phenomena. Any particular repertoire is constituted out of a restricted range of terms used in a specific stylistic and grammatical fashion. (Potter and Wetherell 1988, p. 172)

The concept of interpretative repertoires is aligned with the research ontology and epistemology and allowed me the *see* what I was looking for in the data. It is sometimes useful to draw your conceptual framework as a net of relationships. This will allow you to clarify your concepts and theories and how they relate to each other and to the object of your research. Figure 4.1 shows a basic version of my conceptual framework (for a detailed discussion on constructing conceptual frameworks, I recommend Van der Waldt (2020)).

Choosing your research methods

As mentioned earlier, ontology and epistemology are a set of ideas that guide action, and therefore will also influence the choice of research methods. All research methods have strengths and limitations, and choosing them will depend on, among other things, their alignment with the research's ontological and epistemological assumptions. For example, at the start of my research I designed a methodology that involved questionnaires and interviews. Interviews aligned well with the ontological and epistemological assumptions of my research as I would access the participants ideas and perceptions about teacher preparedness from their own perspectives and they would have freedom to elaborate their answers. I initially considered gathering data from naturally occurring conversations between mentors and newly qualified teachers because they seemed more real and contextualized. However, over time, I realized that these conversations are often unplanned and unscripted which would complicate the recording of data but also the focus of it. I finally decided to use semi-structured interviews (Cohen et al. 2011) because I could control the environment and the topics to discuss, but at the same time it allowed me to explore the ideas underpinning mentors' understandings of teaching. The rationale behind the semi-structured interviews was to let participants expand and elaborate responses, but also to give the interviewer room to explore areas that come up during interviews. The design of the interview guide followed the basic idea that the interview should be a conversation within the limits of the research topic. For this reason, all questions were open-ended in order to provide a framework of reference for participants, but without restraining the answers and the way they could express themselves (Cohen et al. 2011). The interview guide was designed as a 'living' document, setting the structure of the topics to cover, but allowing the interviewer to change the wording of the questions, arrange the themes in different order and add new questions during and after the interview if a topic seemed worth further exploration. Therefore, in most interviews the guide was used as an aide-memoire of the areas to explore while connecting with the participants' answers.

Although the use of semi-structured interviews seemed a good way to capture the participants' perceptions, the use of questionnaires became problematic. Questionnaires tend to be closed tools that use multiple choice, Likert scales and ranking questions (Cohen et al. 2011). What was more problematic for my research was the fact that questionnaires assume that all participants read and understand the questions the same way and that their answers (e.g. agree/disagree, or numbers) mean the same to all participants. These assumptions clash with the research's ontology and epistemology, and the assumption that different people will perceive and understand reality (in this case the questionnaire) in different personal ways. For this reason, I could not trust the answers given in the questionnaire, but I still decided to use it but with a different purpose. First, it was a way of recruiting participants for the follow-up face-to-face interviews when the questionnaire was distributed through social media and mailing lists. Second, the participants' answers would be the starting point of the interviews in which the reasons behind their choices would be explored in more detail. In the end, the data gathered from questionnaires was not directly used in my thesis, only when it was discussed during interviews.

Considering ontology and epistemology in your findings: Discovery vs. production

One of the major challenges research projects within an interpretivist paradigm face is the subjectivity of its findings (Mayan 2023). Then, how do we make sure that our findings are reliable? There are several options to strengthen the data analysis, but sometimes zooming out from the fine details of your data and thinking about the underpinning ideas of your research will bring clarity and security to your arguments. The question I asked myself was, how do ontology and epistemology understand findings? In my research, ontology and epistemology were clear. Although there is a real physical world out there, our understanding of it, how we make sense of it is always mediated by our values, opinions, biases and the current discourses available to us. For this reason, findings are not discovered as if they were independent of our minds, but they are produced by us, the researchers. Although, this realization was unsettling at first because I wanted certainty and find 'truths', it eventually was a relief. My job was not to uncover a universal 'truth', but to interpret how my participants interpreted their world. Once I understood this, I had to find a way to analyse and produce findings that were reliable and traceable.

In order to do DA, I had to analyse beyond the face value of the text and think about the underlying assumptions mentors made, the perspectives they bring into the conversation and the worldviews they use. One of my main concerns was to prevent my biases from *finding* what I expected to find in my data. Sharing my analysis with colleagues allowed me to keep my biases in check and my research becoming more reliable. In a nutshell, my research findings suggests that mentors constructed preparedness to teach using predominantly three discourses: *Instrumentalist, managerial and research* (see a more detailed discussion in Lofthouse and Turu 2022). The discourse about preparedness to teach is not made up of one discourse, but it is the use of these three discourses (instrumentalist, managerial and research) that builds the construct of *preparedness to teach*. In order to justify these findings and minimize claims of subjectivity, I decided to produce a highly detailed findings chapter in which a step-by-step analysis was presented. I presented the unaltered data including my questions and the participants' whole answer. Although this made the writing of the analysis and findings considerably longer, it allowed the reader scrutiny over my analysis and interpretation of the data and as well as allowing them to judge the validity of my findings.

Conclusion

Navigating ontology, epistemology and developing conceptual frameworks is hard but it stands at the heart of social research. As Alvesson (2002, p. 91) brilliantly put it:

> A particular important element in critical research is to avoid seeing the social world as self-evident and familiar [. . .] Research then becomes a matter of defamiliarization, of observing and interpreting social phenomena in novel ways compared to cultural dominant categories and distinctions.

Questioning one's own assumptions and not rigidly positioning researchers within well-defined categories is critical to develop worthwhile research. Having doubts about where my research sat ontologically and epistemologically allowed me to explore different world views and potential areas of inquiry. In my case, one of the hardest parts of the journey, but also the most freeing one, was the realization that it was not about who I was as a researcher or my personal views, but what was best for the research, the participants and to make a meaningful contribution.

Tips for new researchers

- Engage with research philosophy. Do not be afraid of exploring different ontologies, epistemologies and research designs even if they seem irrelevant for your research.
- Read those who challenge your perspectives; they can only enrich your knowledge.
- Grab a coffee with other doctoral students, researchers and academics. A PhD study can sometimes feel very lonely. Most people will be interested in what you are doing, and they might offer their perspective and insight.
- Do not be afraid of sharing your concerns and challenges with your supervisory team. You are at the start of your research career; you are not expected to be an effective and independent researcher. Even the most experienced professors and researchers have all been there at some point or another.

References

Alvesson, M. (2002). *Postmodernism and social research*. Buckingham: Open University Press.
Ambrosio, J. (2013). Changing the subject: Neoliberalism and accountability in public education. *Educational Studies*, 49(4), pp. 316–33.
Biesta, J. (2013). *The beautiful risk of education*. London: Paradigm Publishers.
Burr, V. (2015). *Social constructionism*. 3rd ed. Hove: Routledge.
Chandler, D. E., Kram, K. E., and Yip, J. (2011). An ecological systems perspective on mentoring at work: A review and future prospects. *The Academy of Management Annals*, 5(1), pp. 519–70.
Cohen, L., Manion, L., and Morrison, K. (2011). *Research methods in education*. 7th ed. Abingdon: Routledge.

Debnam, K. J., Pas, E. T., Bottiani, J., Cash, A. H., and Bradshaw, C. P. (2015). An examination of the association between observed and self-reported culturally proficient teaching practices. *Psychology in the Schools,* 52(6), pp. 533–48.

Department for Education [DfE]. (2011). *Teachers' standards.* Available: https://www.gov.uk/government/publications/teachers-standards [accessed 1 June 2023].

Evans, L. (2011). The 'shape' of teacher professionalism in England: Professional standards, performance management, professional development and the changes proposed in the 2010 white paper. *British Educational Research Journal,* 37(5), pp. 851–70.

Fairclough, N. (2013). *Critical discourse analysis: The critical study of language.* Abingdon: Routledge.

Foucault, M. (2002). *The archaeology of knowledge.* Sheridan Smith, A. M. trans. Abingdon: Routledge Classics.

Gee, J. P. (2011). *An introduction to discourse analysis: Theory and method.* 3rd ed. New York: Routledge.

Gove, M. (2013). *Michael Gove speaks about the importance of teaching* [online]. Available: https://www.gov.uk/government/speeches/michael-gove-speaks-about-the-importance-of-teaching [accessed 1 June 2023].

Guba, E. (1990). *The paradigm dialog.* Newbury Park: SAGE Publications.

Klassen, R. M. and Tze, V. M. (2014). Teachers' self-efficacy, personality, and teaching effectiveness: A meta-analysis. *Educational Research Review,* 12, pp. 59–76.

Lofthouse, R. and Turu, M. (2022). Enabling and sustaining early career learning through coaching and mentoring. In: Ovenden-Hope, T. (ed.), *The early career framework: Origins, outcomes, and opportunities.* Melton: John Catt Educational, pp. 275–91.

Maxwell, J. A. (2013). *Qualitative research design: An interactive approach.* Thousand Oaks: SAGE Publications.

Mayan, M. J. (2023). *Essentials of qualitative inquiry.* New York: Routledge.

Mullins, L. J. (2008). *Essentials of organisational behaviour.* Essex: Pearson Education.

O'Keefe, D. J. (2015). *Persuasion: Theory and research.* Thousand Oaks: SAGE Publications.

Pitsoe, V. and Letseka, M. (2013). Foucault's discourse and power: Implications for instructionist classroom management. *Open Journal of Philosophy,* 3(01), pp. 23–8.

Potter, J. and Wetherell, M. (1988). Discourse analysis and the identification of interpretative repertoires. In: Antaki, C. -(ed.), *Analysing everyday explanation: A casebook of methods.* London: SAGE Publications, pp. 168–83.

Potter, J. and Wetherell, M. (2001). Unfolding discourse analysis. In: Wetherell, M., Taylor, S.-, and Yates, S. J., (eds), *Discourse theory and practice*. London: SAGE Publications, pp. 198–209.

Turner-Bisset, R. (2001). *Expert teaching: Knowledge and pedagogy to lead the profession*. Abingdon: David Fulton.

Van der Waldt, G. (2020). Constructing conceptual frameworks in social science research. *TD: The Journal for Transdisciplinary Research in Southern Africa*, 16(1), pp. 1–9.

Winch, C., Oancea, A., and Orchard, J. (2015). The contribution of educational research to teachers' professional learning: Philosophical understandings. *Oxford Review of Education*, 41(2), pp. 202–16.

CHAPTER 5

How Can the Lens of Cultural-Historical Activity Theory (CHAT) Help Conceptualization?

Ciara Molloy

Writing retrospectively about my research, I realized how the journey from topic to research grounded in theory was a significant one. As a primary school teacher embarking on a Master of Education, I was very much an experienced practitioner but a novice academic. My enthusiasm abounded for all things school related, but from a practitioner standpoint and with perhaps a more concrete than conceptual lens. As a teacher, I am acutely aware of how prior knowledge connects to how we process new information. Yet in this instance, my prior knowledge of the world of academic theory and philosophical stances was scant. This world was new and foreign; I had no clear map. I also felt like an imposter during early tutorials looking in on this curious world with the eyes of an outsider. My peers seemed to have a better sense of this material or perhaps were merely better actors than me. I admit that I was deeply submerged in my research journey before I was cognizant of that which would become the backbone of my research study.

The primary focus of this chapter is the journey involved in the unveiling of Cultural- Historical Activity Theory (CHAT) as the cornerstone of my research. The chapter documents the arduous trek I took, which ultimately led me to select and employ this as my chosen theoretical framework. I will attest to how I grappled with the jargon and terminology pertaining to the philosophical foundations of research and how, through intense self-reflection, I uncovered who I was as a researcher. I will endeavour to untangle CHAT for the reader in the context of my own research study and present it in simple terms. I will highlight how it has been used in other varied research studies demonstrating its pliability and versatility as a theoretical lens. I will discuss how having this conceptual framework provided me with the map I needed to conduct a robust research study and elevate my study from novice and inconsequential to legitimate and rigorous. I will explore how all my methodological decisions were influenced by CHAT, and how it was all-encompassing and influenced each sphere of my research.

Contemplating my topic

This research topic emerged from my professional experiences after the Covid-19 pandemic as a teacher in an Irish Primary school and as their appointed Information and Communications Technology (ICT) coordinator. This period revealed the many fragilities of our education system, laying bare many deficits in schools' digital capabilities. Given that no discrete time was afforded to me for the ICT coordinator role, it had always been a personal challenge to balance my time between the two roles. This period, however, truly accentuated how the role had gained excessive weight, both in terms of time and technical skills needed for a competent execution of the role. Most striking was how augmentations in digital infrastructure, and the explosion of digital teaching tools had increased expectations from school stakeholders, as to what could be achieved by the role holder. Covid-19 enforced a fast tracking of digital transformation in schools and leading the expedition was the ICT coordinator.

My experience of how overwhelming the dual roles had become, led to the diagnosis of a significant problem within my school context; a problem that I sensed could be generalizable across other schools. If I collated the experiences of teacher colleagues in other schools who were simultaneously completing the two roles, what commonalities and differences would I find? My personal ruminations began to take shape and what emerged was a deep dive into the role of the ICT coordinator in Irish Primary Schools. The study would be centred on the premise that the expectations and priorities of the role needed to be clarified in order to create effective and functional digital leadership in schools.

Which direction to go?

I was drawn to a more qualitative flavour of research for this topic, as I felt that the data I would gather would be based on human experience, often noted as powerful and sometimes more compelling than quantitative data (Anderson 2010). My professional experience told me that my research sample would have rich and varied insights into the topic. These perspectives of feelings, thoughts, opinions and experiences were what I sought. On the surface, what I wished to discover was how these appointed teachers found space during their teaching day to attend to the multitude of school ICT issues. Did they have the requisite skills to tackle technical issues along with a vision for pedagogical digital integration? What was their experience of the role during the periods of remote learning? The more I reflected on my research topic, the more I came to the realization that I was attempting to reveal those invisible organizational structures, relationships and routines within schools which were heavily influencing the role. I wished to dig under the organization's surface to reveal the dominant culture, relationships and routines, and unearth how these interdependent variables were largely unseen yet were heavily influential on how this role was being executed. Given how the literature concurs that the role of ICT coordinator has many iterations and has been identified as ambiguous, I acknowledge that the initial research study topic was unfocused and had too many possible angles. This disorder required a sorting mechanism to order the chaos. What was required was established theory to render it into a credible study. Ultimately what emerged was my discovery of Cultural-Historical Activity Theory (CHAT), whose application transformed my study.

So, what is CHAT and why did I select it as a framework?

Cultural-Historical Activity Theory (CHAT), more succinctly known as CHAT, is a theoretical framework that has its origins with Vygotsky (1978) and Leont'ev (1978) but has been contributed to by a number of theorists, most recently Engeström (1999). This theory explains how *activities* in organizations operate in relation to the local rules, community and division of labour. These activities are influenced heavily by their cultural and historical contexts. CHAT has been developed as an analytical tool, as its purpose is to promote changes in activity systems (Engeström et al. 1999). The CHAT framework guided my study by documenting and describing the activity system of the ICT coordinator. It identified the contextual conditions and the rules, community and division of labour of the environment where the role holder was performing their assigned functions. It acted as a clarifying instrument for defining and interpreting commonalities and differences in thoughts, values and actions among participants. It put order to the chaos of a large disparate dataset by providing a clear framework to view and interrogate this complex role and to examine the variables influencing perceived technology successes and failures within schools. This was the theory that I chose, although its discovery was not without obstacles. Many robust theories were considered and then sidelined, as they did not fully encompass the parameters of my study.

Introspection to define my research identity

In recollecting my research journey, I acknowledge how my naivety as an early researcher led me to initially prioritize methods and methodology as the building blocks of my study. Owing to the complexity and more conceptual nature of these elusive philosophical foundations, I admit I gave them less consideration than methods in the early stages of designing the research study. Paradigms and philosophical foundations were just terminologies that I didn't fully understand. My mindset was reshaped when I encountered a simple analogy that forced me to rethink my research strategy and ethos. An image of an ice float, (presented in DeCarlo et al. 2021) represented methods as merely the tip of the iceberg. Below the water came methodology and anchoring the iceberg was theory and then philosophical foundations. This clearly explained to me how the deeper you get, the more you can holistically explore your research topic, leading to a higher-quality inquiry. Thus, I needed to discover what my research ethos was. What were my principles, my ethical values, beliefs that shaped how I understood and saw the world? These intangible and intrinsic elements of me as a researcher would subconsciously but acutely influence my research decisions within the study.

Undeterred by the boundaries of my master's programme and its cursory emphasis on philosophical stances and theoretical underpinnings, I took the opportunity to engage in self-reflection to pursue an understanding of philosophies and how they informed the whole research process and to discover who I was as a researcher. The more I read the more I understood that to give my inquiry sufficient depth and direction, I must identify my view of reality (ontology) and my view of knowledge (epistemology). Marsh and Furlong (2002, p. 17) comment on how researchers must try on a lot of theories and philosophies before finding one that fits. They noted how these positions are more like a 'skin than a sweater, they cannot be taken off when the researcher sees fit'. This revealed the innate nature of these views and how contemplating my inner values and core truths was central to the direction that my study would take.

To make sense of my philosophical stance I needed to seek truths about myself and my belief system. I used my 'role as a teacher' as the stimulus to reflect upon and find answers. Teaching is not just my job but a state of mind which permeates all aspects of my life. Teaching offers so many avenues to reflect on and thus provides the ideal mode to consider one's philosophical standpoint. Ultimately, my view of the world has shaped my orientation as a teacher and, reciprocally, my work as a teacher has shaped my view of the world. My values and identity within both professional and personal domains in my life are inextricably linked. I view the world as one of unlimited possibilities, where personal action precedes change. I am action-driven and adaptable. I am open to new knowledge which I will explore and critically assess before accepting or discarding it, and this will shape my future action. I will always consider alternatives and take risks to find the best solution for each situation. Based on this lengthy and in-depth self-reflection, I established very clearly that the fundamental principles of pragmatism resonated with me and seemed to align with my own principles (Tashakkori and Teddlie 2010). Simplistically, I rationalized my understanding by attaching myself to the word 'pragmatic' which paralleled my routine approach to the world.

Pragmatic research unleashed

Armed with a newfound conscious knowledge of my belief system, I embarked on intense reading to verify my initial leanings. Several points resonated with me and strengthened my stance as a pragmatic researcher. I noted how 'pragmatists believe that reality is not static—it changes at every turn of events' (Kaushik and Walsh 2019, p. 3); a point which corresponds with my disposition towards trying new things and thus extending my reality. As a teacher, I see the classroom as a laboratory of possibility where I use experimental strategies for different learning purposes. Pragmatism is based on the proposition that researchers should use the philosophical and methodological approach that works best for the particular research problem being investigated (Tashakkori and Teddlie 2010), based on their worldview. These key principles of pragmatism fitted well with both my own assumptions and the overall aim of the research, which examined the varying contexts, experiences and activities of the specific population of school ICT coordinators. Creswell (2013, p. 13) identified how 'a close tie exists between the philosophy that one brings to the research act and how one proceeds to use a framework to shroud his or her inquiry'. Pragmatism embraces a plurality of methods (Kaushik and Walsh 2019) and is thus regarded as the philosophical partner of the mixed-methods approach (Denscombe 2017, p. 148). The focus is on the problem in its social and historical context rather than on the method, with multiple relevant forms of data collection used to answer the research questions (Creswell and Creswell 2017). With this in mind, and for me to capitalize on my access to a large number of participants, it made sense to adopt a mixed-methods approach for this study.

Evans et al. (2011) advise using a theoretical framework for mixed-methods research. They suggest that it provides a map for 'combining the what with the why in gaining a multidimensional understanding of causal mechanisms' (Evans et al. 2011, p. 278). The theory I sought needed to expose these causal mechanisms and explain the myriad of factors contributing to the workload of the ICT coordinator, the variables influencing how the role was executed, and the changes for effective fulfilment of the role. My conceptual framework needed to analyse these phenomena from a micro level, providing a more detailed understanding of the ambiguities within the role of ICT coordinator. The theory had to apply to a non-linear and non-systematic situation as the context of each research participant differed. This theory must assist in the handling and sorting of my large and disparate data set, to identify commonalities, patterns and emergent behaviours. Overall, I hoped that the theory would help to identify opportunities for improvement and change to the role of ICT coordinator.

So, I identified myself as a pragmatic researcher. I had chosen what I felt was an apt methodology, but that was just the starting point. I still did not have a theory to anchor my study and bring all the stems together. To earn my badge as a pragmatic researcher, I had to embody the beliefs and principles of pragmatism. This meant I needed to consider and discard a medley of theory options before choosing the most appropriate one to scaffold my research problem.

Seeking a conceptual framework: The holy grail of research

The terms 'conceptual', 'theoretical' and 'framework' were often used interchangeably in the literature, which compounded my considerable confusion as to what I was seeking. LeCompte et al. (1993, p. 239) stated that 'theorising is simply the cognitive process of discovering or manipulating abstract categories and the relationships among these categories'. I question their use of the word 'simply' and liken the journey towards theory enlightenment to when one engages in those picture puzzles that reveal a part of an image. By solving a piece, new knowledge is revealed. When each piece has been revealed you finally see the entire image, and it makes complete sense, but without all the information together, it is abstract and perplexing. Building my conceptual framework happened at a glacial pace. A landmark moment for me was reading an article by Osanloo and Grant (2014). This article informally explained how theoretical frameworks had the same function in research as blueprints play in the building of a house, and how it was the foundation from which all knowledge within a research study is constructed. These powerful analogies further communicated how imperative it was to ground my research in theory, as I knew I would never build a house without blueprints!

Reading with new eyes

I regularly went down the rabbit hole of reading, trawling through abstracts seeking appropriate theory, with no clear destination and not necessarily bound for wonderland! Although laborious, it granted me access to many theoretical frameworks in different disciplines which I noted as possible contenders. I began to read with antennae for spotting how authors had threaded their framework through the study. I encountered studies that lacked an explicit framework and how others combined frameworks, to encapsulate all variables of their study. Early iterations of my research questions sought to explain the functions of the ICT coordinator and the desired changes participants wished to realize within their role. Thus, I knew what I wished to reveal on a practical level, but these questions needed strengthening by being scaffolded by established theory. Matching theory to my study involved much second guessing and proved a highly abstract and thought-provoking process. Of relief to me was the discovery that in a qualitative study, one does not necessarily begin with a theory to test or verify. Instead, consistent with the inductive model of thinking, a theory may emerge during later phases, 'shaped by the researcher's experience in collecting and analysing the data' (Creswell 2013, p. 22). My experience coincided with this point, as my survey data (gathered pre-theory) had exposed many themes to guide my search for apt theory.

In this quest, the landscape of my reading was expansive and multidisciplinary. Spanning from leadership studies in education, healthcare and business to theories of change, professional development and digital integration, I contemplated theory centred on digital skills, cause and effect, managing change and the construct of distributed leadership. My disparate search proved fruitful when through seeking theory on distributed leadership, I encountered a study by Ho et al. (2016), which combined this construct with activity theory. Further searches led me to Cultural-Historical Activity Theory (CHAT), which piqued my interest. Other research using the CHAT framework was examined to identify how it had been previously conceptualized. This revealed its wide-ranging applications across many disciplines and activity systems. It fit like a glove with my study.

An abundance of choices

Before I accentuate the merits of CHAT within my study, I will share insights on some theories which I initially considered but then discarded due to their incompatibility. Two theories that I contemplated and critiqued were the theory of Distributed Leadership, and Technological Pedagogical Content Knowledge framework (TPACK).

Distributed Leadership is a practice involving the interactions between leaders, followers and their environment with an emphasis on the importance of context (Hickey et al. 2022). There are three key principles to distributed leadership – autonomy, capacity and accountability. Each is of equal importance, and all are interdependent (Solly 2018). In judging the suitability of distributed leadership theory, I accepted that the role of the ICT coordinator should be a collaborative and distributed endeavour. However, data from my survey revealed how the role was predominantly executed by individual teachers who lacked a support network within their schools. My lived experience of the role within my own school corroborated this data. Consequently, this theory was rejected as a contender.

I noted the inclusion of the TPACK theoretical framework in several studies aligned with mine. Building on Shulman's formulation of *Pedagogical Content Knowledge*, it was extended to include 'Technology'. TPACK seeks to explain the complex interplay between technology, pedagogy and content knowledge in teaching and learning, and proposes that effective teaching and learning require a deep understanding of how these three elements intersect and interact with one another (Mishra and Koehler 2006). It attempts to capture some of the essential qualities of teacher knowledge required for technology integration into teaching, while addressing the complex, multifaceted and situated nature of this knowledge (Mishra and Koehler 2006, p. 1017). I felt that it would be an interesting lens to assess the skill set of my respondent population and match skills to the functions of the role. However, what it lacked was a strategy to expose the inconclusive variables at play within the role of ICT coordinator and also a means of unmasking conduits to affect necessary change. Overall, it did not provide a means for me to probe all the phenomena of my study.

Miles and Huberman (1994) argue that the conceptual framework can be rudimentary or elaborate, theory-driven or commonsensical, descriptive or causal . . . but it delineates the main things to be studied and the presumed relationships among them. (p. 18)

My inexperience as a researcher but experience as an educator enticed me towards the commonsensical; a theory that could be understood, explained in plain English, easily applied and could make sense of a large data set. *Cultural-Historical Activity Theory* (CHAT) provided those components in its flexibility and simplicity. CHAT was the ideal fit for my study for many reasons. Most notable was how the elements of the CHAT model could be matched very clearly to the parameter points of the activity I was attempting to understand. Locating my conceptual framework was a landmark moment in my research journey. The CHAT framework would percolate all aspects of the study systematically, leading me on a more defined route towards my research purpose.

Further chats about CHAT

Cultural-Historical Activity Theory (CHAT) centres on three core ideas; 1) humans act collectively, learn by doing and communicate in and via their actions; 2) humans make, employ and adapt tools of all kinds to learn and communicate; and 3) community is central to all forms of learning, communicating and acting (Vygotsky 1978). In CHAT, the 'activity system' is the basic unit of analysis. It includes the individual, the tools and resources used in the activity, the goals and motives driving the activity, and the social and cultural context in which the activity takes place (Engeström 2001). CHAT spotlights the whole configuration of events, activities, contents and interpersonal processes taking place in an organization (Lim and Hang 2003), thus enabling researchers to analyse complex and evolving professional practices (Yliruka and Karvinen-Niinikoski 2013). In a nutshell, its purpose is to promote changes in activity systems emerging from the self-reflection of their participants (Engeström et al. 1999).

To adequately scrutinize the activity of the ICT coordinator, I needed to situate the role in its cultural and historical context. Foot (2014) explored the applications of CHAT *in* significant detail, referring to how each word in the acronym CHAT is significant. *Cultural* identifies how individuals learn the traditional content of a culture and assimilate its practices and values. *Historical* is linked to cultural in that cultures are grounded in histories and evolve over time (Foot 2014, p. 330) and thus analyses of work practices must be viewed in light of historical developments. *Activity* refers to what people do together and is modified by cultural and historical criteria.

Other applications of CHAT which resonated with me included a study by Lim and Hang (2003) who used CHAT to analyse successes, failures and contradictions in the integration of technology in schools. Their study described the activity systems within and across schools and classrooms, and how larger entities such as policymakers have on them. They identified how taking 'an activity system as a unit of analysis allows one to observe the actual processes by which activities shape and are shaped by their context' (2003, p. 51). CHAT was used as a theoretical framework in a study of school leadership, which recognized how 'culturally developed artifacts have a special status as fundamental mediators of actions' (Hauge et al. 2014, p. 358). Some discourses within these studies aligned with my research objective of exploring an activity with a view to showcasing opportunities for change. This added weight to my belief in CHAT as the appropriate theoretical tool for my study.

CHAT in action

I conceptualized the theory for my study in the following way. Figure 5.1 above presents the triangular CHAT model diagram with its six interdependent components/variables which are reciprocally and simultaneously influencing each other. This model or matrix can be mapped onto any activity in an organization. The *activity system* under analysis in my study is the role of the ICT coordinator who is the *subject* of the activity. Their overarching *object or outcome* is effective digital integration into teaching and learning. Both these variables are influenced by *the division of labour* and the *rules* that structure interaction within the school. *Tools* (including staff development and individual teacher competency building) and *community* shape how the subject (*the ICT coordinator*) orients, thinks and performs in their role. The activity system is not stable but in a constant state of flux with participants negotiating tensions amongst the different elements. Learning or change happens when contradictions among elements are resolved, enabling the subject (the ICT coordinator) to take advantage of an expanded range of actions (Wiske and Spicer 2010, p. 637). Within my study, this framework successfully enabled an interrogation into the role of the ICT coordinator. It is clear

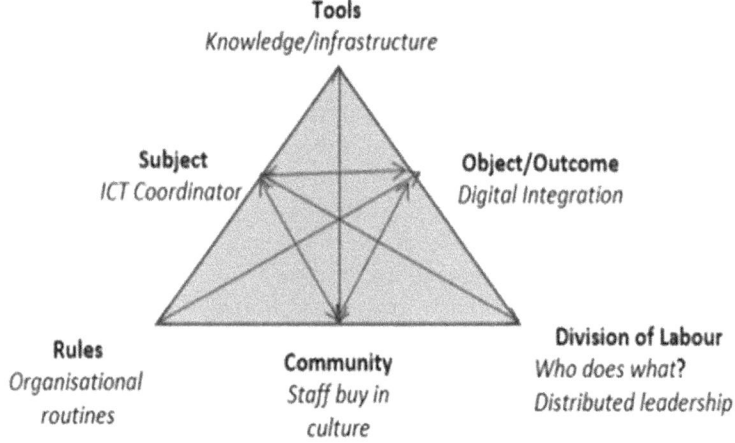

FIGURE 5.1 *Cultural-Historical Activity Theory model (Engeström 1999).*

how this analysis method could be replicated and transposed onto investigations of other activities within a school or organization.

CHAT and its methodological influence

Although this chapter focuses on how CHAT was used to conceptualize digital leadership in primary schools, I think it is imperative to demonstrate its desirability as a framework from a methodological standpoint. The tentacles of CHAT extended into so many methodological decisions within my study, which are outlined below.

> **Determining suitability:** Former research using the CHAT framework was examined to identify how the theoretical framework had been previously employed thus determining its suitability for my research purpose.
>
> **Research problem:** The research problem was situated in its cultural and historical context.
>
> **Research questions:** It had the scope to facilitate the answering of both my research questions. The language of the research questions was influenced by the framework. The use of the words *activity* and *change* are central to the CHAT framework.
>
> 1. What factors influence the **activities** of ICT coordinators in Irish Primary schools?
> 2. What **changes** are necessary at school level and systemic level to better support them in their role?
>
> **Literature Review:** Elements of the CHAT model could be matched to key themes within the literature and subsequently critically analysed and discussed.
>
> **Data collection instruments:** CHAT was used to design the research instruments for data collection. The elements of the CHAT model (tools, rules, community, division of labour) were explored through the questions in the interviews with participants.
>
> **Data analysis:** The elements of the CHAT model were used as initial codes in the early stages of data analysis. As the

files were examined and analysed, other codes emerged and were added.

Findings: The participants offered many suggestions as to how the role of the ICT coordinator needed to change to be effective. I was able to take these perspectives and map them onto the different elements of the framework, thus creating coherent findings. This further clarified the efficacy of the CHAT framework as a model to implement change in activity systems.

In conclusion

The time one invests in crafting a piece of research is significant and the pathway through is often murky. I found the transposition between theoretical and practical to be perplexing and requiring great flexibility of mind and precise knowledge of my chosen topic. I acknowledge how the realization of who I was as a researcher and consequently the discovery of such a befitting theory for my research, was fundamental in connecting the dots between theory and practice and for clearing the pathway through my study. I credit my chosen theory CHAT with enabling me to manoeuvre through the research process in a more streamlined way. Knowing that my pragmatic approach was consistent with how I operate in the real world was very enlightening and reassuring. This strengthened my belief in my thesis and made me cognizant of a much higher register of thought than I had formerly engaged in. My crash landing into the world of academic theory has created so many new synapses in my brain for connecting the how, the why and the what of research. Ultimately the journey demystified the research process for me, built my solid philosophical foundations and positioned me strongly to embark on my next research venture.

References

Anderson, C. (2010). Presenting and evaluating qualitative research. *American Journal of Pharmaceutical Education*, 74(8), 141, pp. 1–7.

Creswell, J. W. (2013). *Qualitative inquiry and research design. Choosing among five approaches*. Thousand Oaks, CA: SAGE Publications.
Creswell, J. W. and Creswell, J. D. (2017). *Research design: Qualitative, quantitative, and mixed methods approaches*. Thousand Oaks, CA: SAGE Publications.
DeCarlo, M., Cummings, C., and Agnelli, K. (2021). *Graduate research methods in social work*. Open Social Work Education.
Denscombe, M. (2017). *The good research guide: For small-scale social research projects*. 6th ed. Berkshire: McGraw-Hill Education, Open University Press.
Engeström, Y. (1999). Activity theory and individual and social transformation. *Perspectives on Activity Theory*, 19(38), pp. 19–30.
Engeström, Y. (2001). Expansive learning at work: Toward an activity theoretical reconceptualization. *Journal of Education and Work*, 14(1), pp. 133–56.
Engeström, Y., Miettinen, R., and Punamäki, R. L. (eds.) (1999). *Perspectives on activity theory*. Cambridge: Cambridge University Press.
Evans, B. C., Coon, D. W., and Ume, E. (2011). Use of theoretical frameworks as a pragmatic guide for mixed methods studies: Amethodological necessity? *Journal of Mixed Methods Research*, 5(4), pp. 276–92.
Foot, K. A. (2014). Cultural-historical activity theory: Exploring a theory to inform practice and research. *Journal of Human Behavior in the Social Environment*, 24(3), pp. 329–47.
Hauge, T. E., Norenes, S. O., and Vedøy, G. (2014). School leadership and educational change: Tools and practices in shared school leadership development. *Journal of Educational Change*, 15(4), pp. 357–76.
Hickey, N., Flaherty, A., and Mannix McNamara, P. (2022). Distributed leadership: A scoping review mapping current empirical research. *Societies MDPI*, 12(1), pp. 1–20.
Ho, J. P. Y., Victor Chen, D. T., and Ng, D. (2016). Distributed leadership through the lens of activity theory. *Educational Management Administration & Leadership*, 44(5), pp. 814–36.
Kaushik, V. and Walsh, C. A. (2019). Pragmatism as a research paradigm and its implications for social work research. *Social Sciences*, 8(9), 255, pp. 1–17.
LeCompte, M. D., Preissle, J., and Tesch, R. (1993). *Ethnography and qualitative design in educational research*. San Diego: Academic Press.
Leont'ev, A. N. (1978). *Activity, consciousness, and personality*. Englewood Cliffs, NJ: Prentice-Hall.
Lim, C. P. and Hang, D. (2003). An activity theory approach to research of ICT integration in Singapore schools. *Computers & Education*, 41(1), pp. 49–63.

Marsh, D. and Furlong, P. (2002). A skin, not a sweater: Ontology and epistemology in political science. *Theory and Methods in Political Science*, 2(1), pp. 177–98.

Miles, M. B. and Huberman, A. M. (1994). *Qualitative data analysis: An expanded sourcebook*. Thousand Oaks, CA: SAGE Publications.

Mishra, P. and Koehler, M. J. (2006). Technological pedagogical content knowledge: A framework for teacher knowledge. *Teachers' College Record*, 108(6), pp. 1017–54.

Osanloo, A. and Grant, C. (2014). Understanding, selecting, and integrating a theoretical framework in dissertation research: Creating the blueprint for your "house." *Administrative Issues Journal: Connecting Education, Practice, and Research*, 4(2), pp. 12–26.

Solly, B. (2018). *Distributed leadership explained. The voice for secondary education* [online]. Available: https://www.sec-ed.co.uk/content/best-practice/distributed-leadership-explained/#:~:text=In%20a%20distributed%20leadership%20approach,them%20ownership%20of%20their%20work. [accessed 30 November 2023].

Tashakkori, A. and Teddlie, C. (2010). *Sage handbook of mixed methods in social & behavioural research*. Thousand Oaks, CA: SAGE Publications.

Vygotsky, L. (1978). *Mind in society: The development of higher psychological processes*. Cambridge, MA: Harvard University Press.

Wiske, M. S. and Spicer, D. E. (2010). Teacher education as teaching for understanding with new technologies. In: Baker, E., McGaw, B., and Peterson, P. (eds), *International encyclopaedia of education*. 3rd ed. Amsterdam: Elsevie, pp. 635-641.

Yliruka, L. and Karvinen-Niinikoski, S. (2013). How can we enhance productivity in social work? Dynamically reflective structures, dialogic leadership and the development of transformative expertise. *Journal of Social Work Practice: Psychotherapeutic Approaches in Health, Welfare, and the Community*, 27(2), pp. 191–206.

CHAPTER 6

Why Do I Need a Conceptual Framework Anyway?

Tanya Davies

This chapter focuses on the challenges I faced designing a conceptual framework for my qualitative ethnographic study. The project, titled: "'But we're not a multicultural school!": Local spaces, cultural difference and the challenges of intercultural education at one Australian secondary school' examined teachers' experiences of doing intercultural work in an Australian secondary school. Being a qualitative ethnographic project meant that I was interested in the local socio-cultural and historical conditions that complicate teachers' intercultural work. I was focused on human experience in the particular space of the research site. My study was a single site ethnography – which I talk about later – with six teacher-participants. In this kind of research, findings were not sought to be generalizable, but rather to demonstrate the complexity of intercultural work in local school settings. This established a particular set of challenges in developing my conceptual framework where my enduring struggle came to define my PhD experience and profoundly shaped my approach to research more broadly. Sharing this experience here has both been cathartic, but also attempts to reassure emerging researchers that intellectual and emotional struggle is a necessary part of the journey.

I start by providing some context to my study, before elaborating on the development of my conceptual framework and how this conceptual work came to constitute my methodology and approach to analysis. By examining the messiness of this process, you may find lessons and solace in my struggles!

Nomadic beginnings: From research topic to conceptual framework

Understanding the origins of a project and what brings you to the questions you are asking can help better understand why you are drawn to research and drive your focus as your project evolves. As a starting point, my supervisors asked me to write a personal account of my central question:

What makes teachers' intercultural work in public (government) schools so complicated?

I talk about this here because it signals how I am situated in relation to the project as well as detailing the broader socio-cultural context of intercultural work in Australian schools. In writing about my relationship to the question I began to understand the kinds of perspectives that interest me and provided insight into the kind of project I might design. As a first task for my supervisors, I wrote about an experience teaching at an outer suburban school in Melbourne, Australia where a white fifteen-year-old male student rifled racialized and sexualized abuse towards me and another student – a recently arrived Afghani young woman, in the school courtyard. I don't have scope to go into the details here, however this experience, although almost ten years before, characterized the ongoing challenges of racism in Australia and how this plays out in schools, giving body to the official curriculum policy imperative that mandates teachers teach intercultural understanding.

As a result of writing through my question it became clear that concepts of race and racism, and culture and difference were central to my research. I began thinking historically about the role of schooling and nation building, about official curriculum as a cultural artefact, and how teachers navigate official curriculum requirements such as the Intercultural Capability (Australian Curriculum and Assessment Reporting Authority [ACARA] 2022) against the backdrop of invasion, white Australia and (anti) humanitarian policy that detains asylum seekers (indefinitely). Race relations in Australia have an ugly history (and present) and racialized behaviour is a normalized part of everyday life (Gunew 2004; Hage 1998, 2014; Wilkinson 2008). For teachers, this is fraught terrain to navigate, and I wanted to understand how these complex histories and socio-cultural intersections shaped teachers' intercultural work in the context of an official curriculum and policy mandate.

In 2014 intercultural and ethical capabilities were formally built into the national curriculum alongside five other general capabilities and cross-curriculum priorities. The inclusion of the general capabilities explicitly acknowledged the role schools play in cultivating disciplinary knowledge and skills for young people to participate in civic, economic and educational life, as well as how schools contribute to social cohesion, democracy and an informed citizenry (ACARA 2022; Education Council 2019; Victorian Curriculum and Assessment Authority 2017). My first point of struggle was how could I, a novice researcher, possibly tackle questions of nationhood, schooling and teachers' work? I found myself really wrestling with big questions of curriculum and policy, Australia's colonial legacy and institutional and everyday racism, and the role of schools in contemporary nation building. I needed to find a way to sharpen my focus and the official Intercultural Capability curriculum became a productive anchor and point of tension for my study. It became clear to me that the curriculum mandate of Intercultural Capability was not *about* an elusive 'other', but rather about negotiating difference (Gilbert 2019; Gorski 2008; Gunew 2004; Priestley and Philippou 2018, 2019; Walton et al. 2013, 2018). And somehow, I needed to find a way to bring together concepts of race, culture and difference alongside curriculum, policy and schooling to make sense of the contradictions and contested positionalities of this space. This was a point of intense struggle.

First in family and imposter syndrome: Unlearning all that I never knew I knew about doing research

I am the first in my family to attend university and the only person in my extended family to engage in higher-degree research. While I am not defined by this, it did mean that I had no experience with the linguistic and semiotic codes of research: I lacked the cultural capital (Bourdieu 1993), so to speak, of the academy and my idea of what constituted research was limited. Indeed, when I embarked on exploring what my conceptual framework might look like I imagined that I would 'find' a pre-existing 'framework' that I could apply directly to my research and that would offer a formulaic guide to answer my research questions. How I laugh at this now! It took time for me to embrace the provisionality of qualitative research, or research which focuses on situated human experience (Denzin 1997). My project, dealing with questions of identity, culture and difference in schools was conceptually complex. Learning how the conceptual framework provided particular ways of thinking about the project's central concerns was an arduous process that confronted everything I thought I knew about being (ontology) and assumptions I never knew I had about knowledge (epistemology).

I embarked on an intense reading programme, which I detail below to demonstrate how the search for the right language to talk about your project takes time and a relentless tenacity. I spent two years reading widely in the field of educational sociology and philosophy to understand the ways the concepts of identity, culture and difference had been conceptualized. This is murky territory. I traversed Bourdieu's (1993) concepts of 'fields' and 'capital'; Derrida's concept of 'differance' (1967; Royle 2003); and Deleuze's (1994; May 2005) difference and repetition. As an English teacher, I was drawn to the work of Bakhtin (1981, 1993) and the dialogic imagination, parallax, and the constitutive other. I brought Bakhtin and Deleuze into conversation with each other, and for a time, also Deleuze and Derrida. I spent uncountable hours reading with highlighters and sticky notes; I presented at my institution's higher-degree research student conference two years in a row attempting to wrangle my conceptual thinking into shape. The problem I

WHY DO I NEED A CONCEPTUAL FRAMEWORK ANYWAY? 103

continued to face was the way that identity and culture is shaped in local spaces, evolves over time and is in constant motion, intersecting and cutting across other aspect of human identity in mobile trajectories.

I needed to make some conceptual decisions, but nothing I had experimented with felt right. My final attempt to make it work drew on feminist theory, particularly situated intersectionality (Anthias 2008; Yuval-Davis 2007) as a way to help explain the complexity of intercultural spaces. Yet this too did not quite *do* what I needed. My difficulty was in the way the notion of an intersection remains fixed, and I still couldn't reconcile the mobility across entanglements of culture, identity and difference. I was two years into my PhD and I *still* didn't have a conceptual framework. I was tired. I felt depleted. And amongst all the theory and reading I had lost sight of what I was trying to do. I took a four-month leave from my PhD and spent this time working through the reading and writing I had done and rather than walking away (although the thought crossed my mind) I confronted the prospect of designing my own conceptual framework. I was riddled with anxiety and self-doubt: Who was I, as a working-class first in family novice researcher to construct my own conceptual framework? Who, in their right mind, would take me seriously?!

As Haraway (2016) encourages, staying with the trouble 'is to become capable ... of response' (p. 1). And for me, staying with the trouble paid off. For me, the hard intellectual grind of surveying the conceptual landscape helped me understand how different schools of thought conceptualize culture, identity and difference; how they are positioned in relation to the broader field of cultural studies and sociology of education; and the kinds of epistemologies and ontologies of knowledge and being that inform them. Importantly, I found the kinds of *orientations* that resonated with me, and when I came to generate and analyse data, this foundation provided a comprehensive map within which I was able to position myself. Indeed, it wasn't until I started generating data that my conceptual framework came together.

Eventually, my conceptual framework had two key strands: culture and difference; and the production of space. I drew from the critical cultural studies work of Hall (1993a, 1993b, 1996, 2007, 2017) and Gilroy (1994, 2004) to conceptualize the intercultural through the self-other relations that constitute being. For Hall, culture is situated within locations of power, where there are no origins, only entanglements of histories that shape the present. This conceptual frame allowed me to anchor the *inter*cultural as spaces *in-between*, and as such, intercultural education about understanding the relational spaces *between* diverse cultural groups and the conditions that have shaped these relations today. For school-level education, this is important as schools are microcosms of the communities they are situated within. The intercultural relations that exist in schools are deeply situated in relationships that exist in space and across time, so examining the conditions that produce particular kinds of intercultural relations in particular school spaces helped me understand what makes teachers' intercultural work in particular school settings so complicated. However, to help me do this work, I needed a theory of space to anchor this conceptualization of the intercultural.

In working with the data, I realized that the relational spaces that my teacher participants occupied *constituted*, rather than provided context to, the possibilities they experienced for doing intercultural work. That is, the kind of intercultural work particular teachers were able to do was *constituted by* the particular relational assemblages of their discipline and their classroom (Davies 2022). To support this theorization, I took up the work of Lefebvre (1936, 1991, 2004, 2005; Lefebvre and Régulier 1985) and Massey (2005) to understand space as relational and socially constructed across three domains – conceived (abstract), perceived (everyday/material) and lived (experience/symbolic). This allowed me to look at the intersections of relational spaces that shape teachers' intercultural work across official administrative spaces – such as official curriculum and policy, and spaces of social interaction, such as classrooms. I found myself *thinking with* these conceptual tools and using the language of Lefebvre and Massey in conversation with Hall to explain how different school spaces constituted different intercultural possibilities. It was only then that I understood how a conceptual framework evolves to work *for* the research question/s and offers a language to discuss and analyse the research problem.

The research questions I finally settled on were:

1) What kinds of experiences do teachers have interpreting, translating and enacting the official Intercultural Capability curriculum?

2) What kind of evidence is there of intercultural work beyond the Intercultural Capability?

3) What role do physical and social spaces play in shaping the intercultural work of teachers?

The approach I took was facilitated by my supervisors who encouraged me to experiment with different theoretical tools, where rather than looking for a prefabricated solution, I was supported to bring concepts together in new ways to think about the challenges of intercultural education anew. This directly contributed to the design and enactment of my research project.

The messy work of doing research: Wrestling with epistemology, ontology and methodology.

Central to the struggles of developing my conceptual framework was understanding epistemology and ontology. It took a long time for me to begin to understand the different ways of knowing (epistemology) and being (ontology), with no easy route to developing a rich understanding. Reading widely in education, sociology and philosophy to develop the conceptual underpinnings of my study helped me position myself in the mire. For me, I understand being as relational. We exist in relation to others in an ongoing and unfinalizable becoming-with between self and other. There is no pure self, rather a messy entanglement of histories and identities situated in networks of power (Bauman 1996; Braidotti 2011; Hall 1996; Haraway 2016; Yuval-Davis 2007). Knowledge is constructed, enacted and embodied through dialogue (Bakhtin 1981), and as such I understand knowledge as situated, framed by the politics of our own location. Understanding how we are ontologically and epistemologically constructed is important for research as it necessarily shapes the decisions we make regarding research project design, the kinds of conceptual tools we take up, the ways we interact with research participants and the research site, and how we approach data. For me, my ontological and epistemological positioning meant that I approached data generation dialogically, that I was an instrument in the research process, that data was understood as situated rather than universal and that findings were always provisional. Importantly, my epistemology and ontology shaped the design of my project. I talk about this next.

Ethnography as a way of being in the worlds of others

My study asks: what makes teachers' intercultural work so challenging? I needed a study design that allowed me to focus on the situated nature of teachers' work. My project was interested in teachers' experiences working across local, social, cultural, historical norms, and the official curriculum and policy mandates from elsewhere. Being focused on experience, an ethnographic design for my study made sense, drawing on institutional (Delamont and Atkinson 1980) and socially contextual (Hammersley 2006) constructions of ethnography. It is closely located in the physical school site while recognizing teachers' intercultural work as more than what happens in their classrooms. Within an ethnographic frame, the intercultural work of my participating teachers is understood as 'enmeshed in a cultural system' (Wolcott 2003, p. 334; see also Campbell and Lassiter 2015) of the school, while simultaneously connected to spaces beyond the school. This approach is distinct from understanding teachers' intercultural work in the context of curriculum mandates where teacher's may be thought to implement curriculum and policy. This had implications for how I approached *doing* the research.

After a challenging recruitment process, six teachers from one site with a range of experience and expertise volunteered to participate in my study. Together, we negotiated classes I would observe on a regular basis as well as other activities I could participate in, such as yard duty and curriculum meetings. Participants engaged in two interviews that bookended my time at the school and three focus groups with their teacher-participant colleagues over the course of six months. I wrote extensive fieldnotes from my observation activities and these were brought into conversation with the formal interview and focus group conversations. Interviews and focus groups were recorded and transcribed, and data were organized around the elements of my conceptual framework.

Data analysis as an enactment of my conceptual framework

One of the key challenges of working conceptually is taking up the language of the conceptual framework to describe and explain the phenomena under investigation. This means thinking conceptually about research processes, data organization and analysis. For me, I used Lefebvre's (1991) framework of the production of space as a high-level organizer. The production of space framework enabled me to identify different cultural 'spaces' in schools, such as: curriculum and policy as conceived (abstract) space; physical spaces such as classrooms as perceived (everyday/material) spaces; and social / relational spaces such as classroom interactions as lived. Organizing data in this way allowed me to use Lefebvre's conceptual language to describe and explain what was happening in the school while also offering an organizing structure. Rhythmanalysis – a methodological tool developed by Lefebvre (2004) to complement his theorization of the production of space – was taken up as a tool to analyse, or palpate, situated social interactions across productions of conceived, perceived and lived space. In this way, rhythmanalysis was employed as a methodological extension of the conceptual framework. This was important to ensure conceptual cohesion across the different aspects of the project (for more on rhythmanalysis see Davies 2023).

Why am I telling you all of this? Well, beyond developing your conceptual framework, creating conceptual cohesion in the way you *employ* the conceptual framework remains an area many emerging researchers struggle with. What I have tried to show is the way my conceptual framework informed research design, methods, data generation and analysis. And that the way I positioned myself within my study was a product of my epistemology and ontology. Conceptual framework, research design and research enactment must be complementary. As such, taking time to conceptualize your project in ways that are generative for you is critical. Even if it takes you two years!

Answering the research questions: Accepting provisionality and unfinalizability

In the frantic months of finalising my thesis for submission I was convinced my study made no contribution to knowledge at all. This experience is not unique, rather it is banal and common! Receiving my examiners' reports was a conduit for understanding the contributions of my study. For me, it was through the shared synthesis of my study, and in particular of my conceptual design, that I was able to recognize what I had done and how it contributes to broader bodies of knowledge.

Answering the question: *What makes teachers' intercultural work so complicated?* in the end was answered in the simplest of terms: it's complicated!

Below are the main points I reported on:

1. Intercultural education is not about understanding an externally produced cultural 'other'. Intercultural education is about understanding how intercultural relations are shaped by the situated ways different cultural groups are positioned in relation to each other. In this way, intercultural education is about understanding the relational spaces *in-between* diverse cultural groups and the networks of power that shape these relations.
2. Intercultural work is fraught with risk and teachers need access to a range of resources to cultivate practices that support the development of intercultural understanding.
3. Situated productions of cultural diversity in local school spaces shape intercultural possibilities. It is the job of all teachers in all schools to understand the normative positioning of 'culturally diverse others' and how this implicates opportunities for intercultural work in their setting.
4. Finally, spatial theory is not widely adopted in educational research and my study makes a conceptual contribution to demonstrate how spatial theory can imagine educational problems in new ways (Comber 2021).

These findings grew out of the labour that cultivated my conceptual framework and enabled me to take up conceptual language to talk about my project and my findings. Getting to the point where I could articulate what I found wasn't easy. I encourage you, embarking on this journey, to approach research from a position of radical openness (hooks 1994). By that, I mean embrace uncertainty and provisionality in all aspects of your project; be creative and imaginative in working with concepts; and take time to experiment with ideas to find those that work for you and your study, there is no single way to do your project!

A PhD is an undertaking that changes you in profound and unexpected ways, at times taking you on a journey into the darkest corners of yourself. Make use of the resources available to you, especially the advice of your supervisors. I had two brilliant PhD supervisors, Scott Bulfin and David Bright, to whom I will be forever thankful for their wisdom and support. Become part of the research community at your institution. Participate in conferences and writing collectives. Take leave when you need it. Be realistic about deadlines. Be open about when the pressure is too much. Ride the highs of every success and ride out the lows knowing they will pass. I wish you the very best in your research journey. No journey follows the same path or arrives at the same destination. Make yours your own and own it!

References

Anthias, F. (2008). Thinking through the lens of translocational positionality: an intersectionality frame for understanding identity and belonging. *Translocations: Migration and Social Change*, 4(1), pp. 5–20.
Australian Curriculum Assessment and Reporting Authority [ACARA]. (2022). *Australian curriculum v8.1 F-10 curriculum: Intercultural understanding* [online]. Available: https://www.australiancurriculum.edu.au/f-10-curriculum/ [accessed 26 November 2023].
Bakhtin, M. (1981). *The dialogic imagination*. Trans. Emerson, C. and Holquist, M. Austin, TX: University of Texas Press.
Bakhtin, M. (1993). *Toward a philosophy of the act*. Trans. Liapunov, V. Austin, TX: University of Texas Press.
Bauman, Z. (1996). From pilgrim to tourist: A short history of identity. In: Hall, S. and Du Gay, P. (eds), *Questions of cultural identity*. Thousand Oaks, CA: SAGE Publications, pp. 18-36.

Bourdieu, P. (1993). *The field of cultural production: Essays on art and literature*. New Jersey: Wiley & Sons.

Braidotti, R. (2011). *Nomadic theory: The portable Rosi Braidotti*. New York: Columbia University Press.

Campbell, E. and Lassiter, L. (2015). *Doing ethnography today: Theories, methods, exercises*. New Jersey: Wiley & Sons.

Comber, B. (2021). Thinking spatially: A springboard to new possibilities. *Australian Geographer*, 52(1), pp. 19–23.

Davies, T. (2022). 'But we're not a multicultural school!': Locating intercultural relations and reimagining intercultural education as an act of 'coming-to-terms-with our routes'. *The Australian Educational Researcher*, ahead of print, https://doi.org/10.1007/s13384-022-00537-0

Davies, T. (2023). Rhythmanalysis as methodology for understanding the social complexity of school spaces. *Research in Education*, ahead of print, https://doi.org/10.1177/00345237231163038

Delamont, S. and Atkinson, P. (1980). The two traditions in educational ethnography: Sociology and anthropology compared. *British Journal of Sociology of Education*, 1(2), pp. 139–52.

Deleuze, G. (1994). *Difference and repetition*. Trans. Patton, P. London: Bloomsbury.

Denzin, N. K. (1997). *Interpretive ethnography: Ethnographic practices for the 21st century*. Thousand Oaks, CA: SAGE Publications.

Derrida, J. (1967). *Writing and difference*. Trans. Bass, A. Milton Park: Routledge.

Education Counil (2019). Alice springs (mparntwe) education declaration. Available at: Alice Springs (Mparntwe) education declaration. (nla.gov.au) (Accessed: 27/05/2024 at 14:57)

Gilbert, R. (2019). General capabilities in the Australian curriculum: Promise, problems, and prospects. In: Reid, A and Price, D. (eds), *The Australian curriculum: Promise, problems, and possibilities*. Canberra: Australian Curriculum Studies Association, pp. 169–177.

Gilroy, P. (1994). *The black Atlantic: Modernity and double consciousness*. New York: Verso.

Gilroy, P. (2004). *After empire: Melancholia or convivial culture?* New York: Routledge.

Gordon, T. (2015). The notion of 'display' in ethnographic research. In: Troman, G., Jeffrey, R., and Walford, G. (eds), *Methodological issues and practices in ethnography*, Amsterdam:Elsevier, pp. 111–30.

Gorski, P. (2008). Good intentions are not enough: A decolonizing intercultural education. *Intercultural Education*, 19(6), pp. 515–25.

Gunew, S. (2004). *Haunted nations: The colonial dimensions of multiculturalisms*. New York: Routledge.

Hage, G. (1998). *White nation: Fantasies of white supremacy in a multicultural society*. London: Pluto Press.

Hage, G. (2014). Continuity and change in Australian racism. *Journal of Intercultural Studies,* 35(3), pp. 232–7.
Hall, S. (1993a). Cultural studies and its theoretical legacies. In: During, S. (ed.), *The cultural studies reader.* Milton Park: Routledge, pp. 277–294.
Hall, S. (1993b). Culture, community, nation. *Cultural Studies,* 7(3), pp. 349–63.
Hall, S. (1996). Introduction: Who needs 'identity'? In: Hall, S. and Du Gay, P. (eds.), *Questions of cultural identity.* Thousand Oaks, CA: SAGE Publications, pp. 1–17.
Hall, S. (2007). *Living with difference: Stuart Hall in conversation with Bill Schwarz.* Queen Elizabeth Hall, London, England. Edited extract published with permission from South Bank Centre Talks Department. Available: https://www.lwbooks.co.uk/sites/default/files/s37_15hall_schwarz.pdf
Hall, S. (2017). *The fateful triangle: Race, ethnicity, nation.* Cambridge: Harvard University Press.
Hall, S., Evans, J., and Nixon, S. (2013). *Representation.* 2nd ed. Thousand Oaks, CA: SAGE Publications.
Hammersley, M. (2006). Ethnography: Problems and prospects. *Ethnography and Education,* 1(1), pp. 3–14.
Haraway, D. (2016). *Staying with the trouble: Making kin in the Chthulucene.* Durham, NC: Duke University Press.
Hooks, B. (1994). *Teaching to transgress: Education as the practice of freedom.* New York: Routledge.
Lefebvre, H. (1936). Nation and Culture. In: Elden, S., Lebas, E., and Moore, G. (eds), *Henri Lefebvre: Key writings, English language.* Trans. Forster, I., Sturrock, J., Guterman, N., and Lebas, E. London: Bloomsbury, pp. 218–226.
Lefebvre, H. (1991). *The production of space.* Trans. Nicholson-Smith, D. Hokoken, NJ: Blackwell Publishing.
Lefebvre, H. (2004). *Rhythmanalysis: Space, time and everyday life.* Trans. Elden, S. and Moore, G. London: Bloomsbury.
Lefebvre, H. (2005). *Critique of everyday life* (Vol. 3). Trans. Elliott, G. New York: Verso.
Lefebvre, H. and Régulier, C. (1985). The rhythmanalytical project. In: Elden, S., Lebas, E., and Moore, G. (eds), *Henri Lefebvre: Key writings, English language.* Trans. Forster, I., Sturrock, J., Guterman, N., and Lebas, E. London: Bloomsburypp. 188-196.
Massey, D. (2005). *For space.* Thousand Oaks, CA: SAGE Publications.
May, T. (2005). *Gilles Deleuze: An introduction.* Cambridge: Cambridge University Press.
McLaren, P. (1992). Collisions with otherness: "Travelling" theory, post-colonial criticism, and the politics of ethnographic practice –

the mission of the wounded ethnographer. *International Journal of Qualitative Studies in Education*, 5, pp. 77–92.

Priestley, M. and Philippou, S. (2018). Curriculum making as social practice: Complex webs of enactment. *The Curriculum Journal*, 29(2), pp. 151–8.

Priestley, M. and Philippou, S. (2019). Curriculum is – or should be – at the heart of educational practice. *The Curriculum Journal*, 30(1), pp. 1–7.

Royle, N. (2003). *Critical thinkers: Jacques Derrida.* Milton Park: Routledge.

Victorian Curriculum and Assessment Authority [VCAA]. (2017). *The Victorian curriculum F-10: Intercultural capability* [online]. Available: http://victoriancurriculum.vcaa.vic.edu.au/intercultural-capability/introduction/rationale-and-aims [accessed 26 November 2023].

Walton, J., Priest, N., and Paradies, Y. (2013). Identifying and developing effective approaches to foster intercultural understanding in schools. *Intercultural Education*, 24(3), pp. 181–94.

Walton, P., Priest, N., Kowal, E., White, F., Fox, B., and Paradies, Y. (2018). Whiteness and national identity: Teacher discourses in Australian primary schools. *Race, Ethnicity and Education*, 21(1), pp. 132–47.

Wilkinson, J. (2008). Good intentions are not enough: A critical examination of diversity and educational leadership scholarship. *Journal of Educational Administration and History*, 40(2), pp. 101–12.

Wolcott, H. (2003). A "natural" writer. *Anthropology and Education Quarterly,* 34(3), pp. 324–38.

Yuval-Davis, N. (2007). Intersectionality, citizenship, and contemporary politics of belonging. *Critical Review of International Social and Political Philosophy*, 10(4), pp. 561–74.

CHAPTER 7

Is Objectivity the Aim?

Ceridwen Owen

In this chapter I discuss the ethical approach that I took in my PhD study (Owen 2020) to demonstrate how you can think about ethics when you are undertaking a research project. The purpose is to demonstrate the role of ethics in the research process and how it can be more than an objective regulatory measure, that are applicable to all studies. I propose that alongside the regulatory measure, ethics is also specific to the project, the individuals, and the time and place.

My PhD study used an ethnography-in-education methodology to examine the everyday work and development of nine early career English teachers, to understand their experience and development (Green and Bloome 2005; Owen 2020). Alongside understanding their experience and development, the aim was to understand how institutions could better support teachers in their transition into the teaching profession.

This chapter is divided into three sections. Section one provides you with an outline of the study, including the rationale, research questions, methodology, and data analysis approach. The purpose of this section is to provide you context for the ethical discussion in the following two sections. In section two, I discuss broad ethical considerations, before linking these to specific concepts that were used during the PhD process to assist me to enact my own ethical position. Finally, in the third section I outline ethics in action, an example from my research that highlights how I used the ethical considerations I had developed.

Study overview

All research projects will have research questions and aims, methodology and an analysis framework. A key learning for me from my PhD journey is that each of these are connected and inform each other, and the research process has ethical considerations embedded throughout. In this section, as I discuss the study, I indicate where I had to consider ethics, so that you can understand the embedded nature of ethics. This is a precursor to the discussion I have in the following section that unpacks the ethical considerations I had and the framework I developed.

Situating the study

When considering how your study fits within the broader research and social context, I encourage you to reflect on what those contexts are and where your study fits. For my study, I started my research journey examining the contemporary education context in Australia.

The contemporary education context in Australia is increasingly focused on measurable outcomes and standards. In the last three decades the standards-based reform agenda has impacted the practice and professionalism of teachers in Australia (Allard and Doecke 2014; Biesta et al. 2015; Breen et al. 2018). This agenda emphasizes 'outcomes, effectiveness, performance standards, service delivery to "clients", customer satisfaction and accountability' (Kostogriz 2012, p. 398). This has reconfigured the work of teachers in their classrooms, but also their interaction with colleagues and the principal team in their schools (Biesta 2015; Kostogriz 2012; Lingard et al. 2017).

In response to this standards-based reform agenda and with the high attrition rates of teachers (Buchanan et al. 2013), my PhD study aimed to better understand the experience of early career English teachers working within the context of standards-based reforms in Victoria, Australia. The hope was that through focusing on the experience of teachers and their narratives and stories, my research could contribute to how institutional structures and supports were tailored to the individual and collective professional needs of English teachers early in their careers. I also hoped to provide a space for participating teachers to collaboratively discuss their work and engage in critical reflection. With this context and hope in mind, I began to examine what research questions would be appropriate.

Research questions

Your research questions connect to the aims of the study but are also informed by, and inform, your methodology and data analysis approaches. Because of this, my research questions changed across the research journey. While these changes were not substantial, I only settled on the final wording of these in the writing up stage. This is an important ethical consideration because if you are not willing to alter your questions, particularly with qualitative work, you may not be open to the data because you are trying to make the data fit the research questions.

The research questions I ended up with were:

1. What is the nature of early career English teachers' everyday professional experience within the context of standards-based reforms?
2. What processes of becoming are evident/possible within these contexts?

Two supporting questions address the specific dimensions of early career English teachers' everyday experience and becoming:

1. How do institutional practices and discourses shape early career English teachers' work?
2. How do early career English teachers negotiate professional and related relationships within and beyond schools, and how do these shape their becoming? (Owen 2020)

Methodology

I selected ethnography-of-education because it enabled the examination of 'teachers' practice and the issues of everyday life in classrooms from the perspective of teachers' (Woods 1996, p. 10), which was the focus of my research questions. Ethnography-of-education is when researchers external to the field use ethnography to study education, whilst ethnography-in-education is undertaken by education researchers, teacher educators, teachers and students (Green and Bloome 2005). As I am an experienced English teacher in secondary schools, as well as being a teacher educator at a university level and an education researcher through the PhD study and other related research projects, I utilized an ethnography-in-education methodology, as it meant I could explicitly recognize my role as the researcher and my background and expertise. Considering your background, experience, and expertise, and the insight you may have during data collection is an important ethical consideration because if you ignore it, you are not recognizing your role and potential bias in interpreting data.

Once I had selected a methodology, I had to consider participant numbers and data collection methods. Determining participant numbers is always tricky and requires consideration for what the research project needs, but also what the researcher or research team can practically manage. Ethnography-in-education is labour intensive and as such I had the practical consideration of how many participants I could manage within the time and word-length constraints of a PhD study. Also, the purpose of the study required a focus on depth, the unique experience of individuals, and breadth, the commonality of experience across individuals. This chapter does not focus on methodology, so I will not go into a lot of detail, but considering the above, I ended up with nine participants.

Data collection

To enable a holistic understanding of teachers' work I needed a range of data collection methods that would be sustainable across an eighteen-month data collection timeframe. Reading other studies and talking with my supervisors was important at this stage of planning, because I had not undertaken research before and so I was only theorizing about how to manage the data. After much consideration and conversation, I included: semi-structured interviews, focus groups and ethnographic observation with participants. I also collected artefacts from the schools, including photographs. The data collection methods I selected provided rich data about participants experience and becoming, but because of the embedded nature of the data collection in the professional lives of participants, they also raised important ethical considerations about the influence I had on them and their workplaces and their influence on me.

Data analysis

The aim of the research, the methodology and research questions guided my choice of analysis methods, which were thematic and narrative analysis. Thematic and narrative analysis are broad approaches and there is nuance related to how these can be used in a study. Again, it is worth taking the time to read how other studies that have used the approach to data analysis you are considering, to understand how they work in practice.

Thematic analysis enabled me to establish broad themes across the data set and across the participants (Barton and Hamilton 1998). Unlike traditional thematic analysis, due to my methodology I used an ethnographic approach to coding, where I was able to assign data to more than one thematic category. My reasoning was that the purpose was not to remove the social or time-space context from the data set, but rather to consider that 'different instances [were] all examples of similar phenomenon' (Barton and Hamilton 1998, p. 69). This approach effectively enabled me to build an understanding of the individual and collective needs of early career English teachers, addressing a key aim of the study.

Yet, the purpose of the study was also to understand the everyday experiences of teachers, which meant that I needed to include another analytical approach. Narrative analysis recognizes that individuals 'lead storied lives' (Connelly and Clandinin 1990, p. 2), and it is through stories that individuals make meaning individually and together (Bakhtin 1981; Benjamin 2007).

Now that I have briefly outlined the research approach to frame the discussion about ethics, in the next section, I discuss the specific ethical considerations of the study.

Ethical considerations

As you may be aware in undertaking research all researchers are required to align with ethical processes. These are regulatory requirements to ensure the protection of all involved and the integrity of the research. Regulatory ethics is an objective form of ethics that is based on apparently stable social, moral, and ethical norms. While social, moral, and ethical norms are an essential part of the human experience (Bakhtin 1993), they are limited in their ability to address the unique experiences of individuals. It is important for research projects to align with regulatory ethics, but researchers need to look beyond regulatory ethics to the specific ethical dimensions that relate to their project.

Due to the ethnography-in-education methodology I used, I had to consider what impact my involvement with participants and my presence in their workplace would have on them in terms of their understandings of work and their relationships with colleagues. While any study that works with participants should be considering the influence on participants, because ethnography occurs across a long period of time, in the case of my study this was eighteen months and requires the researcher to be with the participant in different contexts, it is particularly important.

A dialogic approach to ethics

My ethical framework and my potential influence on participants and their influence on me is underpinned by my epistemological understanding. I believe that there is no absolute truth about human experience because an absolute truth does not, and cannot, include 'diversity of speech and voice' (Bakhtin 1981, p. 25). Bakhtin's identity and dialogic theories highlight the social and nuanced experience of individuals and the process of meaning-making. It positions that we make meaning with others, and we do so through language. The meaning that we make forms our ideologies, where ideologies are views, values and beliefs. From this epistemological, I could never remove myself from the data. In examining the everyday work and becoming of early career English teachers, I could not take an objective approach in terms of observing my participants. It was unavoidable that I would impact their experience and therefore their becoming, as they would mine. Taking this into consideration I decided that rather than attempt to remove my influence, or to merely be an observer, I would choose to be a part of my participants' everyday experience and becoming. I realized that by working with and alongside my participants, I would have the opportunity to gain a somewhat embedded understanding of their experience. This aligned with my methodological approach of ethnography-in-education, where I could bring my position, knowledge, and expertise to the analysis.

Yet, this position required structures to ensure that I could understand, to some extent, my influence and the participants' influence on me. This is where Roth's (2013, p. 103) description of ethics being more than 'values in the mind', was important, as it empowered me to reflect on the 'thought and action, body and mind' dimensions. Two key concepts assist in this process: reflexivity and answerability.

Reflexivity

Reflexivity relates to the 'explicit, self-aware reflection and analysis' (Finlay 2012, p. 317) that the researcher engages in throughout the research process. When deciding to work with and alongside participants in an ethnography-in-education study, reflexivity provided a framework of reflection that assisted in ensuring the relationships I developed with participants, the data set that was formed and the analysis that was conducted was done so with 'integrity of understanding' (ibid, p. 317).

An example of this was my attempt to reserve judgement about the rightness or wrongness of participants actions and choices. Considering my experience in education I had to be careful when thoughts about what I would do would arise. I had to reflect on any judgement that arose to understand what was occurring and why. This can be difficult work and requires ongoing commitment and focus. This was important in the integrity of the relationships I built with participants, as judgement would have been negative to building trust and making meaning with participants. Haverkamp (2005, p. 146) describes this as 'the thoughtful, and sometimes courageous, commitment to creating trustworthy human relationships'. This integrity extended to analysis and the writing process.

Another example is my focus on making the familiar strange. Due to my use of ethnography-in-education it was important that I did not assume the workplaces of my participants were the same as those with which I had engaged as a teacher. Gordon et al. (2007) discuss the difficulty, but added importance, in making the familiar strange when conducting research in schools as they are 'familiar for all of us', either as a student and/or teacher. The role of the researcher, therefore, is to ensure that they are recording that which is 'beyond what "everyone" already knows' (Delamont 2014, p. 11). Due to my experience in schools, I was positioned to do that as I was able to 'access more subtle and underlying aspects of participants' work' (Owen 2020, p. 73). This is because I was able to use my expertise to undertake some of their work, which included working alongside them, and contributing to meetings and planning, to encourage empathy and understanding (Emerson et al. 2011). Yet, this required that I worked to be reflexive, which as stated above, included a process of 'explicit, self-aware reflection and analysis' (Finlay 2012).

Answerability

Answerability raises questions about the individual's responsibility to others and is derived from Bakhtin's earlier work (Bazerman 2004; Bialostosky 1999). Kostogriz and Doecke (2007) describe answerability as the ability and willingness

> to listen and to be open to the Other; it is to be immersed in the discursive space where the self becomes responsive and answerable when face to face with alterity. (p. 13)

This alterity, or otherness, can come from Others such as participants, but also from those within the institutions where participants worked, such as school leaders, colleagues and also policymakers through curriculum and policy documents. There were also the Others that were beyond the participants, such as the theorists and researchers that the participants and I discussed, as well as those that I engaged with in my development of the study. Answerability, therefore, is about transparency but also acknowledgement and integrity.

It is a concept that assisted me in developing a critical consideration of my role with respect to the participants, and the role of the participants in the study, as we worked together. From this concept comes the idea of being 'responsive' and 'answerable' (Kostogriz and Doecke 2007, p. 13) to the participants, society and myself. This is a dialogic understanding of ethics that assisted in my recognition that while the other is not like the self, the self recognizes and responds to the 'other's uniqueness and singularity' (Nealson 1997, p. 129). This linked to my reflexive position and, again, to Haverkamp's (2005) description of aiming to create trustworthy human relationships.

Yet, answerability extended beyond my interactions with participants. For example, it related to the responsibility I, as the researcher, had for the participants' stories, ensuring that both voices were heard. This meant that I needed to find a way for the participants' voices to not always be mediated through mine in the thesis. One step that I took to be answerable to the voices of my participants was to include much of their own words in the thesis, resulting in large sections of their stories being included verbatim. This also led to their voices not being restricted to the data analysis section, as my understanding of theories, methodology and ethics were informed by the meaning-making I was engaged in with participants across the two years of data generation.

Summary of ethical considerations

A process of dialogue between the researcher and participants encourages the researcher to move beyond the regulatory requirements of ethics to consider the specifics of their study and the relationship with participants. I encourage you to take the time to consider your ethical relationship with participants, which may be similar to what I have outlined here if you are using ethnography. Whether they are similar or not, the concepts of reflexivity and answerability may be useful. In my work, this enabled me to engage in a reflexive research process that provided a depth of understanding about the everyday experiences of the nine participants.

In the final section of the chapter, I provide an example of the application of this ethical approach from my thesis so you can develop an understanding of what it looks like in action.

Ethics in action

In the ethics section of my thesis, I used an example of a difficult ethical moment that occurred with a participant, Charlotte. Charlotte was a central participant in the study, which means she was involved in the ethnographic observation. Near the end of the two years of data generation, Charlotte lost a student to suicide, and she shared this information with me over text message. Below is a copy of the exchange:

> *Charlotte:* I lost a student yesterday. Someone I worked closely with, and adored, for three years. He chose to end his life. Third male student in 12 months. I feel like the curriculum is failing these rural kids somehow.
>
> *Ceridwen:* Oh Charlotte. That's devastating. I lost a past student once, a student from before I was a teacher, I taught him Distance Ed once a week through Apple Grove Victoria . . . I remember taking him to the National Gallery, it was the last thing we did together, as he had moved to Melbourne to live with his aunt so away from Apple Grove. He couldn't believe he was there, didn't think it was possible for him. I showed him my favourite paintings, we talked about the stories of paintings. He was thrilled to tell his aunt. He was 16. I remember him chattering away on the tram. I hadn't seen him for 6 months when he took his own life. Over 15 years later I still think of him. Yes, the curriculum as it restricts our ability to build relationships. But also, schools and teachers. The system of schooling where we each play a role. There are those, like you, that still find the place for relationships. But it's also broader, our communities, his family, friends, himself. Everyone is to blame, and no-one is to blame. Rather than blame, I like to think of the possibilities and what was possible while they were with us. That's why I remember the gallery with Devon rather than the times he would go off for lunch and then I would wander the streets of Yea because he hadn't

come back. Or how the system failed him. You provided him opportunities. All my love Charlotte.

Charlotte: Your words bring tears back to my eyes. I did everything I could for him, you're right. I think I feel like I wish (that was grammatically okay) I was there on Thursday to speak with him. To explain that this would pass and to try and convince him to stay. Drugs really stuff these kids – especially those with special needs (Owen 2020, pp. 62–3).

There were a number of ethical considerations that were made before I responded to Charlotte's initial message.

The first related to our relationship and consideration of her intent in sharing the news with me. There was a need for me to be responsive, to provide support and comfort, but was there also a need for me to provide guidance? I was unsure from which position I should be responding to Charlotte as over the nearly two years of data generation we had worked extremely closely together. I had entered her school, classroom and life, as required of an ethnographic study. As such, our relationship was heteroglossic (Bakhtin 1981) and it was unclear if Charlotte was contacting me as a friend, a researcher or a mentor. While she was reporting a school-based event, it was obviously also impacting her personally. Answerability was essential in unpacking the experience for Charlotte and me, and in determining my response.

However, there were other dimensions that also impacted my response. The first is the biographical dimension, where the suicide of Charlotte's student brought up memories of a similar situation that I had experience, making the receiving of the message difficult for me. As I recorded in my thesis, 'when I received it, I was once again awash with all the thoughts and feelings I had experienced over the years since Devon's suicide' (Owen 2020, p. 63). Additionally, were more recent memories of when a colleague confided to me about a similar loss she had experienced. This is an example of the ethical consideration that the researcher has towards themselves and others. I was answerable to Charlotte, Devon and myself. Ethics is not objective, but dialogic in nature; when researchers engage in research with participants, they are dialogically making meaning and that will impact both theirs and their participants becoming.

The ethical understanding I had, the Bakhtinian approach of answerability, and the developing skill I had of reflexivity, did not provide a straightforward answer to Charlotte, as regulatory ethics would attempt to do, but it assisted me in navigating the situation with empathy and integrity, which considering Charlotte's response means that I was able to provide Charlotte with what she evidently needed, even if those needs were not explicit.

Conclusion

Ethics is not just a regulatory hurdle if you are working with participants. It is an important consideration for your entire research project. It is informed by your epistemology and relates to your methodology. Ethics informs your approach to the research process and how you understand your interactions with participants and the potential impact of the research on them and you as a researcher and person. Your decisions about ethics will not match what I have outlined in this chapter, as you will have a different epistemology and methodology.

In this way, ethics is both regulatory and situation specific. The regulatory ethics embedded in institutions is an essential but incomplete part of the research project. Ethics is also specific to the project, the individuals and the time and place. This chapter has demonstrated how in completing research, ethics can be understood as an integral part of the process extending beyond meeting institutional requirements to include the impact of the subjective experience of all the relevant people involved.

References

Allard, A. and Doecke, B. (2014). Professional knowledge and standards-based reforms: Learning from the experiences of early career teachers. *English Teaching: Practice & Critique,* 13(1), pp. 39–54.

Bakhtin, M. M. (1981). *The dialogic imagination: Four essays.* Emerson, C. and Holquist, M., trans. Austin, TX: University of Texas Press.

Bakhtin, M. M. (1993). *Toward a philosophy of the act (V. Liapunov rans).* Austin, TX: University of Texas Press.

Barton, D. and Hamilton, M. (1998). *Local literacies: Reading and writing in one community.* London: Routledge.

Bazerman, C. (2004). Intertextualities: Volosinov, Bakhtin, literary theory, and literacy studies. In: Ball, A. F. and Freedman, S. W. -(eds), *Bakhtinian perspectives on language, literacy, and learning.* New York: Cambridge University Press, pp. 53–62.

Benjamin, W. (2007). The storyteller. In: Arendt, H. (ed.), and Zohn, H., trans. *Illuminations: Essays and reflections.* New York: Schocken Books, pp. 83–110.

Bialostosky, D. (1999). Bakhtin's 'rough draft': Toward a philosophy of the act, ethics, and composition studies. *Rhetoric Review*, 18, pp. 6–25.

Biesta, G. (2015). What is education for? On good education, teacher judgement, and educational professionalism. *European Journal of Education*, 50, pp. 75–87.

Biesta, G., Priestley, M., and Robinson, S. (2015). The role of beliefs in teacher agency. *Teachers and Teaching*, 21, pp. 624–40.

Breen, L., Illesca, B., and Doecke, B. (2018). Stepping inside an English classroom: Investigating the everyday experiences of an English teacher. *Changing English*, 25, pp. 252–63.

Buchanan, J., Prescott, A., Schuck, S., Aubusson, P., and Burke, P. (2013). Teacher retention and attrition: Views of early career teachers. *Australian Journal of Teacher Education*, 38, pp. 112–29.

Connelly, F. M. and Clandinin, D. J. (1990). Stories of experience and narrative inquiry. *Educational Researcher*, 19(5), pp. 2–14.

Delamont, S. (2014). *Key themes in the ethnography of education: Achievements and agendas.* London: SAGE Publications.

Emerson, R. M., Fretz, R. I., and Shaw, L. L. (2011). *Writing ethnographic fieldnotes.* 2nd ed. Chicago: University of Chicago Press.

Finlay, L. (2012). Five lenses for the reflexive interviewer. In: Gubrium, J. F., Holstein, J. A., Marvasti, A. B., and McKinney, K. D. (eds), *The SAGE handbook of interview research: The complexity of the craft.* Thousand Oaks, CA: SAGE Publications.

Gordon, T., Holland, J. and Lahelma, E. (2007). Ethnographic research in educational settings. In: Atkinson, P., Coffey, A., Delamont, S., Lofland, J. and Lofland, L., eds. *Handbook of ethnography.* London: SAGE Publications, pp. 188–203.

Green, J. and Bloome, D. (2005). Ethnography and ethnographers of and in education: A situated perspective. In: Flood, J. I., Heath, S. B., and Lapp, D. (eds), *Handbook of research on teaching literacy through the communicative and visual arts.* Mahway, NJ: Lawrence Erlbaum, pp. 167–180.

Haverkamp, B. E. (2005). Ethical perspectives on qualitative research in applied psychology. *Journal of Counselling Psychology*, 52, pp. 146–55.

Kostogriz, A. (2012). Accountability and the affective labour of teachers: A Marxist-Vygotskian perspective. *The Australian Educational Researcher*, 39, pp. 397–412.

Kostogriz, A. and Doecke, B. (2007). Encounters with 'strangers': Towards dialogical ethics in English language education. *Critical Inquiry in Language Studies*, 4, pp. 1–24.

Lingard, B., Sellar, S., and Lewis, S. (2017). Accountabilities in schools and school systems. In: Noblit, G. W. (ed.), *Oxford research encyclopaedia of education*. Oxford: Oxford University Press, pp. 1–28.

Nealson, J. (1997). The ethics of dialogue: Bakhtin and Levinas. *College English*, 59, pp. 129–148.

Owen, C. C. (2020). Becoming an English teacher: The shaping of everyday professional experiences in early career teaching. Thesis, Monash University.

Roth, W. M. (2013). Toward a Post-Constructivist ethics in/of teaching and learning. *Pedagogies: An International Journal*, 8, pp. 103–25.

Woods, P. (1996). *Researching the art of teaching: Ethnography for educational use*. London: Routledge.

PART II

Up and Running – Grappling with Methodology, Tools, Participants and Ethics

CHAPTER 8

How Can We Design Data Collection to Explore Children's Learning?

Kirstin Mulholland

This chapter shares my experiences of practitioner research, with a particular focus on approaches to data collection. This took place in an English primary context with nine- and ten-year-old pupils and considers my attempts – as both teacher and researcher – to support the development of children's metacognition in maths. This chapter begins by outlining the context for my research, including my rationale and the issues that led me to explore this aspect of practice. It then focuses in upon the challenges surrounding the exploration of the invisible processes of children's learning, and describes my approach to data collection, using pupil views templates to enable insight whilst allowing pupils to express their thoughts and experiences in their own words. This chapter ends by offering reflections regarding my own learnings from these experiences, including considerations for data collection for those seeking to engage in similar research in their own settings.

The research context

In my own primary classroom, I can call to mind many pupils who – although often enthusiastic – had little understanding of the 'why' in maths. Why did they need to use particular approaches and procedures? Why employ multiplication or division to solve a particular problem or puzzle? They couldn't explain their reasoning, and for many children, I believe this stemmed from a lack of understanding of the maths activities they were doing. My pupils didn't really seem to understand what successful learning looked like. Instead, when trying to answer unfamiliar problems, many would resort to guesswork, no matter how wild or inaccurate.

These difficulties are particularly important given the work of Picker and Berry (2000, p. 88) who point out that, for many children, understanding of how maths works is often hidden and invisible, and so it can seem 'more like a power than an ability, which anyone has the possibility to learn'. This resonated with me. I can vividly remember my fifteen-year-old self, feeling completely baffled by certain lessons (Algebra certainly springs to mind!). I remember feeling helpless as those around me seemed to effortlessly move on with the tasks, whilst I felt as though I had reached a ceiling in my learning which no amount of explanations from my friends or teachers could help me breach.

When I first began my own further studies in education as part of a Master's degree, and later doctoral study, this stood out to me as one of the 'problems' within my own practice that I really wanted to try to solve. Further reading uncovered a great deal of evidence emphasizing the value of teaching pupils to think through maths to develop deeper understanding (Boaler 2006; Wright and Taverner 2008). In England, the work of the National Centre for Excellence in the Teaching of Mathematics (NCETM) has since helped this idea to become widespread, forming the basis of the Teaching for Mastery programme which had been used in more than 5000 schools by July 2019 (NCETM 2019).

Developing a conceptual framework

Once I established that pupils must be taught to think through maths to gain deeper understanding, I next needed to identify how best to achieve this. The more familiar I became with research surrounding maths, the more I recognized the potential influence that a range of factors – including cognitive, pedagogic and even emotional concerns – hold upon pupils' experiences of the subject. Perhaps most striking was the strength of feeling that maths seems to inspire. The belief that maths is viewed negatively by many pupils is widespread, with researchers reporting pupils' perceptions of maths as 'boring' (Brown et al. 2007, p. 12), inspiring 'anxiety, feelings of inadequacy and feelings of shame' (Hoyles 1982, p. 368) and, perhaps most tellingly, of mathematicians as 'authoritarian and threatening' (Picker and Berry 2000, p. 88).

One explanation often suggested for this is the idea of 'success' in maths, as well as, crucially, pupils' perceptions of what they are 'capable' of understanding. This is closely linked to attitudes and self-belief, and it seems likely that this plays an influential role in pupils' experiences – and ultimately their levels of achievement – suggesting a 'reciprocal relationship' (Sammons et al. 2008, p. 10) between self-concept and attainment.

As I read more, for me, this highlighted the importance of pupils' metacognition for maths. Metacognition is often defined as 'learning to learn', and involves the planning, monitoring and evaluation of learning strategies to make sure that these are successful (EEF 2018). Many sources suggest the potential benefits of metacognition for pupils' progress and attainment (EEF 2018), as well as for motivation for learning (Lai 2011). For me, developing metacognition therefore meant helping pupils to become more conscious of their own learning, ultimately empowering them to assume increased ownership and control of their own learning journeys.

However, whilst there is some agreement around the importance and potential benefits of metacognition, how to support the development of this in the classroom is rather less clear. Developing metacognition in the classroom can require a shift of focus, away from procedural learning, where pupils follow a set of instructions without understanding the reasons underpinning the selection and use of a particular approach, and towards discussion about the 'why' and 'how' of learning: why does this method work here, why was that mistake made, or how can we improve this particular strategy?

Identifying and clarifying the focus for research

As pupils couldn't explain their thinking, I took this as both my starting point and my goal: by emphasizing the development of pupil talk and explanations, I hoped to encourage pupils to engage more actively in mathematical challenges, approaching them as something which could be decoded and understood, rather than as something unfathomable which could only be solved through guess work and luck. Moreover, the opening of discussions would also allow me, as a teacher, to develop understanding of my pupils' level of mathematical engagement, unpicking misconceptions and, hopefully, thereby helping to inform my pedagogic understanding of how best to tackle these.

I therefore set out to build more frequent opportunities for talk of this nature – metacognitive talk – into our day-to-day interactions during maths lessons. This included adopting a range of different strategies, including modelling my own metacognitive thinking using a 'Think Aloud' approach, supporting pupils' reflections upon learning through questioning, and also by including more frequent opportunities for pupils to collaborate during lessons in order to prompt discussions around learning. I then attempted to explore the impacts of this upon my pupils' perceptions of maths lessons, focusing on two central, related research questions:

1. What are children's experiences of teaching and learning in maths?
2. What do children understand about how learning in maths happens? What is their *metacognition* for maths?

My approach to the research process

As stated earlier, this study arose from challenges within my classroom context, and is therefore grounded in the everyday realities of my own pedagogic practice. This places this study very firmly within the field of practitioner research, however this investigation is also a description of a very specific and localized case of thirty-seven-, nine- and ten-year-old pupils from one school in northern England. It's therefore important to acknowledge that this can be seen in contrast to the current bias towards scientific methods and generalizable knowledge (Pring 2000; Groundwater-Smith and Mockler 2007).

Biesta (2007) summarizes this view by observing that there are those within the field of education who believe that research can provide an objective 'truth' and that it's then possible to translate this directly into a set of rules or routines for teaching which can be applied across classrooms and school contexts 'without any further reflection on or consideration of the concrete situation they are in' (p. 11). However, like many teachers, I believe that 'The variability of educational situations is grossly underestimated' (Stenhouse 1988, p. 44) and that, as a result, knowledge is always heavily dependent upon its context.

For me, as for Stenhouse (1988), education research deals with people; participants rather than subjects. Human responses often vary widely and can be difficult to predict, therefore what may work in one school or with one pupil, may produce a very different impact upon another. However, this line of thinking prompts one obvious question: if each individual classroom is unique, what's the point of seeking to better understand them through education research?

To argue this point, I draw upon Pring's (2000) suggestion that 'uniqueness in one respect does not entail uniqueness in every respect' (p. 258). Although pupils and classrooms are undoubtedly different, there may be similarities which mean that aspects of knowledge can be transferred to a new context. Good teachers don't need to be told what to do (Stenhouse 1988), however this doesn't mean that knowledge of this nature is worthless. This knowledge can 'guide us first in our attempts to understand what the problem might be and then in the intelligent selection of possible lines of action' (Biesta 2007, p. 16), or, as Hall (2009) puts it, prevent us from 're-inventing the wheel' (p. 672). For me, this indicates that research should act not as a 'truth', but instead aim to be informative, perhaps furthering the thinking of practitioners, prompting their own research in their own classrooms.

This means that research, rather than providing an instruction manual to be followed to the letter, instead supplies possible avenues for exploration by describing approaches which may be suitable, together with their successes and probable limitations. Rather than serving as a means of looking backwards – at something which has previously been achieved and attempting to replicate this – it provides a means of using existing knowledge to inform future action, making it possible to assimilate, adapt and build upon previous work, learning from past mistakes to further enhance practice.

The importance of selecting the 'right' data collection tools

It's important to recognize that, if research is to inform the actions that teachers make within their own classroom contexts, the task of generalization is shifted from the researcher to the reader (Rudduck 1985), so that the reader is responsible for determining whether the research is relevant to their own situation. This stance had profound implications for my study; the description of the case thus becomes fundamental, and it becomes the job of the researcher to describe this as objectively – as openly and honestly – as possible (Larsson 2009).

This issue of objectivity strongly influenced my choice of data collection tools. As Stenhouse (1979) explains, 'any description [. . .] rests upon the judgment of him who observes and describes, both in respect of what he selects as worthy of notice and in respect of interpretative perception' (p. 8). Whilst I believe that, to make this research useful to me as a teacher, it was necessary to interpret the findings using my own judgement, I also recognize that, to be relevant for other practitioners, the data must be allowed to speak for itself.

Observations made by those on the outside may be influenced by previously held beliefs or run the risk of being misinterpreted. Unfortunately, this is particularly true when the subject of investigation isn't easily visible to external observers. Metacognition is an internal – and therefore largely invisible – process (Ritchhart and Perkins 2008) and can be difficult to 'see' in action. Therefore, to increase the reliability of my research, I endeavoured to select data collection tools which allowed pupils to express their own experiences in their own words. This also further enhanced the validity of this research through adhering to the principle of dialectics by aiming to reproduce the voices of different people as authentically as possible – and to keep them so genuine and original that the informants can recognize their own thinking in them. (Heikkinen et al. 2012, p. 9)

I considered several different methods for attempting to capture pupils' metacognition, however each of these came with their own flaws. Perhaps the most obvious – or, at least, the method which I tried first – was to observe pupils at work in the hope of identifying metacognitive behaviours and charting any change. This method wasn't without complications. For example, Lai (2011) suggests that strategies which require pupils to 'think aloud' to identify metacognition don't account for actions that children carry out implicitly, meaning that metacognitive knowledge and skills can be underestimated. My attempts to scrutinize video recordings were also problematic. At first, I tried to record a focus group of six volunteers as they worked, however, as well as greatly reducing the number of pupils that I was able to observe in this way, I quickly found that the time needed to transcribe the resulting interactions was unsustainable, particularly when added to the joint demands of my existing roles as teacher and teacher-researcher.

Pupil views templates

Instead, my research supervisors suggested using pupil views templates (PVTs). Originally developed by Wall and Higgins (2006), PVTs are designed to gain insight into pupils' metacognition through providing space for pupils to reflect upon their lived experiences. Consisting of a space for pupils to draw themselves during lessons, along with speech and thought bubbles, PVTs allowed me to collect data from my class as a whole, rather than being limited to a small number of volunteers. Furthermore, data was already in a written format, eliminating the need for transcription. Most importantly, PVTs allowed pupils to articulate their thinking and record this independently, removing the need for these to be interpreted by an external observer. An example of a completed PVT can be found in Figure 8.1.

PVTs are designed to be used by teachers in classrooms. They can be seen as pedagogic in intent because they encourage pupils to reflect upon their thinking, however this leads some to argue that they can't provide true evidence of metacognitive thought. To address this, I draw upon Wall's (2008) argument that evidence from PVTs, in which pupils have demonstrated awareness of metacognitive strategies and their conscious deployment of these, would nevertheless 'surpass any subjective evidence from observation completed by a third person' (p. 32).

I'd also argue that, far from being a disadvantage, the pedagogic nature of PVTs was actually beneficial to this study, serving a dual purpose in prompting pupils to reflect upon lessons, providing not only a form of data collection which allowed me insight into pupils' metacognition, but also – and perhaps more importantly – a teaching tool which encouraged them to do so. In this way, PVTs provided, not just a window for external observers to examine pupils' thinking, but also a mirror to reflect pupils' thoughts and actions, enabling the children themselves to consider their own 'thinking about thinking'.

FIGURE 8.1 *An example of a completed pupil views template (PVT).*

Data collection

Children were given thirty minutes to complete PVTs, although this was flexible to allow all pupils sufficient time to record their ideas. Pupils completed PVTs once each half term for one academic year after a randomly selected lesson. The decision to select focus lessons at random was deliberate and aimed to investigate a wide range of learning opportunities including a game-based lesson on probability; a lesson on mixed word problems in the context of measures; and a practical investigation involving weight. However, whilst it was extremely interesting to gain insight into such a variety of lesson types, there were disadvantages to this choice. For example, the dissimilarity of lessons meant that it wasn't possible to track any kind of progression in children's thinking, meaning that instead it was necessary to use this more simply to provide insight into pupils' thinking at each individual point in time. When planning practitioner research, it's therefore important to carefully consider when data will be collected, fully taking into account all the potential implications of these choices.

In light of the findings of Black et al. (2006), children were informed at the outset of teaching that they'd complete a PVT based on that particular maths lesson. This allowed pupils time for reflection prior to recording their views, and also perhaps encouraged them to think more about their learning throughout the course of the lesson than they may have done ordinarily. The decision to record their experiences of a specific lesson was influenced by the work of Hoyles (1982), who found that an 'approach based on the description of real situations rather than the collection of generalities or opinions was thus felt to be more meaningful to the pupils concerned' (p. 350).

Analysis

To analyse the PVT data, I adopted a general inductive approach to analysis which allowed me to consider the data set as a whole, identifying trends, patterns and areas of potential interest as they emerged, rather than being limited by a predetermined analysis structure (Thomas 2006). This freedom was particularly appealing as it parallels neatly with my belief that education research is most valuable when it 'develops in response to specific problems of practice' (Hiebert et al. 2002, p. 6). Similarly, I believe that this data has been most informative precisely because the details contained within it were used directly to shape its analysis.

Following the procedures outlined by Thomas (2006), data was first prepared in a common format, a series of Word documents. I then read the text closely to familiarize myself with the content, gaining an initial sense of themes and patterns emergent from the text. I subsequently read the pupils' responses several more times to further identify categories or themes. Similar responses were grouped to allow them to be read 'horizontally'; this facilitated comparisons within categories, following the processes previously used by researchers such as Marshall (1999). This process continued until all themes and patterns had been identified, with no further examples presenting themselves.

Findings

The inductive analysis process led to the identification of three key themes. Whilst a more detailed account of these findings can be found elsewhere (Mulholland Shipley 2016), an overview of these themes is shared below:

1. There was a shift in pupils' use of language to describe their learning experiences. For example, over time, pupils used more questions and speculation, and there was also a decrease in simplistic descriptions of learning as 'easy' or 'hard'.
2. As research progressed, pupils' PVTs included a greater proportion of representations of their discussions with peers, suggesting that collaboration and discussions about learning became more frequent over time.
3. However, PVTs didn't include greater proportions of metacognitive comments as the research progressed. Instead, there was a decrease in comments of this nature during the data collection period.

Initially, I was disheartened by these findings, the lack of clarity surrounding the development of metacognition and my resulting inability to answer the second research question for this study. However, more than this, what most struck me about this analysis was that, although it was interesting to explore the information contained within the PVTs in this way, it failed to reflect the richness of the insights these provided about what actually went on in our maths lessons: the conversations my pupils had, who was participating and who wasn't doing their fair share, and the feedback about the tasks themselves. Therefore, I felt that there was yet more to be gained by looking again at the PVTs in their entirety.

The value of embedded case studies

With the support and encouragement of my supervisors, I decided to look again at the PVTs, exploring the templates from specific children on a case-by-case basis. My rationale for this was that, by considering the reflections from pupils as the unique individuals they are, I'd be able to more easily determine the impact that the approach had upon the development of their metacognition. Looking back, I realize that giving myself permission to revisit my data and to look again, and reconsider my next steps accordingly, ultimately deepened my learning and understanding. I therefore decided to incorporate two narrative-based embedded case studies (Yin 2009) to tell the stories of one boy and one girl from my class – Harry and Grace. Through sharing these case studies, I hoped to enrich the evidence collected throughout this research, offering further insight into the experiences of the children in the focus cohort.

In selecting Harry and Grace as the subjects of these case studies, I followed the advice of Pettigrew (1990), who suggests that, considering the limited number of cases which can usually be studied, it's logical to select extreme situations in which the process of interest is 'transparently observable' (p. 275). This is true of Harry and Grace: they intrigued me precisely because they stood out from their peers, rather than being representative of them. They were distinct in terms of the comments they recorded in their books, their contributions to discussions, and, for Grace, in her changing attitudes towards maths. They demonstrated strong metacognitive knowledge and skilfulness, and I hoped that, by gaining a better insight into their thoughts and experiences, I might also be able to better understand how our emphasis upon metacognitive talk may have influenced the development of their metacognition.

I also hoped that these case studies would provide further means of ensuring the authentic representation of Harry and Grace, in keeping with the principles of dialectics (Heikkinen et al. 2012). I therefore adopted a two-column format to present these case studies, with one column containing a narrative of each case, whilst the other contains analysis. This structure was used to more clearly distinguish between the different voices represented. I wanted Harry and Grace to express themselves and their experiences from their own perspective, in their own words, and I felt that the column format provided a physical space to separate their voices from my own interpretation of them. Harry's case study is presented in its entirety elsewhere (Mulholland 2021), however, an example of this format – taken from Grace's case study – is also shared in Figure 8.2 below.

Presenting Harry's and Grace's own representations of their experiences in their own words fulfils one of their fundamental rights, not only according to my beliefs as a teacher-researcher, but also according to the UN Convention on the Rights of the Child which states that any child 'who is capable of forming his or her own views should have the right to express those views freely in all matters affecting that child' (U.N.C.R.C. 1991, Article 12). It also allowed me the opportunity to more deeply explore the wealth of valuable yet unforeseen information that emerged from the PVTs – without following any agenda or preconceived notions – and simply discover whatever I could regarding our shared classroom reality.

Reflections

Overall, my experience of practitioner research through this study helped me to better understand not just my pupils' metacognition, but the research process itself, prompting vital reflections around

DATA COLLECTION TO EXPLORE CHILDREN'S LEARNING 141

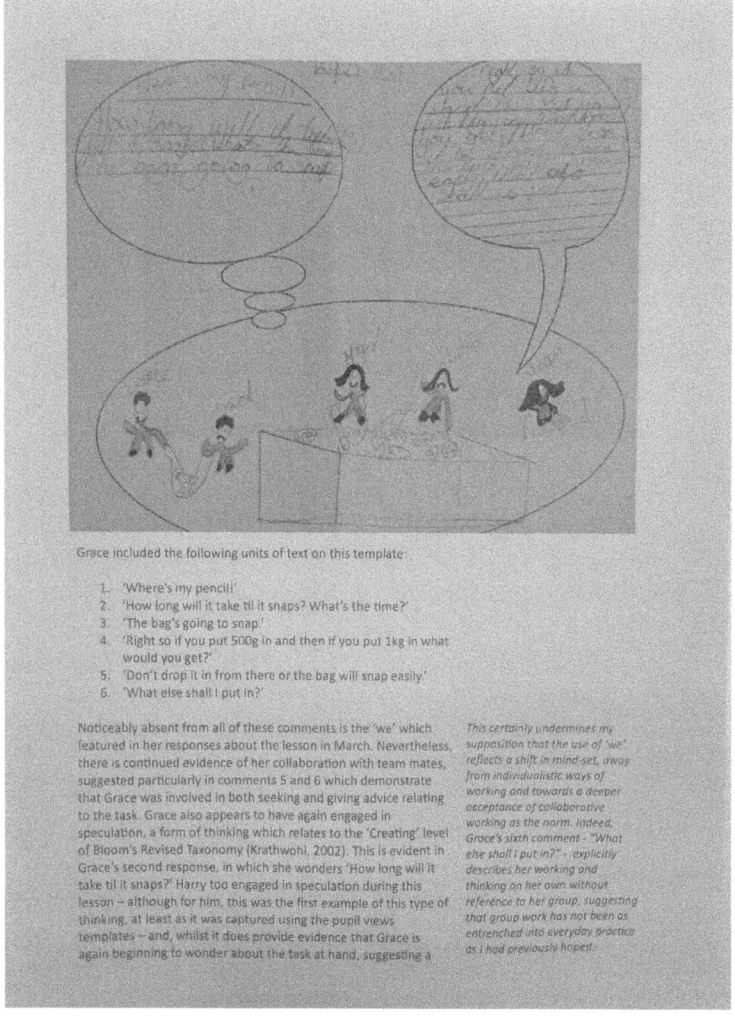

Grace included the following units of text on this template:

1. 'Where's my pencil!'
2. 'How long will it take til it snaps? What's the time?'
3. 'The bag's going to snap.'
4. 'Right so if you put 500g in and then if you put 1kg in what would you get?'
5. 'Don't drop it in from there or the bag will snap easily.'
6. 'What else shall I put in?'

Noticeably absent from all of these comments is the 'we' which featured in her responses about the lesson in March. Nevertheless, there is continued evidence of her collaboration with team mates, suggested particularly in comments 5 and 6 which demonstrate that Grace was involved in both seeking and giving advice relating to the task. Grace also appears to have again engaged in speculation, a form of thinking which relates to the 'Creating' level of Bloom's Revised Taxonomy (Krathwohl, 2002). This is evident in Grace's second response, in which she wonders 'How long will it take til it snaps?' Harry too engaged in speculation during this lesson – although for him, this was the first example of this type of thinking, at least as it was captured using the pupil views templates – and, whilst it does provide evidence that Grace is again beginning to wonder about the task at hand, suggesting a

This certainly undermines my supposition that the use of 'we' reflects a shift in mind-set, away from individualistic ways of working and towards a deeper acceptance of collaborative working as the norm. Indeed, Grace's sixth comment – "What else shall I put in?" – explicitly describes her working and thinking on her own without reference to her group, suggesting that group work has not been as entrenched into everyday practice as I had previously hoped.

FIGURE 8.2 *An example of the two-column analysis format used for the embedded case studies in my thesis.*

how to ensure that the authentic voices of the pupils themselves could best be 'heard'. Whilst I can in no way claim the authority to offer advice for others seeking to engage in practitioner research, I'd like to end this chapter by offering my reflections regarding my own learnings resulting from my experiences:

1. When planning practitioner research, it's important to consider approaches to data collection carefully. In particular, researchers need to determine which perspectives the research is seeking to gain, and how the choice of data collection methods may influence this.
2. If research aims to explore participants' experiences, it's important to think carefully about the extent to which their voices can be 'heard', and the implications of this. Similarly, when researching our own working contexts, it's important to reflect upon any potential influence that participants may experience which may lead them to feel unable to express their views openly and honestly, and how (and even whether) it's possible to mitigate against these.
3. In analysing and presenting research findings, it's important to consider how to ensure that interpretations remain faithful to the original voices of participants, maintaining authenticity and presenting an honest account of the research.

References

Biesta, G. (2007). Why 'what works' won't work: Evidence-based practice and the democratic deficit in educational research. *Educational Theory*, 57(1), pp. 1–22.

Black, P., Swann, J., and Wiliam, D. (2006). School pupils' beliefs about learning. *Research Papers in Education*, 21(2), pp. 151–70.

Boaler, J. (2006). How a detracked mathematics approach promoted respect, responsibility, and high achievement. *Theory into Practice*, 45(1), pp. 40–6.

Brown, M., Brown, P., and Bibby, T. (2007). "I would rather die": Attitudes of 16-year-olds towards their future participation in mathematics. *Proceedings of the British Society for Research into Learning Mathematics*, 27(1), pp. 18–23.

Education Endowment Foundation [EEF]. (2018). *Metacognition and self-regulated learning: Guidance report* [online]. Available: https://educationendowmentfoundation.org.uk/education-evidence/guidance-reports/metacognition [accessed 26 November 2023].

Groundwater-Smith, S. and Mockler, N. (2007). Ethics in practitioner research: An issue of quality. *Research Papers in Education*, 22(2), pp. 199–211.

Hall, E. (2009). Engaging in and engaging with research: Teacher inquiry and development. *Teachers and Teaching*, 15(6), pp. 669–81.

Heikkinen, H. L. T., Huttunenb, R., Syrjäläc, L., and Pesonen, J. (2012). Action research and narrative inquiry: Five principles for validation revisited. *Educational Action Research*, 20(1), pp. 5–21.

Hiebert, J., Gallimore, R. and Stigler, J. (2002). A knowledge base for the teaching profession. *Educational Researcher*, 31, pp. 3-15.

Hoyles, C. (1982). The pupil's view of mathematics learning. *Educational Studies in Mathematics*, 13, pp. 349–72.

Lai, E. (2011). *Metacognition: A literature review*. Always Learning: Pearson Research Report.

Larsson, S. (2009). A pluralist view of generalization in qualitative research. *International Journal of Research & Method in Education*, 32(1), pp. 25–38.

Marshall, M. N. (1999). Improving quality in general practice: barriers faced by health authorities. *British Medical Journal*, 319, pp. 164–167.

Mulholland, K. (2021). Using pupil views to uncover evidence of children's metacognition in mathematics. *International Journal of Student Voice*, 8.

Mulholland Shipley, K. E. (2016). *'I think when I work with other people I can let go of all of my ideas and tell them out loud': The Impact of a Thinking Skills Approach Upon Pupils' Experiences of Maths*. PhD thesis [online], Newcastle University. Available: https://theses.ncl.ac.uk/jspui/bitstream/10443/3282/1/Mulholland%20Shipley,%20K%202016.pdf [accessed 26 November 2023].

National Centre for Excellence in the Teaching of Mathematics [NCETM]. (2019). *Teaching for mastery: What is happening in primary maths, and what next?* [online]. Available: http://www.nwmathshub3.co.uk/news/2019/10/14/teaching-for-mastery-what-is-happening-in-primary-maths-and-what-next/ [accessed 26 November 2023].

Pettigrew, A. (1990). Longitudinal Field Research on Change: Theory and Practice. *Organization Science*, 1, pp. 267–292.

Picker, S. H. and Berry, J. S. (2000). Investigating pupils' images of mathematicians. *Educational Studies in Mathematics*, 43(1), pp. 56–94.

Pring, R. (2000). The false duality of educational research. *Journal of Philosophy of Education*, 34(2), pp. 247–60.

Ritchhart, R. and Perkins, D. (2008). Making thinking visible. *Educational Leadership*, 65(5), pp. 57–61.

Rudduck, J. (1985). The improvement of the art of teaching through research. *Cambridge Journal of Education*, 15(3), pp. 123–7.

Sammons, P., Sylva, K., Melhuish, E., Siraj-Blatchford, I., Taggart, B., Jelicic, H., Barreau, S., Grabbe, Y., and Smees, R. (2008). *Relationships between pupils' self-perceptions, views of primary school and their development in year 5*. London: Institute of Education, University of London.

Stenhouse, L. (1979). Case study in comparative education: Particularity and generalisation. *Comparative Education*, 15(1), pp. 5–10.

Stenhouse, L. (1988). Artistry and teaching: The teacher as focus of research and development. *Journal of Curriculum and Supervision*, 4(1), pp. 43–51.

Thomas, D. R. (2006). A general inductive approach for analysing qualitative evaluation data. *American Journal of Evaluation*, 27(2), pp. 237–46.

Wall, K. (2008). Understanding metacognition through the use of pupil views templates: Pupil views of learning to learn. *Thinking Skills and Creativity*, 3(1), pp. 23–33.

Wall, K. and Higgins, S. (2006). Facilitating and supporting talk with pupils about metacognition: A research and learning tool. *International Journal of Research and Method in Education*, 29(1), pp. 39–53.

Wright, D. and Taverner, S. (2008). *Thinking through mathematics*. London: Chris Kington Publishing.

Yin, R. J. (2009). *Case study research: Design and methods*. Thousand Oaks, CA: SAGE Publications.

CHAPTER 9

What Research Tools Might be Appropriate to Use with Young School-Age Children?

Sinéad Gallagher

Background

This is the story of my research journey that I hope will be of help to you on yours. While the primary focus of my chapter is the methodology and the tools I used, I'd first like to share a little about me. I think it is important to 'set out my stall' by outlining my personal (and theoretical) starting points as authors such as MacNaughton, Rolfe and Siraj-Blatchford (2010) argue that the idea of a researcher who is neutral and disentangled from their research is a myth. Indeed, what we choose to research and how we see the world are influenced by our cultural resources (Cousin 2010). I would encourage you to do likewise. It may be beneficial, at the onset of your journey, to determine your rationale as it may be helpful in providing focus to your research.

From a very young age, I had a love of numbers fuelled by my parents giving me interesting mental maths problems to solve – these involved cows, sheep, dogs, chairs, tables, legs, tails and shopping, to name a few. My (first) career as an accountant stemmed from that love. Later, I decided on a career change – lecturing. During my first year as a lecturer, I found that many of my non-accounting students disliked and had a fear of working with numbers. This phenomenon had not occurred to me – my circle of friends and peers enjoyed working with numbers. Then, volunteering in my children's junior infants' classroom, I perceived that a dislike of, and anxiety towards, maths was not confined to older students. At that stage, I began to review the literature on maths anxiety and attitudes towards maths and this really intrigued me.

And so, fellow researcher, I would suggest that you undertake such an exercise. Think about (and write down) how and why you came to have an interest in the topic you hope to research, share it with a critical friend to illicit their views and review the literature, to determine if a 'gap' exists.

How to find (as opposed to mind) the gap

As I reviewed the literature, various themes emerged. For example, maths pervades many aspects of our day-to-day lives and it can affect those we live and interact with, not just ourselves. Furthermore, over half of the variance in maths achievement can be attributed to experience, biological and environmental factors (e.g. parents/carers views on maths, resources, etc.) not intelligence (Organisation for Economic Co-operation and Development 2007). It was this latter nugget of knowledge that helped me to refine my focus, prompting me to delve deeper into attitudes towards maths, when these materialize and their association with maths anxiety.

After narrowing my focus, I found that negative attitudes act a barrier to learning maths and affect behaviours in class (Adelson and McCoach 2011). Moreover, highly maths anxious individuals tend to steer away from maths courses as early as eleven years of age (Dowker et al. 2016). However, while older children have the choice to opt out of maths courses, younger children may opt out psychologically by 'distancing themselves emotionally and attitudinally' from maths (Larkin and Jorgenson 2016, p. 926), which was another nugget of knowledge.

During this more focused and in-depth phase of my literature review I discovered the studies mainly involved secondary school students who have the ability to opt in or out of maths courses

(Attard 2011). There was a paucity of research conducted with younger children to consider their attitudes towards maths and whether they experience maths anxiety (Eden et al. 2013). This indicated a clear gap in the literature, and so, fellow researcher, I had found my 'gap'.

Having found my 'gap', I wanted to ensure that this was a topic worthy of investigation. Again, I would suggest that you follow a similar route – read extensively in your field of interest and if something 'hits home' for you, do some investigative work to see if this is an area worth pursuing. For me, I felt my research was important; a good basic knowledge of maths provides academic and varied career opportunities (Geist 2010), and poor numeracy skills can result in many disadvantages, including higher rates of unemployment, which have implications for overall health and well-being (Grotlüschen et al. 2016).

It was then time to consider my research questions, what methodology and tools I would use and whether these would align with my worldview. Let's look next at the research questions.

Moving on to your research questions

My initial review of the literature (oh, did I mention that your literature review will continue throughout your research journey?) identified a 'gap' and having deemed it to have merit, I then considered my research questions. Even though I was teaching in higher education, I wanted to undertake research with young children, as children develop emotional reactions to maths prior to entering secondary school and these are hard to change. This was not where I thought my literature review would take me. And that's the thing with research, you may have a general destination in mind, say a country, but the road you travel to get there has many twists and turns – you will not get to see the whole country, just a few highlights.

My initial 'country' or goal was to consider attitudes towards maths and its intersection with maths anxiety. However, first I needed to determine whether the children I would work with were maths anxious. I had to reflect on any potential biases I might have (e.g. gender or cultural biases) that could influence my research questions as well as ethical issues, which are crucial when working with children. These shifted my focus somewhat as I understood that these elements would impact my research questions and the methods I would employ to answer them, as would my worldview or paradigm, which is the next on our whistlestop tour.

Paradigm

So, what is a paradigm? Well, it is a set of integrated theoretical assumptions that underpin how I (and you) see the world. These assumptions encompass ontology, epistemology and axiology which in turn delineate the scope of the paradigms (Hammersley 2012). And what do each of these refer to and what was my position with respect to each, you may ask? Let's have a look!

- Ontology concerns the essence of reality, a researcher's view of reality and whether what I am researching is external to me or not (Saunders et al. 2009). Ontologically, I see children as having multiple realities, construed in their minds, which are formed by their life experiences.

- Epistemology considers the philosophical issues surrounding the nature of knowledge, how phenomenon can be understood, what acceptable knowledge is, how it can be acquired and whether the social world can be studied using the same principles employed in the natural sciences (Bryman 2012). Epistemologically, I believe people are different to other 'objects' and see children as knowledgeable and competent in their own right. I feel young children can provide valuable insights and information on issues which impact them. Moreover, I am of the opinion that children are the best source of information about themselves, rather than a third party.

- Axiology, while linked to my epistemological views, considers the role of my values while undertaking research (Bryman 2012). From an axiological perspective, I believe my values as an educator (mutual respect, dignity, celebrating differences, love of learning, support, hard work, perseverance, growth mindset) came into play when undertaking my research.

These are concepts that you too will have to consider as they will help you to determine your worldview and what methodology and tools are appropriate.

Having thought about and reflected on the various paradigms, I found that I wanted to employ methods that would prioritize children's perspectives on maths and allow me to engage with the children in a way that was sensitive to their unique characteristics. This, in essence, meant I wanted to conduct qualitative (as opposed to quantitative) research. With qualitative research, I would be exploring the children's experiences and perspectives which would entail non-numerical data (notwithstanding my affinity to numbers). However, I wanted to consider the intersection of attitudes towards maths with maths anxiety. And here's where I came to a cross-roads! From my literature review, I knew that the methods employed to determine maths anxiety levels were firmly within the quantitative dominion, with standardized questionnaires being used. As the ability to consider maths anxiety was a key component of my research, I had a choice to make – either make peace with using a quantitative tool or go back to the drawing board, and reconsider my research objectives and questions.

In the end, I adopted a mixed-methods approach which included both quantitative and qualitative research. I appeased my reticence by recognizing that this approach would offer perspectives that would not be available with a solely qualitative or quantitative methodology. The quantitative element allowed me to determine if the children were maths anxious which was my 'jumping off point'. The qualitative (and more substantial) element of my research allowed me to put in context the children's thoughts and beliefs about maths.

Consequently, my research fell within the Pragmatic paradigm which 'embraces plurality of methods' (Hoshmand 2003 cited in Johnson and Onwuegbuzie 2004, p. 16). This paradigm emphasizes the practical application of knowledge in real-world situations. It recognizes that knowledge is not created in a vacuum, but rather in the context of specific social, cultural and historical circumstances. It is also an approach that effectively combines the interpretivist (using qualitative tools) and post-positivist (using quantitative tools) paradigms. One of the main strengths of pragmatism is the ability for new and deeper meaning to come to light as a result of its practical relevance and focus on the problem to be researched

(Feilzer 2010). By engaging such an approach, my hope was to gain a fuller and deeper understanding of young children's perceptions of and attitudes towards maths, not just their level of maths anxiety (if it were present).

My views on children and the data collection methods I used

No doubt you have your own ideas about children's competencies. For me, I view children as competent actors in their own lives who have an important role to play in the present and not just in the future, as adults, which aligns with my epistemology and ontology. I do not think children can be treated as a homogenous group nor do I believe a simple categorization into age brackets can account for differing competencies and cognitive development. Therefore, I felt that it was important to engage with children's diverse competencies and use different mediums of communication, as Clark (2005) proposes. Additionally, different methods were necessary to shed light on different aspects of the research.

If you are hoping to carry out research *with* children, please note that there is little consensus regarding the theories, techniques and methods which should be adopted (Christensen and James 2008). Conducting research *with* as opposed to research *on* children is still a relatively recent concept (Einarsdóttir 2007) and as Christensen and James (2008, p. 1) suggest, there are 'no well tested recipes with formulas guaranteeing a successful result'.

Given my ontology, my views on children and my research questions, the data collection methods I employed were questionnaires, drawings, vignettes/stories and small group interviews. By combining these tools, it allowed me to consider both qualitative and quantitative aspects, for example, if children were maths anxious and why this might be the case. I undertook my primary research in three schools, two of which were co-ed, and with seven different class groups (spanning first through third class). This combination allowed me to compare and contrast schools and year groups. In total, approximately 130 children participated in various elements of the research. I visited each class on a weekly basis and developed a rapport with children in advance of the small group interviews, which were last. This sequence also facilitated a discussion based on a review of the other data sources. I will now explore the data collection methods I used for my research, in the order in which they were employed.

Questionnaires

Though questionnaires are a widely used research tool, young children are not frequently the chosen respondents (Einarsdóttir 2007). Nonetheless, a number of scales were developed to evaluate the level of maths anxiety experienced in younger populations. After a review of these scales, the *Children's Anxiety in Math Scale* (CAMS) (Jameson 2013) was chosen. Having made peace with myself that this was a necessary initial step, albeit not aligned with my worldview, and having secured permission to use the questionnaire from the author, I adapted it for an Irish audience (primarily by including Irish rather than American terminology). Using a tool that has already been devised and tested has many advantages, and perhaps it is something you too might consider.

For me, adopting the CAMS centred on a number of factors; internal consistency was high ($\alpha = 0.86$); the scale was of average length, it used the same 5-point pictorial rating scale throughout, the statements were short and were to be read aloud.

Drawings

The second tool chosen was children's drawings. These are a common non-verbal method employed to uncover young children's views and experiences (Clark 2005) that had not been used previously in research on attitudes towards maths, to my knowledge. Drawing, a popular activity among children (Thomas and Jolley 1998), is perceived as fun and non-threatening (Rubin 1984), takes time and so does not require an immediate response (Dockett and Perry 2005), minimizes the power relationship (Merriman and Guerin 2006) and does not require literacy and verbal skills (DiCarlo et al. 2000). Moreover, drawing is a child-centred research method that 'grants precedence to children's experience and respect to their personhood' (Merriman and Guerin 2006, p. 56). It also offers a different way for children to express their experiences and perspectives, involving children in research as 'producers of knowledge' (Eldén 2012, p. 68). For my research, the children were asked to draw a picture about how maths made them feel, for example, happy, sad, relaxed. The children were also asked to write a short note explaining their drawing.

Vignettes/stories

The third tool employed was a vignette or story. My hope was for this to provide additional context to children's attitudes towards maths and allow triangulation of data. Though some studies use vignettes within a quantitative paradigm, others such as Finch's (1987, p. 112) use of this technique resonates closely with qualitative researchers as it 'leaves space for respondents to define the situation in their own terms'. A review of literature on the use of vignettes clearly demonstrates their ability to capture how meanings, beliefs, judgements and actions are situationally positioned (Hughes and Huby 2002).

For this activity, the children were asked to write a short story about a boy or girl who was about to start school and would have to do maths as part of their schoolwork. The vignette was a hypothetical, yet 'concrete and realistic' example (Bryman 2012, p. 479). This was important as was the fact that the children, having at least two years of formal schooling, would have previously expressed their ideas in writing (Mason and Boscolo 2000). Consequently, asking children to write a story allowed them to participate effectively using their talents (Punch 2002) while being cognizant of the fact that each may have differing competencies, strengths and cognitive development. For example, some children may not like to draw, and their competencies may lie elsewhere.

Small group interviews

Given my interpretive leanings, where I place importance on understanding and interpreting the subjective experiences of children, I felt that semi-structured interviews were an appropriate research tool. This was especially the case as they would allow me to probe children's perceptions on maths. However, as you may know, interviews with children pose both practical and methodological problems encompassing ethical concerns, which span a range of issues. For example, debate abounds as to whether children should be interviewed individually or in groups as well as where the interview should be conducted (Cohen et al. 2011). It was decided to conduct small group interviews in the children's school and the small group element was an effort to dilute the power differential. By conducting the interviews in school, in a place where we could be seen but not heard by other adults, this alleviated some ethical concerns, while also ensuring I did not encroach on the children's private terrain.

Another consideration when interviewing children is their willingness to answer questions. Responses are more likely to be forthcoming where there is good rapport, when children feel their information is confidential and where the interviewer reacts to and follows their lead (Punch 2002; Hill 2006). As the interviews were last, I was by then a familiar figure with an established rapport while the semi-structured nature of the interviews allowed flexibility to follow the children's lead.

As 'multiple viewpoints, perspectives, positions and standpoints' were sought (Johnson et al. 2007, p. 113), the 'initial' children invited to participate in the interviews included some who appeared to like and dislike maths and those at various points on the maths anxiety spectrum. Each 'initial' child was asked to nominate two or three other classmates to take part in the interview with them in the hope that the children would feel more powerful, relaxed and comfortable (Dockett and Perry 2005).

To increase the likelihood of the questions being answered honestly, unambiguous and comprehensible instructions were given in child-appropriate language at the start of each interview (Mayall 2008). And for clarity, please note, the same advice holds true when interviewing adults! Additionally, children were asked whether they agreed or disagreed with a statement before probing more deeply to assess their initial response (Mayall 2008). The children were encouraged to discuss the issues amongst themselves and in this respect the interviews were similar to focus groups. However, the one difference was the fact that they were somewhat more structured than a focus group as there were a small number of questions that I posed to each group. The children were also encouraged to ask questions at any point, which stimulated interaction, but were asked to be respectful of others' views. This less structured, indirect approach to interviewing was adopted as it allowed more flexibility to respond to the children's input (Merriman and Guerin 2006).

The use of the four methods or tools, sometimes called a 'mosaic approach', allowed children to effectively participate in the research and use their competencies in doing so while also answering the research questions. Each time I met with the children, I reinforced the fact that it was their own views about maths that I was interested in. This was fundamental as children may not have experience of adults wanting to be taught by children about their own lives and experiences.

Ethical considerations

While the main focus of my chapter is my worldview and the methodology and tools I employed in my research, I have made passing reference to ethical considerations. For me, these were extremely important because my research involved younger children. As with my worldview, it is not possible to separate my ethical lens from the research process and ethical issues must be considered in advance and alongside methodological issues (Howe and Moses 1999). Furthermore, when the participants are children and are viewed as social actors in their own right, even more complex ethical challenges and responsibilities are present (Einarsdóttir 2007).

Though I will not provide an in-depth review of this aspect of my journey, I suggest that you read Emanuel et al. (2000, p. 2701) seven requirements that answer their question 'What makes research involving human subjects ethical?' and the ten 'topics' which Alderson (1995) recommends when conducting social research with children. In both, the protection from harm of participants and protection of their autonomy are paramount (Bryman 2012) with voluntary informed consent being an important aspect of autonomy (Howe and Moses 1999). Privacy and confidentiality are also vital issues for children when seeking their thoughts and opinions on general matters such as their experience of maths. For example, Alderson and Morrow's (2011, p. 35) suggestion of using the 'Chatham House rules' was employed when interviewing as these rules can be explained clearly even to young children. In essence, the children can talk to other people about what was said in the interview but are asked not to relate the name of the person who said it nor the names of any of the people they were talking about.

The readings mentioned above were helpful to me (and I hope will be to you) when considering methodology, associated ethical issues and gaining ethical approval for my research. The ethical approval process was also illuminating as some nuggets of knowledge were provided from those on the board, given their experience of undertaking research with children.

In conclusion

My research took me on an unexpected journey. Undertaking my data collection with children in primary school was a truly wonderful experience and I loved every minute of it. I am grateful to all those who made my research possible, especially the children themselves. Their enthusiasm was infectious, and I am thankful to them for sharing their knowledge, experiences and stories with me.

Are there things I would have done differently? Yes, but nothing fundamental. And what about the analysis of the data? Well that, I'm afraid, is a story for another day.

I wish you, fellow researcher, every success on your own journey. And if there are some specific pieces of advice I would leave you with it is these; choose a topic you are interested in and are passionate about so that you can enjoy your journey of discovery and be prepared to pivot. You too may encounter a T-junction or crossroads (or even end up on a Cul-de-Sec), just be sure to continue on your journey as the journey itself can be more important than the destination.

References

Adelson, J. and McCoach, D. (2011). Development and psychometric properties of the math and me survey: Measuring third through sixth graders' attitudes toward mathematics. *Measurement and Evaluation in Counselling and Development*, 44(4), pp. 225–47.

Alderson, P. and Morrow, V. (2011). *The ethics of research with children and young people: A practical handbook*. London: SAGE Publications.

Alderson, P. (1995). *Listening to children: Children, social research and ethics*. London: Barnardos.

Attard, C. (2011). 'My favourite subject is maths. For some reason no-one really agrees with me': student perspectives of mathematics teaching and learning in the upper primary classroom. *Mathematics Education Research Journal*, 23(3), pp. 363–77.

Bryman, A. (2012). *Social research methods*. 4th ed. Oxford: Oxford University Press.

Christensen, P. and James, A. (2008). *Research with children: Perspectives and practices*. 2nd ed. London: Falmer Press.

Clark, A. (2005). Listening to and involving young children: A review of research and practice. *Early Child Development and Care*, 175(6), pp. 489–505.

Cohen, L., Manion, L., and Morrison, K. (2011). *Research methods in education*. 7th ed. Oxon: Routledge.

Cousin, G. (2010). Positioning positionality. In: Savin-Baden, M. and Major, C. H. (eds), *New approaches to qualitative research*. London: Routledge, pp. 9–18.

Dicarlo, M., Gibbons, J., Kaminsky, D., Wright, J., and Stiles, D. (2000). Street children's drawings: Windows into their life circumstances and aspirations. *International Social Work*, 43(1), pp. 107–20.

Dockett, S. and Perry, B. (2005). Researching with children: Insights from the starting school research project. *Early Child Development and Care*, 175(6), pp. 507–21.

Dowker, A., Sarkar, A., and Looi, C. (2016). Mathematics anxiety: What have we learned in 60 years? *Frontiers in Psychology*, 7, pp. 1–16.

Eden, C., Heine, A., and Jacob, A. (2013). Mathematics anxiety and its development in the course of formal schooling - a review. *Psychology*, 4(06), pp. 27–35.

Eldén, S. (2012). Inviting the messy: Drawing methods and 'children's voices'. *Childhood*, 20(1), pp. 66–81.

Einarsdóttir, J. (2007). Research with children: Methodological and ethical challenges. *European Early Childhood Education Research Journal*, 15(2), pp. 197–211.

Emanuel, E., Wendler, D., and Grady, C. (2000). What makes clinical research ethical? *Jama*, 283(20), pp. 2701–11.

Feilzer, M. (2010). Doing mixed methods research pragmatically: Implications for the rediscovery of pragmatism as a research paradigm. *Journal of Mixed Methods Research*, 4(1), pp. 6–16.

Finch, J. (1987). The vignette technique in survey research. *Sociology*, 21, pp. 105–14.

Geist, E. (2010). The anti-anxiety curriculum: Combating math anxiety in the classroom. *Journal of Instructional Psychology*, 37(1), pp. 24–31.
Grotlüschen, A., Mallows, D., Reder, S., and Sabatini, J. (2016). Adults with low proficiency in literacy or numeracy. *OECD Education Working Papers, No. 131*. Paris: OECD Publishing.
Hammersley, M. (2012). *What is qualitative research?* London: Bloomsbury Academic.
Hill, M. (2006). Children's voices on ways of having a voice children's and young people's perspectives on methods used in research and consultation. *Childhood*, 13(1), pp. 69–89.
Howe, K. and Moses, M. (1999). Ethics in educational research. *Review of Research in Education*, 24, pp. 21–59.
Hughes, R. and Huby, M. (2002). The application of vignettes in social and nursing research. *Journal of Advanced Nursing*, 37(4), pp. 382–86.
Jameson, M. (2013). The development and validation of the Children's Anxiety in Math Scale. *Journal of Psychoeducational Assessment*, 31(4), pp. 391–5.
Johnson, B. and Onwuegbuzie, A. (2004). Mixed methods research: A research paradigm whose time has come. *Educational Researcher*, 33(7), pp. 14–26.
Johnson, B., Onwuegbuzie, J., and Turner, L. (2007). Toward a definition of mixed methods research. *Journal of Mixed Methods Research*, 1(2), pp. 112–33.
Larkin, K. and Jorgensen, R. (2016). 'I hate maths: Why do we need to do maths?' Using iPad video diaries to investigate attitudes and emotions towards mathematics in Year 3 and Year 6 students. *International Journal of Science and Mathematics Education*, 14(5), pp. 925–44.
MacHaughton, G., Rolfe, S., and Siraj-Blatchford, I. (2010). *Doing early childhood research: International perspectives on theory and practice*. London: Open University Press.
Mason, L. and Boscolo, P. (2000). Writing and conceptual change. What changes? *Instructional Science*, 28(3), pp. 199–226.
Mayall, B. (2008). Conversations with children: Working with generational issues. In: Christensen, P. and James, A. (eds), *Research with children: Perspectives and practices*. 2nd ed. London: Falmer Press, pp.109–24.
Merriman, B. and Guerin, S. (2006). Using children's drawings as data in child-centred research. *The Irish Journal of Psychology*, 27(1–2), pp. 48–57.
Organization for Economic Co-Operation and Development. (2007). *Understanding the brain: The birth of a learning science*. Paris: OECD Publications.
Punch, S. (2002). Research with children: The same or different from research with adults? *Childhood*, 9(3), pp. 321–41.

Rubin, J. (1984). *Child art therapy: Understanding and helping children grow through art*. 2nd ed. New York: Van Nostrand Reinhold.
Saunders, M., Lewis, P., and Thornhill, A. (2009). *Research methods for business students*. 5th ed. Harlow, England: Financial Times/Prentice Hall.
Thomas, G. and Jolley, R. (1998). Drawing conclusions: A re-examination of empirical and conceptual bases for psychological evaluation of children from their drawings. *British Journal of Clinical Psychology*, 37(2), pp. 127–39.

CHAPTER 10

How Do You Choose an Appropriate Data-Gathering Tool?

Christion Hutchinson

Identifying a research area can be challenging, involving deliberation combined with understanding and interpreting new terminologies. This chapter will outline my research journey. My focus throughout this chapter is on data-gathering tools, specifically interviews. I will outline my small-scale research study, situated in one rural school in Ireland, through the lens of an interview.

This chapter details my rationale for my research area and developing my research question. This was central to the research process as it would inform my research focus and design. Based on this, along with my justification, I will explain why I chose a specific methodology and the significance of an interview as an optimum data-gathering tool. This was far from a eureka moment. It involved in-depth reading and reflection. Aligning these elements with my paradigm was essential as they are intrinsically linked. This will be discussed and aligned with my position as an insider researcher. Finally, ethical considerations and how data was analysed will be considered, and the many lessons learned discussed.

What to research and where to start?

Conducting research involves a curiosity, preference or interest. I wanted to identify an aspect related to my work as a teacher of autistic learners. Through many years of experience, I recognize how these learners learn and how to respond to the complexities of teaching this cohort. Interestingly, conversing with colleagues highlighted that perceptions of including this cohort in mainstream classrooms varied, and they grappled with the challenges of including them. Initially, I was surprised as teachers need to know more about ASD to respond to its complexity (Ravet 2015). This has consequences for autistic learners, as autism is among the most common neurological disorders (American Psychiatric Association 2013). The prevalence of ASD has steadily increased over the past three decades (Ravet 2018). These factors, combined with three autism classes in the study school where inclusion occurs daily, signified teachers will have to teach these learners at some point in their careers. Consequently, an aspect worth exploring as it reflects my personal and professional interests, which I maintain is a key consideration for anyone setting out on their research journey.

The exploration of my topic

Establishing the meaning behind key concepts and terminologies is an important element of the research process. An essential factor I needed to consider was establishing the foundations of inclusion. Literature has indicated many stances on the inclusion debate, but the overarching theme lacked clarity (Krischler et al. 2019). How was I to unpack the various interpretations of inclusion? This process was daunting because aligning my views with literature resulted in paradoxes due to interpretation. Therefore, I needed to align an interpretation that matched my beliefs, as it would be impossible to address every variation. To this end, I recognize children's fundamental right to an appropriate education, regardless of ability. My stance aligns with the numerous international conventions (United Nations 1990, 2006) and Irish legislation (Government of Ireland 2004) for all learners to enjoy their human rights and freedoms.

Interestingly, one of my findings indicated that my colleagues acknowledged these rights. However, this right could be in jeopardy without a comprehensive understanding of the concept of inclusion. I needed a holistic view and a narrative on including autistic learners.

Narrowing my focus

An important factor you should consider when you have identified a topic is refining its scope so it is feasible to study. My initial focus was on inclusion, but this is a multifaceted concept with no agreed definition; therefore, too broad to research. Identifying an aspect of this concept that would help address its limitations was important. Through extensive background reading, I found interesting insights into the concept of inclusive pedagogy. The core of inclusive pedagogy relates to adapting the curriculum to meet the needs of all learners and valuing all children equally (Mintz and Wyse 2015). Through reflection, this concept aligned with my thinking and provided a specific focus that helped to shape my research question further.

Developing my research question

Developing a tightly focused research question was essential; to do this, you may need to consider several aspects. In my context, these included addressing the challenges/difficulties teachers experience when including autistic learners in a mainstream class. It could not be answered with a yes or no, and I felt it could be completed in the timeframe. Undoubtedly, limitations would be identified; however, the possibility of supporting teachers in their efforts to include autistic learners was an opportunity that could not be missed. The increasing prevalence of autism suggests teachers will have to teach these learners at some point (Ravet 2018). With these factors in mind, it became imperative I understood 'How can teachers be supported to adopt an inclusive pedagogy for the education of autistic learners in a mainstream setting?'

Choosing a suitable methodology

The next step in the research process requires the selection of a suitable methodology. When identifying an appropriate methodology, consider the data you require to answer your research question. Distinguishing between a quantitative and qualitative approach is essential. A quantitative approach focuses on numerical data (Punch 2013), where responses are limited to the range supplied due to predetermined questions (Leavy 2022). While a qualitative approach is ideal when seeking more information about human interaction (Lichtman 2013). How do you identify the correct method to underpin your research? For example, my research had numerical data present, such as age and experience, but my main focus was human interest. Therefore, a quantitative approach was rejected as I wanted to explore and interpret my colleagues' perspectives based on their opinions and experiences. Based on this, I considered a qualitative research design most suitable.

Within this consideration, I also questioned what specific methodology would be the best option for my research. I considered a case study the most appropriate methodology as they are well established in social sciences. What is a case study, and how could interviews provide the required information? A case study is an empirical inquiry that examines a case within its everyday context when the boundaries between the case and context may not be obvious (Yin 2018). My initial readings identified numerous types of case studies, such as single and multiple cases (Yin 2018). The first step in choosing a case study was determining the type I should use. My research focused on one school's teaching population, a specific group in a specific location; consequently, I considered a single case study acceptable as it aims to capture the details of an ordinary situation (Yin 2018). This aligned with my context, and participants could provide their interpretation of the questions asked.

Once I established a case study would be employed, the next step required was confirming the most suitable research tools. An interview was deemed most appropriate. In reaching this choice, I reflected on the data that I required; I wanted to gather participants' perspectives, and the focus of interviews in a case study is on how and why questions (Yin 2018), ultimately letting participants convey their perspectives in their own words and, subsequently, receive a detailed description (Merriam and Tisdell 2015). This perspective confirmed interviews as the optimal tool, giving me a holistic view, as interviews are an important source of case study evidence (Yin 2018).

The significance of an interview

As is the case for any early researcher, I read widely on the many tools available and what was entailed in employing each. Initial readings indicated an interview is a conversation with a purpose when an interviewer questions an interviewee and then collects information like a conversation (Lune and Berg 2017). This method caught my attention as I had plenty of experience with similar conversations. At first, I thought this could be an easy option. Further reading revealed differences between interviews and conversations (Brinkmann and Kvale 2018). Now, the interview became a more complex issue for me, alerting me I needed to read extensively about this tool to understand its complexities in gathering data as interviews produce knowledge rarely discussed in general conversations (Denscombe 2017). This was significant, as an interview would allow me to get participants' accounts and lived experiences that may otherwise be concealed uninfluenced by external factors, specifically, the absence of other people and the potential to receive privileged information. Albeit, interviews can introduce hidden risks due to a lack of preparation (Denscombe 2017), planning (Bryman 2016) and awareness of the social interactions involved (Braun and Clarke 2013). These considerations were pertinent as I sought my colleagues' viewpoints and experiences, and engaged more deeply with literature that specifically addressed the interview instead of more general research texts. I advise you to do the same; once you clearly understand the variety of research tools, it is important to consult texts that deal exclusively with specific tools.

Advantages of interviews

From the more focused readings I conducted, interviews have many advantages, including receiving a wealth of information (Roulston and Choi 2018), gaining insight (Punch 2013), incorporating participants' perceptions (Silverman 2010), multiple perspectives (Flick 2021), accessibility (Braun and Clarke 2013) and flexibility (Bryman 2016). The advantages for my research meant insights could be explored by providing a platform for participants' accounts and reasoning behind their feelings, actions and opinions, ultimately gaining insights into the participants' views, thoughts and beliefs, and applying them to the bigger picture of inclusion. Although there were significant advantages to employing interviews, limitations were also present.

Limitations of interviews

Literature has outlined several limitations and challenges for researchers using the interview as a research tool. These included being time consuming (Robson and McCarten 2016), having lots of data (Bryman 2016) can be unreliable due to smaller samples (Braun and Clarke 2013), incorporating the Hawthorne Effect, where people are recognized as behaving differently when observed (Denscombe 2017) and be intrusive (Braun and Clarke 2013). These were key considerations, and my research emphasized limitations; time was a factor, and the probability of the Hawthorne Effect was acknowledged. A further potential issue highlights interviewer bias can impact interview reliability (Denscombe 2017). Nevertheless, what did this mean for my research, and could I overcome these challenges, and if so, how? Naturally, due to my prior relationships and interest in the subject, my bias would likely influence the interview schedule. These, combined with the intrusive nature of interviews, signified the necessity to keep language, expression and gestures neutral, supported by the question's wording.

The interviews were recorded, which may have caused unease or discomfort to participants along with my bias. Therefore, objectivity was essential, which is the absence of bias in research (Denscombe 2017). To address my bias, I needed to acknowledge it and ensure reliability. Reliability is when a researcher's method is always consistent (Gibbs 2018). How could I provide this consistency?

The optimum data-gathering tool

Some factors you should consider when choosing a data-gathering tool are based on the information you seek. Initially, observations were considered. However, this method was most likely to produce unreliable results due to the probability of the Hawthorne Effect. I selected interviews because they let me gather information from the participant's perspectives and were convenient. There are multiple types of interviews: unstructured, semi-structured and structured, and variation in the type of interview comes with its own attributes (Punch 2013). So, based on this, you will need to identify what type of interview would best suit your research.

Unstructured interviews are informal conversations with a focus (Lune and Berg 2017). The interviewer's role is exploratory, with no interview schedule (Merriam and Tisdell 2015). Due to these attributes, this type of interview was rejected as I sought specific information that may have been overlooked by utilizing this type of interview. Second, I considered using semi-structured interviews, which allow the interviewer some flexibility by, for example, modifying the sequence, content and administration of questions (Robson and McCartan 2016). This approach incorporates probes supporting follow-up questions based on participant responses (Roulston and Choi 2018). Again, this type of interview was rejected due to the characteristics outlined. I sought participants' insights without deviation and to support standardization and comparability; therefore, I considered a structured interview most suitable.

A structured interview consists of multiple pre-defined questions that do not allow for deviation (Punch 2013). Utilizing structured interviews supported the expression of participants' thoughts without my influence supporting standardization. Participants' viewpoints were accommodated by providing an option for elaboration at the end of each question, accommodating expansion. So, this method let me gather and interpret data from teachers' perspectives. This approach focuses on specifics (Flick 2021), and my specific focus was inclusion. Utilizing this approach supported reliability by asking the same questions in the same order and location.

How my view of the world influenced the design of the interview schedule

A further consideration relates to the researcher's beliefs. Your belief systems will influence how you see the world, your choices and your research design. My belief system played a significant part in my research, guiding my research design and interview schedule. Although I did not know it then, these were my ontological and epistemological positions. It was the first time I encountered these terms, and honestly, they confused me and still do! Nevertheless, what is ontology? Ontology is the study of being, focusing on what is with the nature of existence and the structure of reality (Crotty 2012). What does this mean for research? My research aimed to gain a deeper understanding of how people perceive inclusion. Ontology seeks to answer a question utilizing existing knowledge (Alharahsheh and Pius 2020); therefore, I wanted to interview my colleagues to get their perspectives. I believe everyone has their own perspective, and there is no single reality, as in most cases, their opinions and experiences influence their decision.

This led me to the second concept, namely epistemology. This is concerned with knowledge and how knowledge is perceived. But what did this mean for my research? Epistemology involves knowledge and how we know what we know (Crotty 2012). I grappled with applying this to my research, but I eventually concluded that it is a way of uncovering knowledge to reach reality (Alharahsheh and Pius 2020). For example, inclusion has multiple interpretations, and many scholars take slightly different viewpoints. This is not to say they are wrong, as this is based on their epistemological position.

I believe interactions between people and concepts are context-specific. So, to answer my research question, I needed to consider the data type required to support my analysis. My epistemological position was vital as this provided a framework, specifically, how you will approach your research. I wanted to identify my colleague's perceptions; therefore, interviews would provide the insights I required by accommodating individual expression. Interviews are best suited to experience-type research questions (Braun and Clarke 2013).

Based on my stance, I had one further consideration. Which paradigm did I align with? First, I considered a positivist perspective;

this approach usually focuses on numerical data, experiments and statistics (Cohen et al. 2017). Positivists seek relationships between variables, and this perspective is unsuitable to a social context due to constant conjunction (Robson and McCarten 2016). As noted, I mainly pursued individual viewpoints, so this perspective was rejected. From my background reading, based on the variables outlined, an interpretivist perspective was considered most suitable. An interpretivist perspective allows social scientists group subjective meaning into a single concept (Bryman 2016). The mind creates meaning; therefore, individuals construct interpretations (Crotty 2012). Thus, multiple interpretations of inclusion may be present without a unified understanding. Again, my objectivity was essential, so my views did not indirectly shape the findings. I adopted a single concept of inclusion while acknowledging multiple interpretations to standardize inclusion in my context.

These factors signified the importance of utilizing an interview. I wanted to examine reality from varying standpoints and try to draw it all together to see if there was a consensus and the factors which either contributed to or inhibited this. For instance, the participants were from different backgrounds, such as special class teachers, mainstream teachers and special education teachers; therefore, different perspectives would be expressed. Conducting interviews allowed an examination of current practices from all stakeholders, ultimately providing varied insights and positions on inclusive practice.

The interview schedule

The next step required was designing the interview schedule to get the information I needed. Again, as participants were my colleagues, prior relationships and knowledge had to be considered as this may influence what participants expressed (Dwyer and Buckle 2009). I required a narrative uninfluenced by my input and one I could interpret. From this standpoint, the start of the interview was important. Initially, non-threatening questions were asked to let the participants settle in (Robson and McCarten 2016).

My interview schedule featured forty-one questions and three sections. This may seem like a lot; however, semi-structured interviews usually have ten or fewer questions with multiple prompts. Section one had nine gender, age and career questions, and section two had nine questions designed to gather participants' views. The questions in these sections, apart from the first four, were answered 'yes', 'no' or 'unsure'; consequently, they were quick and easy to answer. The final section had twenty-five scale questions and had an option for elaboration. The questions aligned with the study's aims and objectives, and derived from the literature review's content, ultimately letting the participants interpret the question asked. Importantly, four external teachers piloted the interview to ensure an appropriate timeframe and questions. The interviews were audio-recorded and transcribed for accuracy. A summary was provided to each participant to ensure the findings were factual and supported the study's validity.

Sampling and participants

When considering your sample, you need to ensure the sample represents the study's aims and objectives. For example, since my study focused on one location, the individuals outside that area could not provide a factual account. As a result, non-probability sampling was used, which involves choice when selecting the sample (Merriam and Tisdell 2015). Convenience sampling was used by selecting the closest individuals to participate or those who are accessible (Lune and Berg 2017). Complete collection sampling was utilized as the sample included all teachers within the school (Cohen et al. 2017). I chose this sample as these individuals could provide the information I sought. However, my position as a member of the group I was studying brought its own considerations.

Complexities of being an insider researcher

What is an insider researcher, and how could this impact your research? An insider researcher studies a group they belong to (Breen 2007). When considering my position, I faced a dilemma. Was this a strength or limitation? The participants were colleagues. Therefore, I viewed this as an advantage as I was aware of background information when developing questions that could give me comprehensive information. However, being an insider researcher had limitations you must be aware of if considering its use. For example, it includes greater familiarity, which may impact objectivity (Unluer 2012). I had prior knowledge and could potentially be biased. Therefore, maintaining my neutrality and not letting my bias dominate was critical. I needed to reflect on my own preconceptions and experiences to ensure sensitivity to responses (Roulston and Choi 2018). But why was this important?

I was privy to sensitive information, so bias during data collection and analysis was possible. Being rigorous and transparent through all data collection and analysis stages is essential, ensuring neutral language and avoiding leading, loaded or complicated questions (Robson and McCartan 2016). During the interview, there was a definite risk of assumed understandings and social desirability bias, which is participants' responses are based on their view of what is socially appropriate (Bryman 2016). So, being an insider researcher was far from straightforward – ethical issues must be considered.

Ethical considerations

Ethical and moral issues are central when conducting interviews (Brinkmann and Kvale 2018). Interactions between the interviewer and the interviewee are central; therefore, interviews are immersed in ethical considerations. How can these be overcome? Ethical guidelines provide a framework that supports researchers in considering the possible ethical dilemmas faced in research (Wiles 2012). Before proceeding with my study, ethical approval was granted. My research included various ethical considerations: Informed Consent, Privacy and Data Storage.

The first, informed consent, involves informing participants what they are consenting to (King and Horrocks 2010). For my research, a formal letter was sent to participants outlining the study's purpose, description, risks and benefits, along with what participation involved. Written consent was requested, and withdrawal at any stage was highlighted, avoiding deception and maintaining integrity. These were significant factors due to my position and prior relationships, as my colleagues may have felt coerced to participate (Fleming 2018).

Confidentiality was a second important consideration. Confidentiality is a form of privacy: not disclosing information from a participant, which could result in identification, signifying the importance of anonymity (Cohen et al. 2017). For my research, pseudonyms were given to participants to protect their anonymity. Confidentiality was assured as data was kept strictly private. All information was encrypted; hard copies were stored securely.

Data analysis

Using interviews as a data-gathering tool will result in significant data. One challenge I faced was deciding what to do with the data. Qualitative data was gained from nearly all questions, resulting in comprehensive data I had to interpret as an interpretivist. Analysis relies on interpretation, so multiple interpretations can be made when analysing data (Cohen et al. 2017). To address this possible variation, I used Braun and Clarke's (2013) six-step thematic analysis while cognizant of my research question, bias and objectivity. I interpreted transcripts by reading and re-reading to identify themes and patterns, which was time consuming. To ensure the themes were relevant and useful, reverting to my research question was critical (Seth et al. 2022). The emerging themes were derived from literature and responses during interviews. Coding supported analysis by identifying and labelling data (Punch 2013).

The analysis of quantitative data brought its own challenges as quantitative data was gained from all questions. I had to translate these responses into relevant categories. I used the Statistical Package for Social Sciences (SPSS) to support this interpretation. Initially, this was challenging as I had no experience using this software. I would advise practice and a trial-and-error approach to master the package. The quantitative data collected was analysed and categorized into frequencies and percentages for each question, allowing for comparison.

Conclusion

At times, I was unsure of what I was doing and whether my research would yield beneficial results. Fortunately, my colleagues agreed to be interviewed, which accommodated honest, factual accounts and utilizing an interview allowed the comparison of varying viewpoints and applied them to the bigger picture of inclusion. This identified that teachers have competing priorities. This signified the necessity of policies providing a seamless enactment for all learners. Would I do things differently? Yes, but not intrinsically linked to the research process. Conducting research can be all-consuming, and time for oneself is crucial. Remember, Rome was not built in a day. Take time for yourself, and do not be too hard on yourself. Take the highs with the lows. Finally, do not work in isolation; a critical friend can provide support and direction as they look at your work from a different perspective.

References

Alharahsheh, H. H. and Pius, A. (2020). A review of key paradigms: Positivism vs Interpretivism. *Global Academic Journal of Humanities and Social Sciences*, 2(3), pp. 39–43.
American Psychiatric Association. (2013). *Diagnostic and statistical manual of mental disorders*. 5th ed. Arlington, VA: American Psychiatric Association.
Braun, V. and Clarke, V. (2013).*Successful qualitative research: A practical guide for beginners*. London: SAGE Publications.
Breen, L. J. (2007). The researcher 'in the middle': Negotiating the insider/outsider dichotomy. *The Australian Community Psychologist*, 19(1), pp. 163–74.
Brinkmann, S. and Kvale, S. (2018). Doing interviews. In: Flick. U. (ed.), *The SAGE qualitative research kit*. 2nd ed. London: SAGE Publications, pp. 1- 185pp. 1- 185..
Bryman, A. (2016). *Social research methods*. 5th ed. Oxford: University Press.
Crotty, M. (2012). *The foundations of social research. Meaning and perspectives in the research process*. London: SAGE Publications.
Cohen, L., Manion, L., and Morrison, K. (2017). *Research methods in education*. 8th ed. London: Routledge.
Denscombe, M. (2017). *The good research guide. For small-scale social research projects*. 6th ed. England: Open University Press.
Dwyer, C. S. and Buckle, J. L. (2009). The space between: On being an insider-outsider in qualitative research. *International Journal of Qualitative Methods*, 8(1), pp. 54–63.

Fleming, J. (2018). Recognising and resolving the challenges of being an insider researcher in work-integrated learning. *International Journal of Work-Related Learning*, 19(3), pp. 311–320.

Flick, U. (2021). *Doing interview research: The essential how-to guide*. London: SAGE Publications.

Gibbs, G. R. (2018). Analysing qualitative data. In: Flick, U. (ed.), *The SAGE qualitative research kit*. London: SAGE Publications.

Government of Ireland. (2004). *Education for persons with special educational needs act (EPSEN)*. Dublin: The Stationery Office.

King, N. and Horrocks, C. (2010). *Interviews in qualitative research*. London: SAGE Publications.

Krischler, M., Powell, J. P., and Pit-Ten Cate, I. M. (2019). What is meant by inclusion? On the effects of different definitions on attitudes toward inclusive education. *European Journal of Special Needs Education*, 34(5), pp. 632–48.

Leavy, P. (2022). *Research design quantitative, qualitative, mixed methods, arts-based and community-based participatory research approaches*. 2nd ed. New York: The Guilford Press.

Lichtman, M. (2013). *Qualitative research for the social sciences*. London: SAGE Publications.

Lune, H. and Berg, L. B. (2017). *Qualitative research methods for social sciences*. 9th ed. London: Pearson.

Merriam, S. B. and Tisdell, E. J. (2015). *Qualitative research: A guide to design and implementation*. 4th ed. San Francisco, CA: Jossey Bass, Wiley.

Mintz, J. and Wyse, D. (2015). Inclusive pedagogy and knowledge in special education: Addressing the tension. *International Journal of Inclusive Education*, 19(11), pp. 1161–71.

Punch, K. (2013). *Introduction to social research quantitative and qualitative approaches*. 3rd ed. London: SAGE Publications.

Ravet, J. (2015). *Supporting change in autism services: Bridging the gap between theory and practice*. London: Routledge.

Ravet, J. (2018). 'But how do I teach them?': Autism and initial participant education (ITE). *International Journal of Inclusive Education*, 22(7), pp. 714–33.

Robson, C. and McCartan, K. (2016). *Real world research. A resource for users of social research methods in applied settings*. 4th ed. United Kingdom: Wiley.

Roulston, K. and Choi, M. (2018). Qualitative interviews. In: Flick, U. (ed.),*The SAGE handbook of qualitative data collection*. London: SAGE Publications, pp. 233–51.

Seth, S., Chadha, N. K., and Bhatia, H. (2022). *Qualitative methods a practical journey into research*. India: Friends Publication.

Silverman, D. (2010). *Doing qualitative research*. 3rd ed. London: SAGE Publications.
United Nations. (1990). Treaty no. 27531. In: *Conventions of the Rights of the Child* [online]. Available: https://treaties.un.org/Pages/ViewDetails.aspx?src=IND&mtdsg_no=IV-11&chapter=4 [accessed 12 Feburary 2022].
United Nations. (2006). Treaty no. 44910. In: *Convention on the Rights of Persons with Disabilities*[online]. Available: https://www.un-ilibrary.org/content/books/9789210603911s004-c037?mlang=en [accessed 10 February 2022].
Unluer, S. (2012). Being an insider researcher while conducting case study research. *The Qualitative Report*, 17(58), pp. 1–14.
Wiles, R. (2012). *What are qualitative research ethics?* London: Bloomsbury.
Yin, R. K. (2018). *Case study research and applications: Design and methods*. 6th ed. Thousand Oaks, CA: SAGE Publications.

CHAPTER 11

How Do You Design and Use a Questionnaire to Answer Your Research Questions?

Caoimhe Donovan

This chapter first explores the inspiration behind my decision to write a research study based on student engagement and experience of asynchronous learning during the Covid-19 pandemic in Ireland. The primary focus of this chapter is on the process of choosing a suitable research tool. This begins by examining how I arrived at my conceptual framework, the theories consulted and how I chose my research questions before explaining my research methodology. This chapter then explores how I chose my research tool and how I designed and used a semi-structured questionnaire. Finally, I discuss the extent to which I answered my research questions and will conclude with a list of hints and tips.

First, to introduce myself, I am a post-primary Home Economics and Irish language teacher based in Limerick, Ireland. During 2020 and 2021, while completing my professional master's in education, my teaching qualification, I engaged in a period of online teaching and learning in March 2020, when schools nationwide were instructed to close because of Covid-19. However, as the virus worsened schools were instructed to close again in January 2021 but for a much longer period (Covid-19 – statement from the Department of Education and skills (2020)). Therefore, just like many Irish teachers at the time, I engaged in both synchronous (live) and asynchronous (pre-recorded) teaching, having had no previous experience and very little knowledge on how to navigate online learning for students aged twelve to eighteen years.

An online learning environment refers to any setting that delivers instruction via the internet to learners separated by time and/or distance (Chen and Yang 2010). In my opinion, students are not used to being separated from their teacher or classmates by time, distance or both, therefore it is important to consider how best teachers can accommodate this type of learning. There are two types of online learning: synchronous and asynchronous learning. Let's look at what these terms mean in more detail. Synchronous learning requires the attention of teacher and students simultaneously, offering some opportunity for teacher-student or student-student interaction (Salmon 2013). Pre-Covid-19 this type of classroom interaction was expected. Whereas asynchronous learning allows for flexibility as materials are readily available (Hrastinski 2008), meaning students can access class materials online at any given moment.

Through this ongoing engagement in online teaching and learning, my interest in the online asynchronous learning environment grew and I realized I wanted to explore it further. I noticed through my own practice, teachers were engaging with online learning in very different ways, and I wanted to investigate the effects this new online learning phenomenon was having on young Irish students in terms of their motivation, self-belief and academic performance. Therefore, as part of my master's qualification, I conducted research which compared the impact of asynchronous learning and face-to-face learning on the motivation, self-efficacy beliefs and academic performance of first-year Home Economics post-primary students. I feel this research is relevant for current practice as even though Covid-19 occupies less presence in society today, online learning allows us to accommodate students who cannot attend school for example students who are compromised with an illness, in hospital or in detention centers, etc. My hope is that you gain an insight into my research journey as I endeavoured to explore how best to support students in an asynchronous learning environment and how it affected this cohort of students during the Covid-19 pandemic, which was an extremely challenging time for all teachers and students.

Why did I choose to investigate the asynchronous learning environment?

In my opinion, finding a purpose when writing is so important, especially for you as researchers as it forms the basis of your study. Reading articles and publications around my area of interest helped me to find a gap in the literature and attempt to solve it. Through reading and researching synchronous and asynchronous learning and from my own personal experiences being involved in online teaching during the Covid-19 pandemic, I realized that there was very little literature surrounding second-level online learning, particularly in the Irish context, where I was based. Establishing a gap in literature was a key first step in my research journey and gave relevance to my chosen area of research. Also, as online learning is a relatively new teaching and learning platform at second-level education in Ireland in particular, I feel there was insufficient education and training given to teachers and students in relation to online teaching and learning, further justifying my research. During 2020 and 2021 many teachers in Ireland and in other jurisdictions had to teach synchronously, asynchronously or adopt a mix of both methods. Teachers and learners faced further challenges due to connectivity issues, not having access to a device at a particular time and the nature of the subject being taught. However, many teachers had to use asynchronous teaching with little to no education or training in how to deliver content in this setting that would support, engage and motivate the learner.

Having reached a decision on what I wanted to research and why, I engaged in extensive reading to enable me to refine my focus, and to identify key concepts that would shape and inform the methodology and data-gathering tools. As my literature review took shape, I read extensively on research conducted on online asynchronous learning platforms. I became informed on how to create successful and impactful pre-recorded videos while most importantly reflecting on the students' experience of this platform in comparison with the ordinary face-to-face environment. I sifted through a lot of information to try to find literature that aligned with my work, however I felt bombarded with information. I knew at this point that I would need to refine my focus through themes. As I read, I began to jot down reoccurring themes and the more I read, the more knowledge I gained regarding these themes. The three themes I felt aligned with my work were student motivation, self-efficacy beliefs and academic performance. I felt these themes were broad enough to offer lots of scope to my writing but also correlated as Pajares (2008) alludes to the fact that student motivation, self-efficacy beliefs and academic performance are interconnected as when students have high self-efficacy and self-belief, it drives their motivation, which in turn influences their academic achievement (Pajares 2008). However, I was eager to compare these three themes in the online and face-to-face classroom, and address the research gap which exists in the post-primary online learning context so if we engage in periods of online learning again, we have more knowledge as educators in the successful and most effective delivery of online content. Choosing these themes also helped me move closer to choosing my methodology and tools, however I still had more to do before moving onto those next steps.

How I arrived at my conceptual framework

As a new researcher, before deciding on a methodology and data-gathering tools, I needed to try to locate my work within a wider conceptual framework as this would guide my research, ensure my themes aligned but also help me understand my stance as a researcher and what concepts are important to me. This was a difficult step for me as my focus was on the three different themes of motivation, self-efficacy and academic performance. My first step on my quest to find a suitable conceptual framework was to research the work of educational theorists in these areas which aligned with my work. Self-efficacy is an integral part of learning as reiterated in the work of Bandura (1997) who claims that student's self-efficacy beliefs can predict motivation and performance. However, this was notably absent in the online asynchronous classroom. Therefore, I feel guiding and supporting the learner is extremely important and this is reflected in the work of Vygotsky (1978) and Maslow (1943) which is why I chose their work. Maslow's Hierarchy of Needs model (1943) sheds light on student motivation and self-efficacy which links in with my work very well while, Vygotsky's Zone of Proximal Development (1978) aligned with my work due to the supportive role of the teacher in developing student self-efficacy.

I also considered the work of B.F Skinner's (1938, 1957) Theory of Operant Conditioning as he believes that teacher praise of positive behaviors will increase student motivation and the removal of the stimulus associated with the negative behaviour will encourage the learner not to repeat the behaviour (Seifert and Sutton 2018). However, I rejected this theory as due to the nature of asynchronous learning and pre-recording videos, teacher praise is notably absent which was a large issue in my study.

The search for theories continues

Due to the complexities associated with online learning, I consulted many theories to investigate and compare student motivation, self-efficacy and academic performance. These theorists were instrumental in shaping my work for many reasons. Through my research I learned that motivation is best understood when a variety of theories are investigated (Mansfield 2010). Therefore, I chose to research different motivational theories and draw conclusions from applying these theories to the face-to-face and online classroom. This fostered a much wider scope of understanding of what motivates students to learn. I found the work of Deci and Ryan's (1985) Self-Determination Theory interesting as it was supported in the face-to-face classroom but unsupported in the online classroom. This theory supports the belief that learners' growth and productivity stems from them satisfying their autonomy, competence and relatedness needs. However, this was notably absent in the online classroom due to the lack of social presence from the teacher and other peers.

I began to broaden my research even further which helped me discover the work of Dweck's Achievement Goal Theory (1986) and Vroom's Expectancy-Value Theory (1964). These theories helped me establish that sometimes students' motivation is unaffected by being on an online or face-to-face platform. Achievement Goal Theory by Dweck (1986) helped me understand that both online and face-to-face students are motivated by future goals and Expectancy-Value Theory by Vroom (1964) helped me discover that both online and face-to-face students are motivated to learn if they see value in the content being taught.

Bandura's (1997) Social Cognitive Theory also formed an integral part of this study as it showed that students' self-efficacy beliefs are notably absent in the online classroom, thus highlighting the importance of teacher and social presence. Brame (2016) alluded to the fact that the construction of video clips forms an integral part of the success of asynchronous learning (Brame 2016), therefore I used the Koumi framework of pedagogical principles (2013) and Sweller's Cognitive Load Theory (1988) to structure the creation of the videos which ensured the validity of my work. As you can see, by researching my three chosen themes, I was able to select and justify a range of theories which were key to informing my understanding of the challenges and issues associated with my research which in turn brought me closer to choosing a methodology and data collection tool.

Finalizing my research questions

As my research consists of three themes, I drafted three research questions as this would allow me to investigate each individually and draw conclusions, but it would also allow me to investigate the interconnectedness of these themes. Again, by choosing my research questions, I was another step closer to choosing my methodology and data-gathering tool.

My final research questions were as follows:

1. What factors influence the extent to which asynchronous and face-to-face learning impacts on the motivation of learners?
2. What factors impact on the learner's ability to practice self-efficacy in asynchronous learning and face-to-face learning environments?
3. How are learner grades impacted by using face-to-face learning and asynchronous learning environments?

Choosing a research paradigm

Having chosen my research questions, I then needed to consider my stance as a researcher through choosing a research paradigm. At first, I did not understand what this meant but I started to read about various research paradigms as according to Lincoln et al. (2011) this would guide my actions and define my worldview as a researcher. I started to read about the Pragmatic paradigm and the more I read, the more I felt this paradigm aligned with my work. I feel I am a practical-minded person and according to Creswell and Plano Clark (2011) this method of inquiry is most suited to practical-minded researchers. I learnt that pragmatic research aims to produce knowledge that is useful and actionable to help solve problems (Corbin and Strauss 2008; Feilzer 2010). These principles focus on emphasizing actionable knowledge, recognizing how experiences are interconnected and viewing inquiry as an experimental process (Kelly and Cordeiro 2020). My choice of pragmatism as a research paradigm was influenced by wanting to offer useful and actionable knowledge around the area of asynchronous learning at second level due to the gap in the literature surrounding this area. Pragmatism helped me unpack different aspects of the research questions to enable me to better choose a suitable methodology that would allow me to investigate student experience and find the useful and actionable knowledge I desired so I could offer insight to the wider educational community. In my study I focus on comparing the face-to-face classroom with the asynchronous online classroom, considering student thoughts and experiences to understand what elements of the online classroom need improving.

Searching for a suitable methodology

At last, I was searching for a suitable methodology for my study. I learnt that pragmatism is often associated with mixed methods of inquiry (Creswell and Clark 2011) which is a combination of qualitative and quantitative data. Quantitative research examines a set variable through a narrow lens whereas qualitative research examines patterns and relationships through a wider lens (Brannen 2017). Being a Pragmatist, I needed to know the 'what' and the 'why' of each of my research questions. Therefore, I knew at this point, I would be needing both quantitative and qualitative research data to answer these questions. I realized that quantitative data could tell me the 'what', it would tell me what motivates students to learn in terms of intrinsic motivation, Self-Determination Theory (SDT) by Deci and Ryan (1985), Achievement Goal Theory by Dwek (1986) and Expectancy Value Theory by Vroom (1964). Quantitative data was also useful in helping me understand the student's self-efficacy beliefs, for example, did they feel praised and encouraged by the teacher? It was also useful in providing data to compare academic performance of students in the asynchronous class in comparison with the face-to-face class. However, it would not tell me the 'why' and again being a Pragmatist, I wanted to fully understand student experience, so I needed data telling me the 'why'.

My next task was to hone in on a specific methodology. Merriam (2009) describes the research methodology as the lens through which the researcher views the study at hand (Merriam 2009). Choosing a suitable methodology is an important element in research as it directly affects the research tools and analysis. When choosing my methodology, I asked myself a few questions. How can this particular methodology help fulfill the aims and research questions of my study? Who are the key individuals who will participate in the study to answer the research questions? What kind of data can this methodology provide? What research tools are most likely to provide me with the type of data that will help answer the research questions? In the beginning I considered Action Research as it was much associated with improving teacher practice which was in keeping with my study however upon further inspection, I realized it was too vast for the type of research I wanted to do as I knew from answering the above questions that I would have a small sample size and would be gathering data from one point in time, unrepeated. Learning this about my study led me to research Case Study methodology, which according to Cohen et al. (2018) provides 'a unique example of real people in real situations, enabling people to understand ideas more clearly' (p. 376). I also felt it was in line with the Pragmatists perspective as it involves gathering information to solve an issue in the real world. I also feel it is important to research the benefits and limitations to specific research methodologies as this allows you to make an informed decision while also allowing you an opportunity to minimize the disadvantages of using this methodology from impacting your study. In my study, for example, one of the limitations of using Case Study methodology is that it only provides one set of data to draw all the conclusions from (Stockemer 2019). To try to limit the impact of this on my data analysis, I used both closed-ended and open-ended semi-structured questions so I could gather as much student opinion and experience from the open-ended questions as possible, therefore using one tool to gather two types of data.

Choosing my research tool

In choosing my research tool I asked myself two questions. What kind of information do I want to find that will help me answer the research questions and how would I analyze that information? I was also aware that the participants of the study were students ranging in age from twelve to thirteen years old, so I needed to choose a research tool suitable for them. I chose a survey because it is quick and easy to carry out (Stockemer 2019) which was important to me considering the age group of the participants and it is also accessible and easily disseminated (Wellington 2015) which was important for my study, given the Covid-19 restrictions at the time. I then began reading about a cross-sectional survey which aims to collect data about a specific population at one point in time (Hall 2011). I felt this type of survey aligned with my work as I was only gathering data from a single, non-repeated forty-minute class. Therefore, this type of survey would provide me with a 'snapshot' of the cohort of students I was investigating (Cohen et al. 2018). It is important when choosing a research tool to fully investigate it to ensure it will provide you with the correct data to answer your research questions.

This led me to investigate the advantages and disadvantages of the most suitable research tool, before making the final decision or choice. Considering I wanted quantitative and qualitative data I chose to encompass both open-ended and closed-ended questions, as I thought that by having a mix of open-ended and closed-ended questions, it would result in a better understanding of the learners' feelings towards the face-to-face and the online learning environment. Through researching open-ended questions, I learnt that it may be difficult to control extraneous load when analyzing the questions (Stockemer 2019). Extraneous load is the cognitive load which does not assist in reaching the desired outcome (Brame 2016). Therefore, I decided upon a semi-structured questionnaire to limit this as it contains a mix of both open-ended and closed-ended questions (Cohen et al. 2018). A semi-structured questionnaire is described as having a very clear focus and sequence which allows participants to respond in their own terms due to the open-ended structure of the questionnaire (Cohen et al. 2018).

How to design and use a semi-structured questionnaire

Once I had decided upon a semi-structured questionnaire comprising six questions (Cohen et al. 2018), my focus quickly settled on the construction of the questionnaire. There are many elements to consider before ever beginning to draft questions. I found the work of Cohen et al. (2018) and Stockemer (2019) particularly useful when beginning to research questions; however, I later also consulted the work of Olson et al. (2018) and Cowles and Nelson (2015) for more information. When beginning to construct the questionnaire, I first had to consider the age cohort of the respondents as if the questions were too difficult to understand they would not answer them and if they were too long it could result in disingenuous answers, and they may become disengaged which could affect the validity of the responses (Cohen et al. 2018). The length and complexity of the word choice impacts question difficulty and has a knock-on effect on the respondent's ability to comprehend and respond to a question (Olson et al. 2018). Using common simple language is recommended to ensure the questions can be understood by the majority (Stopher 2012). This was particularly important for my study considering the respondents were aged between twelve and thirteen years old. It is also recommended to avoid double-barrel questions or questions containing double negative/positives as it confuses the respondent again making it more likely for them to skip the question completely (Stopher 2012). I found the work of Cowles and Nelson (2015) very beneficial, as they discuss the key elements of writing appropriate survey questions, common question pitfalls to avoid and offer advice on using open-ended and closed-ended questions in your survey (Cowles and Nelson 2015). The style of questioning was also considered and what type of answers each question would generate. I learnt to include a range of different styles of questions to help generate a range of answers. For example, I incorporated ranking questions as according to Stockemer (2019) they are useful in gathering participant opinions in a quantitative format. I used likert scales as Stockemar (2019) maintains that they are useful to determine the participants opinion, as the scale ranges from not likely at all to very likely, therefore producing quantitative data. I also used multiple choice questions as I felt they suited the age cohort but as Stockemer (2019) points out, they are quick to answer but typically restrictive in terms of choice. I added an open question to allow for students to explain their reasoning behind their choice. I avoided any dichotomous questions as they produce a quick 'yes or no' answer meaning they do not give sufficient information and do not add value to the questionnaire (Cohen et al. 2018).

As stated previously, I chose to include both open-ended and closed-ended questions to result in a better understanding of the learners' feelings towards the face-to-face and the online learning environment. Open-ended questions allow for respondents to give any response; close-ended questions ask respondents to represent their response on a given scale (Olson et al. 2018; Singer and Couper 2017). Some research maintains that close-ended questions are more appealing as they are less burdensome to answer (Singer and Couper 2017). It is also important to consider the amount or total number of questions in your survey and the positioning of questions within the questionnaire as Gummer and Roßmann (2015) and Olson et al. (2015) both maintain that due to fatigue, questions at the latter end of the questionnaire are more likely not to be answered (e.g. Gummer and Roßmann 2015; Olson et al. 2018). However, to try to avoid this and to accommodate for the young age group of the respondents, I designed a short questionnaire with a mix of both open-ended and closed-ended questions. I also found it useful to work backwards and think about the type of answers I wanted to receive first and then begin constructing questions utilizing all the research I have just talked about in order to produce the most useful and accurate answers.

Questionnaire piloting

Piloting the questionnaire was crucial to test for inaccuracies and potential issues (Dillman et al. 2014). It was also useful to gather information regarding the time it takes to complete the questionnaire and if the questions are phrased in the right way to generate the desired answers (Cohen et al. 2018). These are all very important elements to consider. Piloting the questionnaire allowed me to eliminate ambiguity and identify gaps (Cohen et al. 2018) which I then altered before giving the questionnaire to the students. It is a very important and worthwhile step in the process of developing your questionnaire.

Questionnaire administration and ethical issues involved

It is vital to consider ethical issues in your research project to protect participants and researchers from unnecessary harm (McKenna and Gray 2018). The BERA Guidelines for Educational Research (BERA 2018) and General Data protection Regulation (GDPR) were adhered to during this research project. There were many ethical issues raised in this research study. The participants of this study were under the age of eighteen and therefore required parental consent and their own consent to participate. This was achieved by sending a parental consent form home to parents with the approval of the principal. Storing of the data also raised ethical concerns, as according to BERA (2018) the participants are entitled to know how I'm using the data, why I'm using it and whom the data will be available to (BERA 2018). Therefore, the consent forms were stored in a locked drawer and the questionnaire data in a password-protected file on OneDrive. Guidelines were also followed in relation to participants voluntarily consenting (BERA 2018), therefore many students decided not to opt in.

Questionnaire analysis

Analyzing the data correctly is a very important part of a research study as if your data is not valid and reliable, the study will be unsuccessful. It was obvious to me to use a form of thematic analysis as I had already used three themes throughout the study thus far: student motivation, self-efficacy beliefs and academic performance. However, considering motivation was quite a large theme, it would have been too difficult to analyze the data as a singular theme, so it was split up into further themes. This would make it easier to draw conclusions later in the study. Considering I had gathered both quantitative and qualitative data, I decided to do the analysis separately. I used percentages to analyze the quantitative data as Cohen et al. (2018) believe it allows for a clear comparison of results (Cohen et al. 2018). This data is also organized under the themes previously mentioned and represented visually using bar charts and pie charts. I then used deductive coding to analyze the quantitative data as is often used if the researcher is looking at a particular theory (Vogt et al. 2014). This applied to my study as I was looking specifically at the three themes of motivation, self-efficacy and academic performance. Again, I illustrated the data using graphs and I used direct quotes from the qualitative data to strengthen my presentation of findings. Finally, I started to draw conclusions from my analysis and began to make recommendations for future practice. In my opinion, this last step is essential as it allows you time to reflect on the process.

Answering my research questions

As I approached the end of my research, I reflected on aspects I could do differently if this study was to be carried out again sometime in the future. As mentioned previously my research questions focus on the three recurring themes of motivation, self-efficacy beliefs and academic performance. Considering my work is a comparative study, I found it beneficial to look at the similarities and differences which appear in the face-to-face learning environment and the online asynchronous learning environment.

When I consider the extent to which I answered my first research question 'What factors influence the extent to which asynchronous and face-to-face learning impacts on the motivation of learners?' I learnt that online and face-to-face students seem to be similarly motivated in terms of intrinsic motivation, achievement goal theory and expectancy-value theory. This was evident from the closed-ended questions asked in the survey. It was also clear that online students are lacking in motivation regarding social goal theory and SDT which is unsurprising considering the lack of social presence. However, in understanding this was an issue in the online learning environment, I was then able to make a recommendation to enhance social goal theory and SDT in the online learning environment. By choosing to use the semi-structured questionnaire, it gave the respondents scope to express themselves, which I feel really captured the element of student experience. The questionnaire was short, but all questions were carefully constructed and relevant, which I feel also contributed to the success of my chosen tool.

In considering my second research question 'What factors impact on the learner's ability to practice self-efficacy in asynchronous learning and face-to-face learning environments?' I was surprised by the alarmingly obvious results that students in the online classroom felt their self-efficacy needs were very unsupported. This was represented through a mix of both closed-ended and open-ended questions, both of which offered a clear insight into student experience of the online environment. This highlighted an area for future research as online learning continues to be used by second-level students for various reasons. Finally, my third research question 'How are learner grades impacted by using face-to-face learning and asynchronous learning environments?', I realized at this point my results were too similar to provide a conclusive answer to this question.

As a Pragmatist, I set out at the beginning of this journey to represent student experience and produce research that is useful and impactful (Corbin and Strauss 2008; Feilzer 2010). Considering the difficult circumstances in which this data was collected, that is, during Covid-19, I feel I have achieved this. However, upon reflection, I feel this study should be carried out again in the future, using a much larger sample size as I would like to investigate this topic using a wider perspective. I would also include more open-ended questions to ensure I really capture the full experience of the students. The use of a questionnaire as my research tool provided me with useful and impactful information however, I would strongly advise any researcher choosing this tool to place emphasis on constructing the questionnaire as this is pivotal in helping you receive the data you desire. Piloting the questionnaire was also a key moment for me as it helped me recognize and alter any misconceptions.

What I've learned – hints and tips

- Spend time at the beginning of your research journey ensuring you have a clear aim, identify the elements you wish to research, identify your personal/professional relevance of the area you wish to study and all the possible ethical issues. This first step is important as it will help align your thoughts if you are unsure how to start the process.

- When you begin to read and research, keep referring to your title and research questions to ensure you are staying on-track with your research.

- Before starting to write a large section such as the literature review/methodology write the list of headings you hope to use and bullet point what you hope to talk about under each heading. This will ensure there is a flow to your work, that you avoid repetition and it also helps organize your thoughts by giving a rough idea of what your work will look like.

- Ensure your research sources are reliable and current.
  I found it useful to support my writing with more than one reference, that is, two authors/theorists who have similar ideas/beliefs. It is also sometimes useful to provide a contrasting opinion as having both complementing and contrasting opinions will create more scope and interest for you as a writer.

- If using a questionnaire, ensure you have thoroughly researched how to use this tool effectively as every question must be carefully constructed to ensure you get an accurate and relevant answer.

- Piloting the questionnaire is a very worthwhile and useful step as it will highlight any issues that may not have been obvious to you previously. Ensure you reflect on this process and pilot the questionnaire on a similar age group to your intended participants.

References

Bandura, A. (1997). *Self-efficacy: The exercise of control*. New York: Freeman.

British Educational Research Association [BERA]. (2018). *Ethical guidelines for educational research*. 4th ed. London: British Educational Research Association.

Brame, C. J. (2016). Effective educational videos: Principles and guidelines for maximizing student learning from video content. *CBE-Life Sciences Education*, 15(4), es6.

Brannen, J. (2017). *Mixing methods*. 1st ed. London: Routledge.

Chen, K. and Yang, S. (2010). Motivation in online learning: Testing a model of self-determination theory. *Computers in Human Behavior*, 26, pp. 741–52.

Cohen, L., Mannion, L., and Morrison, K. (2018). *Research methods in education*. 8th ed. London: Routledge-Falmer.

Corbin, J. and Strauss, A. (2008). *Basics of qualitative research: Techniques and procedures for developing Grounded Theory*. Thousand Oaks, CA: SAGE Publications.

Cowles, E. and Nelson, E. (2015). *An introduction to survey research*. New York: Business Expert Press.

Creswell, J. W. and Clark, V. L. P. (2011). *Designing and conducting mixed methods research*. 2nd ed. Thousand Oak, CA: SAGE Publications.

Deci, E. and Ryan, R. (1985). The general causality orientations scale: Self-determination in personality. *Journal of Research in Personality*, 19(2), pp. 109–34.

Department of Education and Skills. (2020). *Covid-19 – statement from the Department of Education and skills* [online]. Available: https://www.gov.ie/en/press-release/ee5e2b-covid-19-statement-from-the-department-of-education-and-skills/ [accessed 22 October 2023].

Dillman, D., Smyth, J., and Christain, L. (2014). *Internet, phone, mail, and mixed-mode surveys: the tailored design method*. 4th ed. New Jersey: Wiley.

Dweck, C. S. (1986). Motivational processes affecting learning. *American Psychologist*, 41, pp. 1040–8.

Feilzer, M. (2010). Doing mixed methods research pragmatically: Implications for the rediscovery of pragmatism as a research paradigm. *Journal of Mixed Methods Research*, 4(1), pp. 6–16.

Gummer, T. and Roßmann, J. (2015). Explaining interview duration in web surveys: A multilevel approach. *Social Science Computer Review*, 33(2), pp. 217–34.

Hall, J. (2011). *Encyclopedia of survey research methods, Sage Research Methods* [online]. Thousand Oaks, CA: SAGE Publications. Available: https://methods.sagepub.com/reference/encyclopedia-of-survey-research-methods/n120.xml. [accessed 25 April 2023].

Hrastinski, S. (2008). Asynchronous and synchronous e-learning. *Educause Quarterly*, 31(4), pp. 51–5.

Kelly, L. M. and Cordeiro, M. (2020). Three principles of pragmatism for research on organizational processes. *Methodological Innovations*, 13(2), pp. 1–10.

Koumi, J. (2013). *Pedagogic video design principles-Instructivist exposition with constructivist learning opportunities* [online]. Available: https://www.academia.edu/3083904/PEDAGOGIC_VIDEO_DESIGN_PRINCIPLES_Instructivist_Exposition_with_Constructivist_Learning_Opportunities?source=swp_share [accessed 18 April 2021].

Lincoln, Y. S., Lynham, S. A., and Guba, E. G. (2011). Pragmatic Controversies, Contradictions, and Emerging Confluences, Revisited In: Denzin, N. and Lincoln, Y. S. (eds), *The SAGE handbook of qualitative research*. Thousand Oaks, CA: SAGE Publications, pp. 97–128.

Mansfiled, C. (2010). Motivating adolescents: Goals for Australian students in secondary schools. *Australian Journal of Educational & Developmental Psychology*, 10, pp. 44–55.

Maslow, A. H. (1943). A theory of human motivation. *Psychological Review*, 50(4), pp. 370–96.

McKenna, L. and Gray, R. (2018). The importance of ethics in research publications. *Collegian*, 25(2), pp. 147–8.

Merriam, S. B. (2009). *Qualitative research: A guide to design and implementation*. San Francisco, CA: Jossey-Bass.

Olson, K. and Smyth, J. D. (2015). The effect of CATI questions, respondents, and interviewers on response time. *Journal of Survey Statistics and Methdology*, 3, pp. 361- 396.

Olson, K., Smyth, J. D., and Ganshert, A. (2018). The effects of respondent and question characteristics on respondent answering behaviors in telephone interviews. *Journal of Survey Statistics and Methodology*, 7(2), pp. 275–308.

Pajares, F. (2008). Motivational role of self-efficacy beliefs in self-regulated learning. In: Pajares, F. (ed.), *Motivation, and self-regulated learning: Theory, research, and applications*. New Jersey: Lawrence Erlbaum Associates Publishers, pp. 111–139.

Salmon, G. (2013). *E-tivities: The key to active online learning*. 2nd ed. Oxfordshire: Routledge.

Seifert, K. and Sutton, R. (2018). Motivation theories on learning. In: West, R. E. (ed.), *Foundations of learning and instructional design technology: The past, present, and future of learning and instructional design technology [online]*. EdTech Books. Available: https://open.byu.edu/lidtfoundations/motivation_theories_on_learning?book_nav=true#chapterTitle [accessed 25 April 2022].

Singer, E. and Couper, M. (2017). Some methodological uses of responses to open questions and other verbatim comments in quantitative survey. *MDA Methods, Data, Analyses*, 11(2), pp. 115–34.

Skinner, B. F. (1938). *The behavior of organisms: An experimental analysis*. New York: Appleton-Century.

Skinner, B. F. (1957). *Verbal behavior*. New York: Appleton-Century-Crofts.

Stopher, P. (2012). *Collecting, managing, and assessing data using sample surveys*. Cambridge: Cambridge University Press.

Stockemer, D. (2019). *Quantitative methods for the social sciences: A practical introduction with the examples in SPSS and Stata*. Switzerland: Springer International Publishing.

Vogt, W. P., Vogt, E. R., Gardner, D. C., and Haeffele, L. M. (2014). *Selecting the right analyses for your data: Quantitative, qualitative, and mixed methods*. New York: Guilford Publications.

Vroom, V. H. (1964). *Work and motivation*. New York: Wiley.

Vygotsky, L. S. (1978). *Mind in society: The development of higher psychological processes*. Massachusetts: Harvard University Press.

Wellington, J. (2015). *Educational research: Contemporary issues and practical approaches*. London: Bloomsbury Publishing.

CHAPTER 12

How Do You Use Semi-structured Interviews and Fortune Lines?

Kathryn McCrorie

My initial research experience began when I transitioned from secondary school teaching to a position as a teacher educator at a Scottish university's School of Education. I embarked on a small-scale Master's practitioner enquiry in Supporting Teacher Learning, fully aware of my novice researcher status (Berliner 2001). The assignment topic and focus of this chapter is the relationship between student teachers on school placement and their mentor. What specifically interested me was the potentially problematic relationship that can manifest during school placement, with students struggling to connect with mentors. Mentoring requires both mentor and mentee to proactively engage in a highly complex relationship (Hudson 2016). When the relationship is ineffective, placement can become challenging, with some students withdrawing from the course. My role made me aware of the variety of students' experiences and I was seeking authentic approaches to prepare students for this potential situation. I wanted to use research tools that both supported students and captured their experiences. The initial objective was to inform my practice, improving students' readiness for placement, whilst feeling all Professional Graduate

Diploma in Education (PGDE) students could benefit from learning to manage mentors (Maynard 2000).

This chapter addresses what I learned as the assignment evolved. At points, I have 'retrofitted' my thinking, based on what I know now, to hopefully help you avoid some of my missteps. As an early researcher, I made some decisions based on limited knowledge and understanding. Continuing my studies by embarking on an EdD, I am more aware of research literature, seeing where I got it right and what I would change in retrospect. I discuss how I selected the tools I employed: fortune lines and semi-structured interviews. I knew my research was to be based on supportive, coaching conversations with students and after some reading established that my desire to make sense of the relationship between the mentor and mentee was an ethnographic case study. Initially exploring the significance of mentor–mentee relationships on school placements and the research question devised for the assignment, the subsequent section will address the appropriateness of the tools to capture student experience. Finally, reflecting on the extent to which these tools enabled me to answer the question and what I would change if I undertook a similar research project in the future.

But first, some context (it will help make sense of the chosen tools): A brief explanation of mentoring within Scottish Initial Teacher Education (ITE)

A significant factor in the success of ITE student placements is the relationship with the school mentor (Hudson 2016). Scottish ITE students are allocated a mentor or supporter when they commence school placement. Student feedback showed me that many mentors were not mentoring in ways I had assumed or experienced in my school role. My assignment was a practitioner enquiry based on an aspect of my role. From the outset, I knew a negative mentor–mentee relationship, which has such an impact on students, was what I wanted to explore. Students can feel isolated on placement, and I saw an opportunity to examine their experiences. The good news is I am still exploring related issues; there's always more to investigate.

The focus of my research was based on an omission, as the mentor–mentee relationship was not explicitly discussed with students. The assumption was that mentoring was a good thing, widely understood by all participants. Whilst your research focus may lie in a different field, exploring hegemonic assumptions (Brookfield 2017) in your area is a distinct possibility. The PGDE modules I taught on made no specific mention of mentor–mentee relationships, lacking guidance on what this meant in practice. My hunch was that finding out more about how this felt for students would enable me to be more supportive and therefore my research required me to explore experiences beneath the image students projected.

With these emerging tensions at work, I decided the focus for this enquiry would be to challenge existing assumptions around ITE mentoring. As pupils are at the centre of effective teacher-professional learning, so my learning is intrinsically bound to student experience (Timperley et al. 2007). This echoes Hall and Wall's focus on the duality of teachers being responsible for their learning as well as that of their students (2019). I felt I could influence the preparedness of students for placement by explicitly discussing mentoring relationships and the potential of an unproductive relationship with their mentor. It was apparent that the experiences of my PGDE students were not uncommon and merited further exploration.

I now had a broad area of enquiry but needed to narrow this to be more manageable. An initial task was to clarify terminology as it will be for you too. Reading key articles and examining definitions enabled me to have a stronger understanding of the field. It also enables more accurate and productive searching in databases. Decide on your terms and ensure you use them consistently. Using key terms, I carried out a short literature review on mentoring within ITE programmes. This enabled me to devise a research question and move me one step closer to deciding on a methodology and tools that would be most appropriate.

How did the research question evolve?

My question developed from the reading indicated above, whilst also reflecting on my practice and improving outcomes for ITE students. My initial research question, 'Does discussion around mentoring prepare students to better cope on teaching placement?' was too broad and binary. When I considered more precisely what I wanted to do, I reviewed and refined the focus. This process took time, and many re-drafts to reflect what it was I was actively seeking to do. The final research question became:

To what extent does explicit discussion around the mentoring relationship before placement enable Initial Education Students (ITE) deal with a challenging mentor–mentee relationship?

Deciding on a framework

I wanted to explore what would happen if I were explicit in discussing mentoring relationships with students in advance of placement, echoing Hudson's (2016) view that mentees have a role to play. I also wanted to model myself as a researcher, developing this aspect of practice for students who undertake theoretical practitioner enquiry as part of the PGDE. I read over key articles, seeking inspiration. After considering a range of approaches I decided upon Timperley et al. Inquiry and Professional Knowledge model (2007). Still wrestling with 'proper' research terms I found Timperley's model accessible, reflecting the plan-do-review I employed in teaching. The first stage was to identify students' learning needs, which I based on experiences of former students who had experienced highly managerial, controlling mentors. My objective was to raise awareness of this potential issue and to make students aware of support and strategies.

Research design and tools

How did I decide on my methodology?

The module I was studying was based on practitioner enquiry and so the research I was carrying out reflected this. Practitioner enquiry can be hard to conceptualize, ranging from your way of being as a teacher to a finite project (Wall 2018). I had a foot in both camps, constantly questioning but also with a research assignment to do. Indeed, frequently asking 'What if...?' and 'What happens when...?' (Wall 2018) had run on a loop through my head as a schoolteacher and reflected an enquiry approach that felt right for me as a researcher. At this stage of my research, I was questioning assumptions I had made as a teacher; this is a normal part of being a researcher. You no longer take anything at face value! Be prepared for this and see it as a necessary part of developing a robust position. I wanted to know how I could use my role to support all students but specifically to develop tools to help those who were struggling. This was the starting point for my practitioner enquiry research.

How did I plan the project?

To design the project, I wanted to work with students as co-researchers. Teaching had shown me a constructionist methodology (Bryman 2016) that worked in my classroom (and now lecture hall); I wanted this reflected in my research. Each student has an understanding of the mentor–mentee relationship based on social processes (Gergen 2022). I was looking for an approach that allowed for honest reflection and needed research tools to enable this. I hoped to develop a participatory approach to research (Cohen et al. 2018), working with the students to ultimately affect change. Understanding the experience could only be developed through shared exploration as opposed to remaining separate (Baumfield et al. 2013; Stenhouse 1981). My objective was not, therefore, to develop a definitive approach to the preparation of students for placement, but to find out more about the reality of the mentor–mentee relationship during placement (Hall 2009).

My research was for a relatively short assignment so I had to consider scale as will you. I returned to my literature review and noted research on mentoring ranged from single case studies to large cohort studies. Focussing on problematic placement relationships, I decided to adopt a case study approach, centring on the social phenomena of the mentor–mentee relationship, working with three to four students facing difficulties on placement (Merriam 1998). I had not considered naming what I was doing; this was not an expectation of the assignment. In retrospect, I know I was adopting an ethnographic case study approach, seeking to understand the experiences of the students, and capturing this through artefacts and interviews (Kramer and Adams 2017). Knowing my methodology, I was then able to decide how I would collect data.

Research tools: Finding the right tool for the job

Knowing I was carrying out a qualitative project based on the views of students, I had to explore the best way to capture their thoughts and feelings. With little experience in research, I found using reference books such as *Research Methods for Understanding Professional Learning* (Hall and Wall 2019) and *Creative Research Methods in Education* (Kara et al. 2021) helpful to consider what was out there. Taking time to consider the outcome you want (data) and how you will capture this (tools) are key to ensuring the research is effective. Below I outline the two tools I used, sharing how I used them and the benefits and challenges that arose.

Research tools: Fortune lines

I wanted to know how students felt in relation to working with their mentor and sought a tool which would capture this. Fortune lines are a qualitative approach and visual method that provide a structure to enable reflection on a process over time (Higgins et al. 2001). As such, they can track feelings, and this is what I asked students to do in relation to the mentor relationship (see Figure 12.1 as an example).

Fortune lines originate in the work of Rush, who explored them as a tool to track the arc of a story with children in literacy classes (Rush 1986 cited in White and Gunstone 1992). They can be used in a variety of creative ways both as research and pedagogic tools (Wall 2018). At their most basic the x-axis is time with the y-axis capturing the emotion, success, among others. This can then be developed with annotations and symbols to reflect greater detail (White and Gunstone 1992).

The aim of fortune lines in my research was to enable students to record their feelings, keeping the fortune lines formative with a feeling emoji on the y-axis, rather than using a summative numeric

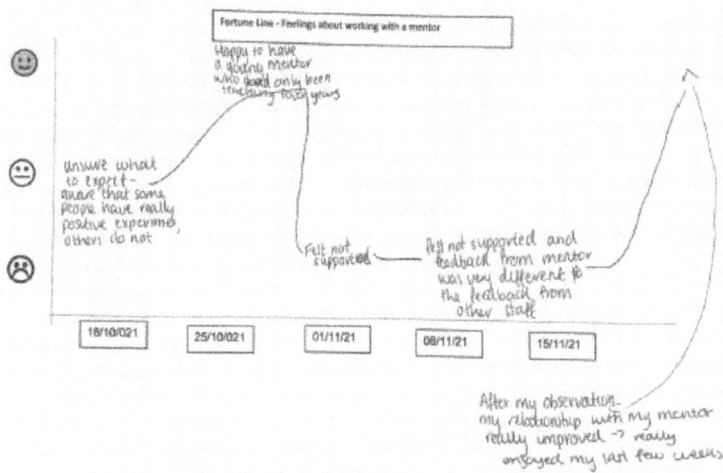

FIGURE 12.1 *School Placement Fortune Line (2021).*

scale (see Figure 12.1). The *x*-scale commenced prior to placement to capture students' feelings in advance of meeting their mentor. It was suggested that they add to their line weekly, showing any changes in their feelings about the mentor–mentee relationship. Fortune lines are flexible and have a place in many qualitative studies where you are seeking to record data over time.

In deciding which tool to use it is important to consider what works within your context. This approach was very low-tech, with students able to access their fortune line and add to it weekly. I was fortunate as my 'research group' comprised students I taught so I was able to speak to them all and introduce the concept of fortune lines in a seminar (Hall and Wall 2019). You may not be working with people you see regularly so need to consider this in your planning. As Kortegast et al. (2019) observe,

> Incorporating visual methods and representations into research opens possibilities for deeper understandings of how individuals experience institutions of higher education. (p. 3)

Students are used to quantitative evaluations, but I was seeking an emotional response, which could be lost in questionnaire (White and Gunstone 1992). Fortune lines are effective at showing changes in feelings around happiness and self-confidence (Özarslan and Çetin 2014), corresponding to Prosser's second category of visual data as participant-generated (Prosser 2007), reinforcing the student's individual experience rather than my interpretation as a researcher.

There were challenges associated with using this approach. I was conscious that despite the collaborative research design, there was the potential that students may feel they were being asked to do 'extra' (Stenhouse 1983), seeing fortune lines only as being part of my research. However, PGDE students are expected to develop a reflective stance, incorporating a variety of lenses (Brookfield 2017) and this visualization of their mentor–mentee relationship has the potential to support their developing reflections. Further, as students need to evidence this evolution, the fortune line gave them a concrete artefact to reference. Fortune lines were a potential addition as a future pedagogical approach for the students and this cross-over between pedagogy and research increases the accessibility of certain tools (Woods 1986; Wall 2018). I was seeking to support the students but also capture their experiences for my enquiry. I was aware of the tensions within this and did not make the fortune lines a mandatory element for students. Consequently, several did not complete them. This is always a potential source of friction; why should people support us by engaging with our research?

Semi-structured Interviews

In carrying out your research one tool will often be insufficient to gather the data you require, only taking you so far. Often it is the process of triangulation, combining and contrasting data from additional tools that clarifies your findings. Ideally, you will build this into your research design, but you may only become aware of this as the research progresses. It was apparent from early in my research process that fortune lines alone would be insufficient to explore the impact of explicit discussion of the mentor–mentee relationship. Discussion around the reflections was needed to both explore key points but also to ensure pastoral support for those students who had faced challenges with the mentor–mentee relationship. The aim was to allow the student to explore the relationship with their mentor, reflecting on the problems and (hopefully) finding their solutions and strategies ready for their next placement. At the end of the placement, the students who had encountered problems were asked directly if they wanted to discuss their experience in a semi-structured interview and were explicitly told that this would contribute to my research. I extended the invitation to the wider class and two students with a more positive experience agreed to be involved.

I chose semi-structured interviews (Bryman 2016) to encourage a natural, conversational approach based on the relationship that had developed over the semester. I had three prompt questions based on previous experience, the literature review and students' discussion on campus. In ethnography, you, as the researcher, are part of the field you are exploring and therefore discussing with a few prompts reflected normal practice for students. A structured interview (Cohen et al. 2018) would have limited the authenticity of the interaction with strict adherence to a questionnaire and no scope for follow-up questions whilst an unstructured interview would make thematic analysis more challenging for me as a new researcher. The interviews ultimately had much in common with focused interviews (Bryman 2016) as I sought to be as non-directive as possible, enabling the student to shape the conversation. This is another feature of ethnography, the researcher should be open to change, based on what they observe rather than adhering to a tight series of questions with no scope to pick-up on points that arise (Kramer and Adams 2017).

The interviews were recorded on Zoom. Using Zoom meant the students were able to arrange a suitable time around school placement. It was also beneficial to me as a researcher as I could easily access a transcript. Each participant was given time to share their experience without interruption, using the fortune line as an artefact to structure their narrative acting as an 'aide memoir' (Hall and Wall 2019, p. 83). This was a helpful approach, allowing the student to develop the fortune line, exploring the trends and the events that changed the trajectory (see Figure 12.1). To explore the experiences further I then asked a series of open questions, prepared in advance, and the other participant could join in, exploring areas of similarity and difference. These questions (or interview guide) formed the basis of prompts rather than the formal, repeated questioning of a structured interview (Bryman 2016). I had revisited my research question to ensure the data I generated would help to answer it; it is easy to lose sight of this, regardless of the scale of your research.

In an ethnographic study trust, curiosity and naturalness are key attributes (Cohen et al. 2018) which I felt took precedence over the order/structure of the interaction. This definitely led to messy data (long transcripts with elements of answers scattered throughout) which is not for everyone.

The use of flexible, open questioning allows for 'access to people's ideas, thoughts and memories in their own words' (Blee and Taylor 2002, p. 93) which were key to my desire for greater understanding of the student experience. This was the case as the students were honest and detailed in their reflections. I was able to use the narrative as a data source but missed deeper understanding from the social interaction. This is something to consider in your own work. The convenience of auto-transcription loses the nuance of the social nature of the moment as the researcher becomes concerned only with the data being generated (Cohen et al. 2018). As a novice researcher, I did not set any time limits and 'went with the flow'. On reflection, setting a clear time frame would have been helpful. I also became aware of the power dynamic within our relationship as one student asked, 'Is there anything in particular you'd like us to say?' This is something to be aware of in your research. Ethnography requires a relationship between the researcher and participants but when the participants are invested, they may want to 'get it right' for you.

Ethical considerations

No reflection on research can ignore ethical issues as they are a key part of the research process and design. However, this is not the substantive focus of this chapter and so I will briefly reflect on how ethics related to the methodology and tools I used. As a practitioner enquiry carried out as part of my day-to-day teaching, I did not require formal ethical approval but did need to adopt an ethical stance in working with my students. Always check with your tutor or supervisor to ensure you comply with your institution's expectations and requirements. To ensure informed consent for my research, the enquiry was explained early in the semester during a seminar and blank fortune lines were shared close to the students' placement. All students were invited to share their fortune lines, but I stressed that this was not mandatory, that is, students could withdraw by not returning them to me. Students were made aware of my intention to 'make public' (Stenhouse 1981) my findings, and that they would be shared with both tutors and other students on the course, but that the content would not be attributable to any one person or to a specific placement school.

Analysis: What to do with the data?

As a novice researcher, I lacked experience in data analysis. I would recommend planning analysis in tandem with your tool choice; this would be my approach if I were to repeat the research. I reviewed my findings by looking at the general trend of feelings in the fortune line and the narrative from the interview transcript but with no clear structure. I knew I wanted to see if there were commonalities in the students' experiences so read through the transcripts and identified common issues to which I attributed colours and highlighted the transcripts accordingly. It transpires that this was a very rudimentary version of the thematic analysis outlined by Braun and Clarke (2006). I reviewed the highlighting (coding) and gradually collated codes into three themes. Thematic analysis fits well with an ethnographic study, using the transcripts as data. I have subsequently carried out a systematic literature review and branched out, using post-its for coding. The process of data analysis will be specific to your research but don't be afraid to experiment and find what works for you (and your data).

Conclusions and key learning

Did these tools enable me to answer my question, 'To what extent does explicit discussion around the mentoring relationship before placement enable Initial Teacher Education (ITE) students to deal with a challenging mentor-mentee relationship?' Overall, I learnt a lot from this enquiry; not all of it related to mentoring and some of the learning was what not to do next time!

Fortune lines proved to be an effective tool to capture the feelings of students about mentor relationships and I would recommend them as a tool to capture the temporality of feelings.

Before the seminar, which introduced the concept of a mentor–mentee relationship, the majority of students had not considered this as an aspect of placement. Those who had assumed that the relationship would be positive. The seminar had the unintended consequence of raising anxiety levels for some. In part, this was due to the strong views of former students who shared their experiences. Whilst the fortune lines showed the changes in feelings, as a novice researcher I did not exploit the full potential of the data they contained. Reading in preparation for this chapter has made me realize that I should have synthesized an analysis of the fortune lines in tandem with the narratives from the interviews (Özarslan and Çetin 2014). Since carrying out the enquiry fortune lines are now part of the Practitioner Enquiry module taken by all PGDE students.

Were semi-structured interviews the best tool for the job? Ultimately, despite my clumsy approach, they allowed me to dig more deeply into the data generated by the fortune lines. Using the fortune lines as a starting point focused the discussion, acting as a prompt. The students were keen to share their experiences, but the responses were broad and at times emotional due to the problems several of them had encountered. I found it challenging to keep the focus on the impact of introducing the potential problems with a mentor steering the interview (Kvale 1996), whilst also giving the students the space to unpack their experiences and to feel heard. When researching with co-workers or your students consider the potential blurring of roles and jurisdictions; can you keep them separate? I thought I had but the emotional nature of some of the experiences made this a false dichotomy for some.

The methods did therefore achieve what I hoped, generating reflections about the mentor–mentee relationship and the impact of discussing this before placement. Combining the fortune lines and the interviews worked well, reflecting the mediated fortune line interviews discussed by Hall and Wall (2019). My lack of experience was most evident in thematic analysis where I had the fortune lines and the transcripts and only then realized, I needed to do something with them! By having a clear research design you will avoid this situation and start with the end in mind. My biggest takeaway was that any future research should build data analysis into the planning stage.

References

Baumfield, V., Hall, E., and Wall, K. (2013). *Action research in education: Learning through practitioner enquiry.* 2nd ed. London: SAGE Publications.

Berliner, D. C. (2001). Learning about and learning from expert teachers. *International Journal of Educational Research,* 35(5), pp. 463–82.

Blee, K. and Taylor, V. (2002). Semi-structured interviewing in social movement research. In: Klandermans, B. and Saggenborg, S. (eds), *Methods of social movement research.* Minneapolis: Minnesota Press, pp. 92–117.

Braun, V. and Clarke, V. (2006). Using thematic analysis in psychology. *Qualitative Research in Psychology,* 3, pp. 77–101.

Brookfield, S. (2017). *Becoming a critically reflective teacher.* 2nd ed. San Francisco: Jossey-Bass.

Cohen, L., Manion, L., and Morrison, K. (2018). *Research methods in education.* 8th ed. New York: Routledge.

Bryman, A. (2016). *Social research methods.* 5th ed. Oxford: Oxford University Press.

Gergen, K. J. (2022). *An invitation to social construction: Co-creating the future.* 4th ed. London: SAGE Publications.

Hall, E. (2009). Engaging in and engaging with research: Teacher inquiry and development. *Teachers and Teaching: Theory and Practice,* 15(6), pp. 669–81.

Hall, E. and Wall, K. (2019). *Research methods for understanding professional learning.* London: Bloomsbury.

Higgins, S., Baumfield, V., and Leat, D. (2001). *Thinking through primary teaching.* Cambridge: Chris Kington.

Hudson, P. (2016). Forming the mentor-mentee relationship. *Mentoring & Tutoring: Partnership in Learning,* 24(1), pp. 30–43.

Kara, H., Lemon, N., Mannay, D., and McPhersonet, M. (2021). *Creative research methods in education: Principles and practices.* Bristol: Policy Press.

Kramer, M. and Adams, T. (eds.) (2017). *The SAGE encyclopedia of communication research methods (Vol. 4).* Thousand Oaks, CA: SAGE Publications.

Kortegast, C., Mc Cann, K., Branch, K., and Latz, A. O. (2019). Enhancing ways of knowing: The case for utilizing participant-generated visual methods in higher education research. *Review of Higher Education,* 42(2), pp. 485–510.

Kvale, S. (1996). *Interviews: an introduction to qualitative research interviewing.* Thousand Oaks, CA: SAGE Publications.

Maynard, T. (2000). Learning to teach or learning to manage mentors? Experiences of school-based teacher training. *Mentoring & Tutoring*, 8(1), pp. 17–30.

Merriam, S. (1998). *Qualitative research & case study applications in education*. San Francisco: Josey-Bass.

Özarslan, M. and Çetin, G. (2014). An investigation of students' views about enzymes by fortune lines technique. *Asia-Pacific Forum on Science Learning and TTeaching*, 15(1), pp. 1–19.

Prosser, J. (2007). Visual methods and the visual culture of schools. *Visual Studies*, 22(1), pp. 13–30.

Rush, R. T. (1986). *Occupational Literacy Education*. International Reading Association, 800 Barksdale Rd., PO Box 8139, Newark, DE 19714-8139 (Book No. 969, $6.75 member, $10.25 nonmember).

Stenhouse, L. (1981). What counts as research? *British Journal of Educational Studies*, 29(2), pp. 103–14.

Stenhouse, L. (1983). Research as a basis for teaching. In: Stenhouse, L. (ed.), *Authority, education & emancipation: A collection of papers*. 22(3), 211–215. Surrey: Heinemann Educational Books.

Timperley, H., Wilson, A., Barrar, H., and Fung, I. (2007). *Teacher professional learning & development; Best evidence synthesis*. New Zealand: Ministry of Education.

Wall, K. (2018). Building a bridge between pedagogy and methodology: Emergent thinking on notions of quality in practitioner enquiry. *Scottish Educational Review*, 50(2), pp. 3–22.

White, R. and Gunstone, R. (1992). *Probing understanding*. Abingdon: Routledge.

Woods, P. (1986). *Inside schools; ethnography in education research*. Abingdon: Routledge.

CHAPTER 13

How Does Your Choice of Participants Influence Your Research Study?

Kathryn McClure

In this chapter, we will explore a critical aspect of the research process that often doesn't get discussed – how your choice of participants influences the entire research process. This is especially crucial for novice researchers who are just embarking on their first experiences of research.

I was a teacher in a small complex Additional Support Needs (ASN) school in the heart of Scotland. In this educational setting, we educated young people with various learning differences who required extra support to thrive within education. Among my students, some had the diagnosis of autism or autism spectrum disorder (ASD). These young people use Restrictive Repetitive Behaviours (RRBs) which are a series of repetitive movements, actions or routines that are unique and are a way of self-soothing or self-stimulation (Manor-Binyamini and Schreiber-Divon 2019). These behaviours while they help autistic individuals self-regulate, could also stand as barriers to their learning and engagement (Harrop et al. 2014). My curiosity about RRBs led to me question: What did the school team understand about these behaviours? What attributions did they hold regarding the staff's influence on these behaviours? And, importantly, did these behaviours remain consistent over time?

The reason for this exploration was simple yet profound. I had developed a deep understanding of how autistic young people harnessed RRBs as their coping mechanisms. Now, I wanted to uncover if this understanding was a universal insight within my working environment. I couldn't ignore the stark reality that the inability to carry out these actions could trigger distressing behaviours, disrupting not only their learning but also impacting their mental well-being, as highlighted by Higashida (2013). So, there I stood, an educator with a mission. My journey was not just one of teaching but of understanding, exploring, and, ultimately, sharing insights that could make a difference in the lives of these extraordinary young individuals.

The quest for clarity: The research question

Before we dive into the world of participants, let's talk about the foundation of your research –the research question. Think of it as the guiding star that leads your research voyage, illuminating the path you'll follow in the vast universe of academia. It all begins with something you're curious about in your professional realm, something you believe can be improved. Often, you might have a broad topic in mind, but turning it into a focused research question is the real challenge. The journey begins with your curiosity and a desire to improve your professional practice, whether it's in your classroom or within your school. You might start with a broad topic in mind, but the challenge lies in crafting a focused research question that will serve as the foundation of your entire research endeavour (Coe et al. 2021; Cohen et al. 2018). It's normal for this step to be a bit daunting. Begin by reflecting on what you've learned and what intrigues you in your professional context. What questions have emerged as you've delved into your practice, your learning and the existing literature? Your research question will take shape through this process of exploration, inquiry and introspection. Consider what you've absorbed as a novice researcher. What stands out in your professional practice and surroundings? What sparks your curiosity? Your question will gradually crystallize through the interplay of your interests, newfound knowledge and the ideas drawn from the vast realm of literature.

From passion to research question: My journey

Let's explore my journey as an example. I was working with autistic young people, a profoundly rewarding experience that piqued my curiosity. I noticed that these individuals exhibited Restrictive and Repetitive Behaviours (RRBs), a notable aspect of autism spectrum disorder (ASD). RRBs are those repetitive actions, movements or routines that autistic individuals use as coping mechanisms, but they can sometimes hinder their learning. What intrigued me further was the field of Attribution Theory (Bandura 1997). This psychological theory fascinated me, especially how it related to my work with autistic young people. I wanted to understand how attributions–explanations or interpretations we make about behaviour–applied in the context of RRBs among this specific group (Bandura 1997; Woolfson and Brady 2009).

To shape my research question, I delved into a wide literature search. I explored research on Attribution Theory and its connection to autistic young people (sources like Brady and Woolfson 2008; Harrop et al. 2014; Welsh et al. 2019; Woolfson and Brady 2009). What I found was revealing: most studies centred on autistic young people in mainstream schools. There was a gap in research when it came to attributions related to autistic young people in specialized provisions or special schools.

This gap in knowledge intrigued me further and provided a clear focus for my research. It was at this point that I made a crucial decision–to choose my participants from the staff in specialized provisions and Additional Support Needs (ASN) or special schools. Why staff? Because they directly experienced the challenges posed by RRBs, and they could offer valuable insights. Working directly with autistic young people as research participants wasn't practical. The barriers included communication differences, varying levels of understanding and the complexity of self-reflection. These factors would have made it challenging to gain meaningful insights from them about RRBs. As I continued my research journey, I uncovered another intriguing aspect. There was a scarcity of research on autistic young people with complex communication differences–a group specifically taught at my school. This became the third dimension of my research question, further narrowing down my choice of participants to those working within complex ASN schools.

Crafting your research question: The gateway to participant selection

The development of your research question is a transformative process. It's not just about formulating a question; it's about selecting the right participants to answer that question effectively. Your research question serves as a compass, guiding you in setting inclusion and exclusion criteria for your participants. These criteria create the boundaries that define who will take part in your research and who won't. In your journey as a novice researcher, remember that your participants are not mere subjects but active contributors to the rich tapestry of your research. Their experiences, insights and perspectives are the threads that weave a compelling narrative, making your research a valuable quest for knowledge.

From question to participants: The linkage

Here's where the magic happens. Your research question essentially shapes the selection of participants. In essence, your research question and your participants are inextricably linked. Only when your question is crystal clear can you determine who can best help answer it.

But why did I choose school staff as participants? I was already working with these young people, and I had a unique insight into RRBs. The next step was to delve into Attribution Theory, a concept that fascinated me. My research was now veering towards understanding people's attributions about RRBs.

A literature search helped me fine-tune my research direction. I noticed that most studies focused on autistic young people in mainstream schools, leaving a gap in understanding RRBs in specialist provisions. This niche became my new focus. As my research refined, so did my participant selection. Staff in complex ASN schools became my target. They were directly involved with autistic young people with complex communication differences, which was a specific group within my school. This meticulous choice ensured that my research was sharply focused.

Setting the boundaries: Inclusion and exclusion criteria

Research is all about clarity. Inclusion and exclusion criteria are the guardrails of your research. They define who your research is about and who is not. In my case, I was specifically looking at the staff's perceptions of RRBs in autistic young people within a complex ASN school. This guided the inclusion criteria: staff working in a complex ASN school with experience in handling RRBs.

It was essential to define these criteria to keep the research focused on those with the knowledge and skills that were vital to answering my questions. In research, you're hunting for answers, and you want the right people on your team. My research's focus on a specific setting meant that not all staff members were eligible. Working in different settings could influence their attributions towards RRBs, so I had to ensure my participants were relevant to the context I was exploring. When you're defining inclusion criteria, think about who possesses the information you need. In my case, my colleagues were the best fit for my research. This practice is often called 'Backyard Research', where you use your colleagues and your working environment for research (Creswell and Creswell 2018).

Backyard research: Pros and cons

Conducting research with people you know well has both advantages and challenges. The relationship between the researcher and participants can influence responses, known as the Hawthorne Effect (Parsons 2021). Participants might tailor their answers to what they think the researcher wants to hear. To counter this, I anonymized the results, ensuring my presence was not felt during the questionnaire process. I was also not aware of who had responded, reducing potential bias. The choice to engage with people you know, 'Backyard Research', can be incredibly convenient, especially when researching in your familiar setting. As a teacher, I had access to willing participants among my colleagues, which made the process smoother.

Ethical considerations: The compass of research

Before collecting any data from participants, ethical considerations are paramount. Consent is the centre of ethical research (BERA 2018). It involves gaining approval from not only the participants but also the relevant authorities, such as your school or institution. Informed consent means giving a clear description of the research study, the participant's role and what's expected of them. In my case, I needed consent from both the school and the individual participants. I first sought permission from the school's Head Teacher and then approached the staff for questionnaire participation. Gaining informed consent was a straightforward process through a questionnaire, where participants read a participant information sheet and consented by proceeding.

For those who are considering researching with young people or children, the process can be more complex, involving consent from parents or carers. Sometimes, the term 'assent' is used for children. They carry out a task if they agree (assent), but if they refuse, it's considered non-consensual (Cameron and Murphy 2007). Anonymity is another vital aspect of ethical research. It protects participants from potential negative consequences of participation. Using pseudonyms or codes can maintain anonymity when participants' names are required in your research.

Navigating data collection methods: A novice researcher's compass

As a novice researcher, embarking on the path of data collection can be both exciting and daunting. Just as a sailor needs the right tools and a well-drawn map to navigate uncharted waters, you, too, require the appropriate methods for your research journey. Let's consider data collection methods, specifically tailored for novice researchers like you.

A spectrum of data-gathering methods

In the realm of research, there's an array of data collection methods at your disposal: interviews, observations, journaling, questionnaires and the use of audiovisual materials (Creswell and Creswell 2018). While these methods have proven effective in various studies, it's essential to understand that these options represent just the tip of the iceberg in the vast sea of research possibilities.

Matching methods with participants

Selecting the right method is akin to choosing the right boat for your voyage. However, keep in mind that your choice must align with your participants. They are not passive entities but active contributors, and your chosen method should resonate with them. Consider the accessibility of your chosen method to your participants. Language, cognitive abilities, literacy levels, understanding, and technological proficiency all play a significant role. For instance, if you're conducting interviews with individuals who have language differences, it's crucial to adapt your questions to ensure they can express themselves effectively.

Seeking guidance from the literature

Imagine the research landscape as a treasure map, and you're on a quest for the most valuable methods. Undertaking a literature search in your research area is akin to consulting seasoned explorers who have traversed similar terrains. In my own journey, I discovered research that utilized vignettes to measure attributions of education staff regarding Restrictive and Repetitive Behaviours (RRBs) in autistic young people (Wanless and Jahoda, 2002; Kesterson 2012,

Welsh et al. 2019). These vignettes presented real-world scenarios, allowing participants to respond based on their experiences. Vignettes offer a standardized way to present information to all participants, ensuring a level playing field (Veal 2002). These short, descriptive stories provide a common reference point for everyone involved. As a novice researcher, the value of consistency in data collection cannot be overstated.

To simplify the process further, I opted for digital questionnaires created using Microsoft Forms. This choice came with several benefits. First, it eliminated the risk of missing consent on the first page, as the questionnaire was designed to progress only if consent was given. Additionally, using technology reduced the time and stress for participants. They could access the questionnaire at their convenience by simply clicking on a link in their email.

Empowering participants in your research journey

As a novice researcher, your methods should not just collect data; they should empower your participants to share their valuable insights. Think about what you want to learn, how participants can best share this information, and the simplest and most effective way to collect the data you need. As stated previously, participants are more than data sources; they are partners in your research. Their experiences, perspectives and contributions shape the course of your study. In selecting and adapting your data collection methods, consider how these tools can be wielded to ensure that participants actively engage and collaborate in your research journey.

The final act: Ethical closure with participants

When your data collection and analysis are complete, it's essential to let your participants in on the results and conclusions (BERA 2018). This is their chance to provide feedback and contribute to the research's outcome. Their participation is not just valuable; it's fundamental. In my case, I offered to share my completed research with my colleagues who had participated. Even though there wasn't much interest in reading the full report, some participants were curious about the results and engaged in discussions. This was the last engagement with my participants as the role of researcher. This completed my research, and I thanked the participants for their valuable input.

Conclusion

As you venture into the realm of research, with your guiding star, the research question, illuminating your path, you are now ready to set sail in the world of participants. In this voyage, participants are not mere subjects; they are your companions, active contributors to the rich tapestry of your research. Their experiences, insights and perspectives are the threads that weave a compelling narrative, making your research a valuable quest for knowledge.

Your journey begins with a question, an inquiry sparked by curiosity, a desire for improvement and a quest for understanding. The research question is your lighthouse, providing clarity and direction. It shapes the path you'll follow and the choices you'll make, including the selection of the participants who will accompany you on this expedition. From question to participants, the link is unbreakable. Your research question shapes the selection of participants, guiding you towards those who can best help answer it. Your participants are your allies in unravelling the mysteries of your chosen topic. They hold the key to unlocking the insights you seek. It's essential to recognize that your participants are more than data sources; they are partners in your research. Their unique perspectives and experiences bring life to your work. They help you connect the dots and draw a more comprehensive picture of your research landscape.

Your journey doesn't stop with participant selection. The development of your research question also influences the establishment of inclusion and exclusion criteria. These criteria define who joins you on your expedition and who remains on the shore. It's your way of setting boundaries that ensure your research stays on course. As you embrace your role as a novice researcher, remember that you're building bridges between your inquiry and those who hold the answers. Your participants are your co-authors in the story of your research. Their voices will echo through your findings, enriching your work. So, to all novice researchers embarking on this quest, remember that your research journey is a shared adventure. Your participants are your fellow travellers on this intellectual odyssey, and their contributions are invaluable. Treat them with respect, protect their rights and engage them as partners. Your quest for knowledge will be more rewarding for it.

References

Bandura, A. (1997). *Self-efficacy: The exercise of control.* New York: W.H. Freeman.

Brady, K. and Woolfson, L. (2008). What teacher factors influence their attributions for children's difficulties in learning? *British Journal of Educational Psychology,* 78, pp. 527–44.

British Educational Research Association [BERA]. (2018). *Ethical guidelines for educational research.* 4th ed. London: British Educational Research Association.

Cameron, L., & Murphy,J. (2007). Obtaining consent to participate in research: the issues involved in including people with a range of learning and communication disabilities. *British Journal of Learning Disabilities,* 35(2), 113-120.

Cameron, L., Murphy, J., Cameron L., and Joan, M. (2007). Obtaining consent to participate in research: The issues involved in including people with a range of learning and communication disabilities. *British Journal of Learning Disabilities,* 35, pp. 113–20.

Coe, R., Waring, M., Hedges, L.V., and Ashley, L.D. (2021). *Research methods and methodologies in education.* London: SAGE Publications.

Cohen, L., Manion, L., and Morrison, K. (2018). *Research methods in education.* 8th ed. Abingdon: Routledge.

Creswell, J.W. and Creswell, J.D. (2018). *Research design.* London: SAGE Publications.

Harrop, C., McConachie, H., Emsley, R., Leadbitter, K., Green, J., and The PACT Consortium. (2014). Restricted and repetitive behaviours in autism spectrum disorders and typically development: Cross-sectional and longitudinal comparisons. *Journal of Autism and Developmental Disorders,* 44, pp. 1207–19.

Higashida, N. (2013). *The reason that I jump.* London: Hodder & Stoughton Ltd.

Kesterson, J.S. (2012). *The effects of labelling and teacher knowledge of autism on attributions made about students with autism spectrum disorder.* Doctoral Dissertation, Oklahoma State University.

Manor-Binyamini, I. and Schreiber-Divon, M. (2019). Repetitive behaviours: Listening to the voice of people with high functioning autism spectrum disorder. *Research in Autism Spectrum Disorders*, 64, pp. 23–30.

Parsons, H. M. (2021). What happened at Hawthorne? In: Parson, H. M. (ed.), *Behavioral theory in sociology.* New York: Routledge, pp. 323–57.

Veal, W.R. (2002). Content specific vignettes as tools for research and teaching. *Electronic Journal of Science Education*, 6(4), pp. 1–37.

Wanless, L. K., & Jahoda, A. (2002). Responses of staff towards people with mild to moderate intellectual disability who behave aggressively: A cognitive emotional analysis. *Journal of Intellectual Disability Research*, 46(6), 507-516.

Welsh, P., Rodgers, J., and Honey, E. (2019). Teachers' perception of Restricted and Repetitive Behaviours (RRBs) in children with ASD: Attributions, confidence, and emotional response. *Research in Developmental Disabilities,* 89, pp. 29–40.

Woolfson, L. and Brady, K. (2009). An investigation of factors impacting on mainstream teachers' beliefs about teaching students with learning difficulties. *Educational Psychology,* 29(2), pp. 221–38.

CHAPTER 14

How Can You Address the Power Imbalance between Researcher and Participants?

Alison Weatherston

As a very experienced education professional, but novice researcher, I was somewhat daunted by the requirement to undertake practitioner enquiry as part of postgraduate study. Working in a national organization, I was particularly worried about not being school-based and how my professional role would impact on the research participants, who were new headteachers. In reality, the experience proved to be deeply rewarding, a genuine privilege and one which is shaping my continued research as a doctoral student. The process was particularly significant in supporting a growing identity of myself as researcher, sensitively balancing my professional role and positioning as a research student.

Professionally, as a specialist in professional learning for leadership, I have an imperative to understand the learning needs of aspiring headteachers. As a former primary headteacher, I also have a personal drive to ensure that their learning experiences are as supportive as possible, that we are getting it right for them. Motivated by this professional and personal interest, my enquiry was aimed at enhancing my understanding of aspiring headteachers' broad experiences, specifically exploring the career pathway of a group of new headteachers who had recently completed the national Into Headship programme (Education Scotland 2023a). The enquiry was approached through a lens of 'what's going on', rather than 'what happens if?' (Baumfield et al. 2013, p. 39), particularly what influenced the headteachers towards aspiring for headship and the role played by professional learning. I hoped to identify turning points and support mechanisms in their career decision making, to better understand the complexity of their career trajectories and inform my practice in support of aspiring headteachers.

Immediately apparent was the potential for an imbalanced power dynamic, as participants would know and relate to me as working for a prominent educational organization in Scotland. Teacher-researchers will often encounter tensions and dilemmas in carrying out doctoral research in their area of work (Czerniawski 2023). The issue of power and positionality is common, where the researcher can be perceived as being in a more senior or privileged position than the research subjects. This was compounded by an awareness of the challenges facing school leaders during the COVID-19 pandemic. It was important to ensure that my research would not add to participants' already complex workload and that they would feel supported rather than obligated to take part.

Through describing my own experience as a practitioner-researcher, I hope to exemplify some of the possible decisions and processes you might encounter when concerned about your positionality in relation to your research participants. Fundamentally, my approach was to maintain a focus on the centrality of the participants, as active and engaged in researching their own professional story. While leading and owning the research, my role had to include ensuring that the participants had autonomy over elements in the data collection processes, promoted through a participative methodology.

Providing background to the enquiry, the chapter begins by outlining both the context for leadership learning in Scottish education and the conceptual framework that prompted me towards finalizing the research question. Details follow of the carefully considered planning, implementation and evaluation of a research methodology that aimed to provide deep insight into the headteachers' experiences, while remaining ethically sound. In conclusion, my reflections on my learning as a novice researcher are proposed to support and stimulate your own reflections.

Knowing your context: Background to the research and the conceptual framework

In sharing my story and exploring the significance of my positionality, it will be helpful for you, the reader, that I outline the context of the research, specifically, the processes and structures for headteacher development in Scotland. Having a professional responsibility to lead professional learning for aspiring headteachers, my enquiry was motivated by a desire to highlight the holistic nature of headteacher development in Scotland. Recent legislative changes had brought one aspect into focus, the national programme for headteacher development, Into Headship (Education Scotland 2023a), and I was becoming frustrated by what was, in my view, an apparent narrowing of perspective. Recognising that there might be value in developing a deeper understanding of the broader experience of becoming a headteacher in Scotland, I planned to engage new headteachers directly in an enquiry. Given my professional role, it could be argued that I was in a privileged position in relation to my research participants.

Scottish education has a politicized context, dominated by policy drivers and initiatives aimed towards closing the poverty related attainment gap, bringing significant levels of associated accountability (Scottish Government 2022). Approaches to professional learning for leadership development are varied, with local authorities, regional improvement collaboratives and private providers offering a range of experiences and opportunities across different career stages.

However, professional development towards becoming a headteacher has a national programme, Into Headship. This established programme is delivered in close collaboration between seven universities across Scotland, local authorities and the national organization, Education Scotland. Participants undertake continual critical self-reflection while leading strategic change within their own context, supported by an experienced headteacher mentor. Successful completion awards participants the Professional Standard for Headship (GTCS 2023a), a mandatory requirement for all headteachers in state-funded Scottish schools (UK Government 2019). This recent introduction of the legislative requirement to hold the Standard for Headship, had provoked concern amongst some stakeholders that having to complete Into Headship might become an additional barrier to headteacher recruitment.

Within this context, the conceptual framework for my enquiry was shaped through critical consideration of Sachs's (2016) proposal of dominant models of teacher professionalism, democratic and managerial. She argues that managerial professionalism focuses on performance and accountability, while democratic professionalism focuses on collegiality and collaboration (Sachs 2016). These models provided an interesting lens to consider headteacher development within the Scottish policy context.

How did I identify the conceptual framework for my enquiry and why was my positionality significant? Being fully funded by the Scottish Government towards attainment of the mandated GTCS Professional Standard for Headship (GTCS 2023a), annual reporting for the National Improvement Framework is based on participant numbers (Scottish Government 2022). With an element of compliance over engagement with the programme, and this statistical approach to reporting, this could be considered to show a 'managerial' (Sachs 2016, p. 419) approach to headteacher development. In my view, this represents an apparent lack of attention towards more holistic aspects of career development.

Indeed, my literature review had suggested that the decision to become a headteacher and transition into post is multifaceted. It involves a complex transformation towards developing professional identity as school leader, described as including a range of elements: role-conceptualization; socialisation; self-efficacy; role identity (Browne-Ferringo 2003; Crow et al. 2017; Purdie 2014; Rhodes 2012). Furthermore, Rhodes (2012) highlights that individual change involves critical challenges, phases and degrees of transformation and intrinsic and extrinsic motivating factors. He argues that the development of school leaders should go beyond 'a perfunctory approach' (p. 443) of identifying required skills and behaviours to a more holistic approach that includes building self-belief.

The design of the Into Headship programme reflects these broader elements, balancing practical and academic requirements and aligned with Sachs's (2016) democratic professionalism. Flexibility is integral to established national programme parameters, to account for the diverse school leadership roles and contexts across

Scotland. Participants analyse their individual context, identifying a focus for strategic change. Peer networks are established and maintained for participants and recognized as a key support, as is the designated headteacher mentor role. These elements support aspiring headteachers towards activist professionalism (Sachs 2003), enabled to challenge dominant discourse. Evaluative evidence suggests that engagement with Into Headship significantly increases participants' confidence in their strategic leadership of school communities (Education Scotland 2022).

Going beyond my personal sense of frustration, exploring the wider career trajectories of teachers presented an opportunity to highlight this 'democratic' (Sachs 2016, p. 419), collegial and collaborative nature of headteacher development in Scotland, beyond a managerial focus on statistics and assumptions around its mandatory nature. To fully investigate the complexity of professional identity transformation (Rhodes 2012), I felt it would be important to capture the voices of those who had recently become headteachers, linking theory to practice.

Throughout my career in education, I believe I have modelled Sachs's (2016) 'democratic professionalism'. Strong, equitable working relationships have been a central pillar of my practice. Despite this conviction, Braun and Clarke (2013) warn that participants can think of the researcher, 'as an "expert" and for some participants your status as researcher will override other aspects of your identity' (p. 89). Being newly appointed headteachers, who knew me from my professional role, there remained an inherent risk that the research participants themselves would perceive my position of researcher as a privileged one.

Knowing yourself as researcher: Towards understanding your positionality

In trying to overcome the potential for a power imbalance, it is key to maintain a reflexive approach across all aspects of the planning and implementation of the research process. This reflexivity includes being transparent with yourself in considering both your positionality in terms of role and your subjectivity, the influences and interactions that shape your individual practice

(Hall and Wall 2019). This encouragement for practitioner-researchers to adopt a 'reflective orientation' in making decisions about their research, 'identifying for yourself what is making some choices more or less likely, from a personal, professional or epistemological perspective' (Hall and Wall 2019, p. 48), shaped my research from the outset.

Reflexivity remained a key feature at every step of my research process; in defining the question, planning the methodology, collecting data, analysing data and sharing the findings. These steps are illustrated in the following sections, and you may find them useful to consider when planning your own research.

The importance of recognizing your ontological and epistemological stances

Like me, you might find that, as an experienced education professional, you have a touch of imposter syndrome as a researcher, and I initially struggled with identifying my ontological and epistemological perspectives. However, committed to Hall and Wall's 'reflective orientation' (2019, p. 48), taking some time here was instrumental in deepening my self-awareness of my researcher identity and positionality. Cited in Cohen et al. (2018), Bettez argues that research knowledge is affected by such positionality, 'how we see ourselves and others' (p. 306), and influenced by various factors, including cultural values and beliefs and status as insider or outsider. Critical reflection on my practice and engagement with relevant literature, for example, Braun and Clarke (2013), Cohen et al. (2018), Leavy (2017) and Schubotz (2020), supported reaffirmation of my professional values, or 'how I see myself'.

This reflective process enabled me to surface some deep-rooted professional interests, values and motivations. Reflecting on Sachs's (2016) arguments, I confirmed my tendency towards a democratic view of professionalism, valuing the meaningful participation of learners in their experience being a recognizable feature of my practice as a class teacher, head teacher and national officer. I attach significance to stakeholder views and observations, rather than privileging statistical data and performativity measures. Being solution-focussed, I tend to seek collaborative approaches in overcoming challenges.

My emergent understanding was that this aligned with an ontological position of 'relativism' (Braun and Clarke 2013, p. 27), that the outcomes of research are dependent on individuals' interpretation of experiences. My epistemological stance aligned with a constructivist view, that knowledge is shaped by the interaction of individuals with others and their environment, (Braun and Clarke 2013; Schubotz 2020) and that 'knowing' includes both 'experiential and practical knowledge' (Schubotz 2020, p. 26). Rather than a definitive truth, this would be relative to the unique perspectives based on participants' individual contexts, investigating 'the messiness of real life' (Braun and Clarke 2013, p. 20), appropriate to the complexity of career development.

Designing your research to reflect your stance and account for your positionality

This attention to developing critical self-awareness of you as a researcher is time well spent, flowing naturally into a research design process that resonates with your values and motivations. Having arrived at the decision that constructivism was a paradigm I was happy to embrace, I felt it was important to position the participants as co-researchers of their own story, supported to investigate their personal transition to headship. As far as possible, they should contribute to the synthesis of findings, feeling a sense of ownership over them, as Kara argues, 'constructing research with participants rather than using participants for their research' (2017, p. 45). Committed to this view of the headteachers as co-researchers, a narrative approach to the methodology emerged (Cohen et al. 2018, p. 664). Participants would be encouraged to tell their own stories through individual interviews, with my focus on supporting their active participation and deep reflection through high-quality interaction.

The significance of the wording of the research question in considering the positionality of the participants

Refining the research question was a significant first step in ensuring the privileging of the voice of the research participants, while meeting the purpose of highlighting broad career experiences. After several re-drafts, it emerged as; 'What influences do new headteachers in Scotland identify as being significant in their transition towards headship?'

The wording of the question indicates the centrality of voice, signalling that the influences will be identified by new headteachers themselves. Beyond professional learning, the term 'influences' highlights the multifaceted nature of leadership identity transformation. Echoing this holistic process, 'transition' also suggests active decisionmaking, led by individuals, rather than just the acquisition of a promoted post.

Considering ethical requirements as a support for your research design

Having finalized your research question you will turn your attention towards the planning and implementation of approaches that resonate with your unique ontological and epistemological stance. In seeking to minimize the opportunity for an imbalanced power dynamic, careful attention to ethical requirements was instrumental in clarifying the detail of these approaches. Resonating with my values, Braun and Clarke's (2013) suggested core ethical principles– respect, competence, responsibility and integrity (p. 62)– proved helpful. However, my understanding was deepened through more systematic consideration of each of BERA's recommended researcher responsibilities– consent, transparency, right to withdraw, incentives, minimizing harm, privacy and disclosure– towards developing 'an ethic of respect' (BERA 2018, p. 6), with the headteachers as active participants.

Taking account of these ethical requirements, it was incumbent on me to establish an inclusive, equitable culture that supported the participants to feel authentically heard and their voice enabled. In highlighting that the shape of research is typically determined by the researcher, Cohen et al. (2018, p. 136) advocate giving participants an element of control over the decision making and that it is researcher's responsibility to develop rapport and trust. Although I hoped this was consistent with my practice, in planning the research methodology, establishing and nurturing trusting relationships became an essential element.

Identifying appropriate tools and techniques to support your methodological choices

In designing your research, you should also seek appropriate techniques for data collection that will resonate with your epistemological stance. In my case, this was concerned with ensuring a positive relational ethos in support of the headteachers' narratives. As advocated by Hall and Wall (2019), I spent 'some time thinking about how different voices can be facilitated and how approaches and tools might privilege or inhibit them' (p. 221). With this in mind, I found myself naturally leaning towards the interviews being coaching conversations. From my experience as a leadership coach, I knew this would be an effective way to build the necessary rapport and trust and aligned with my values.

Coaching and mentoring approaches are well established in Scottish education and recognized as a continuum of support for ongoing professional development (GTCS 2023b). Fundamental to this continuum is non-directive coaching, which aims to encourage 'an individual to explore their own context and take responsibility for professional actions' (Education Scotland 2023b). This is supported through a reflective and focussed conversation, supported but not led by the coach, aimed at illuminating lived experience through open-ended questioning and responsive listening towards realistic goal-setting. As I was experienced in using non-directive questioning and active listening to enhance self-awareness, this felt like a 'good fit' with my aim to establish an open and inclusive approach to the interviews.

While suggesting that the development of headteacher identity 'involves growing and sustaining a narrative', Crow et al. (2017, p. 271) caution that the relationship between interviewer and interviewee affects how headteachers will relate their stories. I was confident that the coaching approach to developing the narrative would be an appropriate way to establish and support relational trust, ensuring that each interview was a confidential one-to-one conversation.

As co-researchers, I aimed to ensure that the participants were as involved as possible in determining the shape of their coaching conversation and the recording and analysis of its outcomes. In supporting their preparation for the coaching conversation, visual timelines were suggested to scaffold the dialogue (Hall and Wall 2019, p. 82), but also proved a useful technique to give the participants some autonomy over the direction of the conversation.

In my coaching experience, visual timelines have proved a powerful way of illuminating otherwise hidden insights into previous experience. Plotting feelings on an axis against points on a career path axis provides prompts for reflection and discussion, highlighting career highs and lows. For research that involves telling a personal story, reflecting on significant events, this method can capture the complexity of lived experience, beyond the scope of more structured methods, such as questionnaires, and are particularly useful when exploring changes over time and associated emotions (Hryniewicz et al. 2014; Sheridan et al. 2011; Mazzetti and Blenkinsopp 2012). Utilizing this approach meant that participants had control over this element of the conversation, creating and keeping their own visual timeline and choosing which parts to share in conversation.

Overcoming the potential for a power imbalance: Implementing open and transparent approaches

In developing relational trust, it is important to be open and transparent about your role in relation to the participants, beginning with your initial contact with the sample. In my case, this involved clarifying and reiterating my specific role as a student-researcher role at every opportunity. The target participant group for my sample was newly appointed headteachers who had most recently gained the Standard for Headship. As a group, we had met in person before pandemic restrictions, so had an established connection towards developing rapport. However, that had been through my professional role, with an inherent risk that they might feel an imperative to participate.

To promote the voluntary nature of the research and aiming to be transparent about my different role here, my first invitation to prospective participants was through my student email address, rather than my professional one. Consistent with other research requests to my organization, I contacted all target participants, outlining the scope of my enquiry. With my priority being that research participants were willing volunteers I remained open-minded about sample size and membership. However, it was important to ensure that potential participants were fully aware of the parameters of their role in the research from the beginning and could make an informed choice about their involvement. A vital step here, which is worth considering for your own research, was to invite the interested volunteers to an online introduction session, with no strings attached. The session outlined the enquiry's rationale, methodology, planned outcomes and use of data, supported with a summary information sheet. The session aimed to put participants at ease and address concerns, towards the avoidance of making excessive demands. I felt assured that those who continued through to the data collection were fully aware of what their commitment entailed.

The importance of being transparent about your positionality to support voluntary participation is essential. Remaining conscious of positionality, it is also worth seeking opportunities to reiterate your role and position. In my case, I shared my own timeline as an example, modelling openness and transparency, and several of the group commented that they appreciated this honest approach. Deciding what element of your experience to share is an important consideration and one that should reflect the research question, while also nurturing trust and mutual respect. It supports the position of participants as co-researchers, with the researcher prepared to model what is being asked of the participants, in the spirit of reciprocity.

Using tools to enhance the active engagement of participants in data collection

The data collection techniques described here were generated in response to the reflexive thinking and careful consideration of ethical requirements. I recommend spending time drafting and refining tools that are aimed at answering the research question, using the literature review that informed the research question to guide you. My examples illustrate how I supported the participants to have some ownership and control over the data produced, while remaining focussed on the research question.

Committed to the headteachers as 'active collaborators' (Braun and Clarke 2013, p. 64), encouraging their agency in the process of data collection, participants were invited to choose what to share from their timeline and reflect on my subsequent retelling of their story, through the questioning and summarizing involved in the coaching conversation.

However, while remaining open and non-directive, the coaching conversations needed an element of structure to focus on the enquiry question and ensure equity across participants. A coaching conversation protocol was generated, to structure the conversation, reiterating the aim and ethical principles of the enquiry and provide questions to guide the conversations. For example, as part of 'telling me the story of your timeline'

- What made the high points distinctive from the others?
- How did you feel about yourself and your role?
- What was key to the decision to apply for headship?
- What particular challenges did you identify? Why were they a challenge? How did you feel about yourself and your role?
- What supported you through them? How did you know it was no longer a challenge?
- Can you identify the moment when you identified as a school leader? What contributed to that?

- How did your self-efficacy and self-belief show up on the journey– if you were to draw a new line for them, what would it look like?

Beyond this structuring of the conversation, we had to find a way to capture the essence of the coaching conversations. Heeding Braun and Clarke's (2013) caution that the researcher's interpretation of others' experience can become their 'story of the story' (p. 64), the participants had a critical role in confirming the outcomes of the coaching conversation for analysis. Guided by elements identified by Rhodes (2012) as key to individual leadership transformation (p. 445), designing a proforma was central to this process, as shown in Table 14.1. Completing the proforma was participatory, using a digitally shared screen. Participants directed the order of its completion and were given the opportunity to review it following the coaching conversation, ensuring their ownership of the data.

The coaching conversation outcomes were analysed using a thematic analysis approach (Braun and Clarke 2013), involving several stages of reading and categorizing of the data. Using the proforma to capture the outcomes facilitated this process and determined common themes. In terms of answering the research question, it was evident that the coaching conversations had enabled the new headteachers to explore their career path in depth, identifying a number of influences towards becoming a headteacher.

Learning from my experience: Reflecting on approaches

In conclusion, what advice might I offer to you, in considering your positionality and potential position of power in relation to your research participants? Throughout, the nature of the participants' engagement was a continued focus for reflexive thinking. Of critical importance was the need to establish respectful working relationships, with headteachers as equal and active participants. Their insights shaped the enquiry tools, they were co-researchers of their story in the recording of the coaching outcomes, and they contributed to the strategic nature of the enquiry with their reflections on the key messages. It is my firm belief that, in

TABLE 14.1 Coaching Outcomes Proforma (Self-designed)

What have you learned today about your transition to headship?
What was significant in developing your understanding of the role and responsibilities of a HT?
Can you identify any changes in your behaviour or attitude?
Can you identify any particular stages in your identity transformation?
What was key to your decision to become a headteacher?
What are your internal motivators?
What are your external motivators?
How do you overcome challenges?
What knowledge and strategies will you continue to use to support you?
How should this new knowledge be used this to support future aspiring headteachers?
Anything else? Do you have a pseudonym you would like me to use?

supporting participants to give open and honest perspectives on their career experiences, the commitment and time spent was essential towards overcoming positionality and addressing a power imbalance.

Reflecting the conceptual framework, the findings seemed to confirm that the development of Scottish headteachers is a complex transformation involving a growing sense of self-belief, evolving identity and practical experience, dependent on much more than one specific piece of professional learning. This small group of headteachers suggested their transition into headship as a gradual transformation, influenced through critical self-reflection and increasing self-confidence, supported by strong relationships with encouraging colleagues, experience and specific professional learning.

The participative approaches supported the new headteachers to interrogate their experiences and encouraged their recognition of how factors affecting self-belief and confidence had impacted on their practice and experience. Constructing their visual timeline and engagement in the coaching conversation promoted deep self-reflection on their leadership trajectory and career experiences in general. They each expressed gratitude for the opportunity for self-reflection afforded by the enquiry, building on their experiences on Into Headship. They appreciated a fresh appraisal of their leadership strengths, given recent operational challenges through the pandemic, resulting in renewed commitment to support the learning trajectory of their colleagues and to provide that mentoring role, encouragement and affirmation that they so valued.

The methodology and findings resonated with my own professional values and ways of working, and I recognize the strong possibility that my own career experiences have influenced me as a researcher, with a commitment to supporting criticality and nurturing trusting relationships towards building the leadership capacity of others. This manifests as a constructivist stance, with a continuing commitment to minimizing a power imbalance. This enquiry deepened my knowledge and understanding of the experiences of the aspiring headteachers that I work with, supporting my critical reflection and strategic thinking. While undoubtedly informing my professional role, this has provided a stimulus for deeper investigation and refinement of research methodology.

References

Baumfield, V., Hall, E., and Wall, K. (2013). *Action research in education.* 2nd ed. Thousand Oaks, CA: SAGE Publications.

Braun, V. and Clarke, V. (2013). *Successful qualitative research: A practical guide for beginners.* London: SAGE Publications.

British Educational Research Association [BERA]. (2018). *Ethical guidelines for educational research.* 4th ed. [online]. London: British Educational Research Association. Available: https://www.bera.ac.uk/publication/ethical-guidelines-for-educational-research-2018-online [accessed 12 August 2023].

Browne-Ferrigno, T. (2003). Becoming a principal. Role conception, initial socialisation, role-identity transformation, purposeful engagement. *Educational Administration Quarterly,* 39(4), pp. 468–503.

Cohen, L., Manion, L., and Morrison, K. (2018). *Research methods in education.* 8th ed. New York: Routledge.

Crow, G., Day, C., and Moller, J. (2017). Framing research on school principals' identities. *International Journal of Leadership in Education,* 20(3), pp. 265–77.

Czerniawski, G. (2023). Power, positionality, and practitioner research: Schoolteachers' experiences of professional doctorates in education. *British Educational Research Journal,* 49, pp. 1372–1386.

Education Scotland. (2022). *National Into Headship programme evaluation report* [online]. Available: https://professionallearning.education.gov.scot/media/2336/into-headship-evaluation-report-alma-harris-sept-22.pdf [accessed 12 August 2023].

Education Scotland. (2023a). *Into Headship* [online]. Available: https://professionallearning.education.gov.scot/learn/programmes/into-headship/ [accessed 12 August 2023].

Education Scotland. (2023b). *What is coaching and mentoring?* [online]. Available: https://professionallearning.education.gov.scot/learn/coaching-and-mentoring-matters/what-is-coaching-and-mentoring/ [accessed 12 August 2023].

General Teaching Council for Scotland [GTCS]. (2023a). *The standard for headship: An aspirational professional standard for Scotland's teachers* [online]. Available: https://www.gtcs.org.uk/wp-content/uploads/2021/09/standard-for-headship.pdf [accessed 12 August 2023].

General Teaching Council for Scotland [GTCS]. (2023b). *Unlocking the potential of professional review and development* [online]. Available: https://www.gtcs.org.uk/wp-content/uploads/2021/08/professional-review-development-guidance-2020.pdf [accessed 12 August 2023].

Hall, E. and Wall, K. (2019). *Research methods for understanding professional learning*. London: Bloomsbury Academic.

Hryniewicz, L., Griffiths, V., and Thompson, S. (2014). Living graphs as a methodological tool representing landmarks in the professional development of teacher educators. *TEAN Journal*, 6 (1), pp. 30–40.

Kara, H. (2017). *Research and evaluation for busy students and practitioners: a time-saving guide*. 2nd ed. Bristol: Policy Press.

Leavy, P. (2017). *Research design: Quantitative, qualitative, mixed Methods, arts-based and community-based participatory research approaches*. New York: Guildford Press.

Mazzetti, A. and Blenkinsopp, J. (2012). Evaluating a visual timeline methodology for appraisal and coping research. *Journal of Occupational and Organisational Psychology*, 85, pp. 649–65.

Purdie, J. (2014). *Key factors in early headship development in the Scottish secondary school sector: An analytical autoethnography*. EdD thesis [online], University of Glasgow. Available: https://theses.gla.ac.uk/5718/ [accessed 13 August 2023].

Rhodes, C. (2012). Should leadership talent management in schools also include the management of self-belief? *School Leadership & Management*, 32 (5), pp. 439–51.

Sachs, J. (2003). *The activist teaching profession*. Buckingham: Open University Press.

Sachs, J. (2016). Teacher professionalism: Why are we still talking about it? *Teachers and Teaching*, 22(4), pp. 413–25.

Schubotz, D. (2020). *Participatory research: Why and how to involve people in research*. London: SAGE Publications.

Scottish Government. (2022). *Achieving excellence and equity: 2023 National improvement framework and improvement plan* [online]. Available: https://www.gov.scot/binaries/content/documents/govscot/publications/strategy-plan/2022/12/achieving-excellence-equity-2023-national-improvement-framework-improvement-plan/documents/achieving-excellence-equity-2023-national-improvement-framework-improvement-plan/achieving-excellence-equity-2023-national-improvement-framework-improvement-plan/govscot%3Adocument/achieving-excellence-equity-2023-national-improvement-framework-improvement-plan.pdf [accessed 2 September 2023].

Sheridan, J., Chamberlain, K., and Dupuis, A. (2011). Timelining: Visualizing experience. *Qualitative Research*, 11(5), pp. 552–69.

United Kingdom Government. (2019). *The head teachers education and training standards (Scotland) regulations* [online]. Available: https://www.legislation.gov.uk/ssi/2019/217/contents/made [accessed 13 August 2023].

CHAPTER 15

How Do You Address Ethical Issues When Engaged in Online Research?

Diana Tremayne

In this chapter I discuss my learning experiences from my doctoral study into the online professional learning of Further Education (FE) teachers with a particular focus on ethical issues and how these were explored and addressed throughout the study. The first section provides the context and rationale for the study and outlines the research topic and research questions while also highlighting how ethical aspects came to the fore from the beginning. In section two I discuss how the various ethical considerations impacted on the methodological choices I went on to make and outline how the netnographic approach I took was helpful in addressing ethical issues. In the final section I reflect on how ethical issues continued to shape both the data collection and analysis phases of the study and how the ethical and participatory stances taken were significant features of the study as a whole.

Setting the scene: Establishing the research topic

The majority of my professional life has been spent working in further education in England, both as a teacher of English for Speakers of Other Languages (ESOL) and as an advanced practitioner. A large part of this role involved supporting staff through coaching, mentoring and delivering professional development. In 2016 I was fortunate enough to be offered a bursary to undertake doctoral research at Leeds Beckett University with a focus on online communities for professional learning as well as teacher agency.

I was already active in using Twitter (now known as 'X') for my own professional learning and was keen to explore this area further as I was aware of how valuable it had been personally. Research into the role of online teacher-learning communities in professional learning was becoming more common but had not yet really explored further education. My own experiences and this gap in the research helped to eventually shape the focus of the study on a weekly Twitter chat which is aimed at FE educators working in the UK. The study considered how participation in the chat supports professional learning and potentially also the development of teacher agency.

As I was already a regular participant in the Twitter chat my role was very much that of an insider researcher where I was involved in the site which was being studied and therefore became both the 'subject of [the] study and the participant object being studied' (Kanuha 2000, p. 441). My position as an insider researcher alongside the fact that I was conducting online research meant that the consideration of ethical issues came to the fore strongly from the start of the study. This was explored through a netnographic approach (Kozinets 2015) which is discussed in more detail in section two. This approach helped me to gain both 'inside' and 'outside' perspectives on the site and to provide a rich picture of this online teacher-learning community while at the same time helping to ensure a strong focus on ethical considerations.

Why informal online teacher-learning communities?

Although large numbers of teachers engage with Twitter and other forms of social media, professional learning remains subject to narrow interpretations which focus on the 'physical action' of teachers (Evans 2019, p. 6). A tendency towards audit cultures and standards frameworks within education (Kennedy 2011; Colley et al. 2003) means that informal or self-directed learning is frequently marginalized and that training within organizations is often seen as a 'tick box' exercise (ETF 2018, p. 64). This is in contrast to the potential for mutual growth and new thinking with others (Cochran-Smith and Lytle 1999) which communities of teachers (both online and offline) may offer. In the FE context the importance of collaboration between colleagues and opportunities for informal professional dialogue is highlighted in recent research as a significant way to support opportunities for teacher agency (O'Leary et al. 2019). However, both informal learning and research into FE have been described as unrecognized or invisible (Eraut 2004; Solvason and Elliott 2013) and I was keen to try to redress this to at least some degree through the research and share the role online teacher-learning communities can play in professional learning.

Online spaces offer opportunities for teachers to develop networks and communities in new ways which can enable them to 'grow their own' professional learning (Lieberman and Pointer Mace 2010, p. 86) outside of organizational constraints. An increasing number of studies explore the role of Twitter in professional learning and development (e.g. Carpenter et al. 2020; Nochumson 2020; Wesely 2013) but there was little which explicitly considered this in relation to the development of teacher agency. Exploring a specific Twitter chat also enabled in-depth analysis of the richness of interactions and a focus on the importance of informal talk both online and offline.

With the emphasis on conducting research into an online space while also foregrounding the voices of its participants, it was necessary to reflect on how best to achieve this in an ethical manner from the start of the study. Ethical approval applications often tend to be completed in the relatively early stages of research, perhaps before methodological ideas have been fully developed or refined, and it is key to think of these not as a tick box exercise but as an opportunity to explore different approaches to ethical concerns.

One important early consideration was in relation to consent which, although key in all research, becomes particularly complex in relation to online spaces where people may be operating in what are essentially 'public' spaces but often 'maintain strong perceptions of privacy' (Markham and Buchanan 2012, p. 6). The Twitter chat which I was exploring was accessible to anyone, but it was important to remember that those participating would not necessarily have considered that their data could be used for research purposes (BERA 2018) and that some of what was shared could potentially be sensitive.

Framing the research questions

Although the research questions themselves do not directly address ethical issues, they were framed to help ensure that both 'inside' and 'outside' perspectives on the site could be gained and this involved different ethical considerations. The questions aimed to explore both the practical aspects of how teachers participate in online teacher-learning communities such as Twitter chats and to dig deeper into what this participation means in terms of supporting professional learning and teacher agency. The three questions were as follows:

> RQ1. How do teachers participate in online teacher-learning communities?
>
> RQ2. How does this participation support professional learning?
>
> RQ3. How might online teacher-learning communities support the development of teacher agency and inquiry?

RQ1 explores the 'outside' perspective on participation more through observation and required reflection on how to collect online data in as ethical a way as possible. RQs 2 and 3 looked at more of an 'inside' perspective through both participant observation and interviews and this meant that different issues came to the fore in relation to anonymity and my insider position. Although the basic research questions did not change significantly from early on in the study, I think that how I reflected on these questions, and how they related to ethical issues did evolve and become clearer as the research and writing up progressed.

Grappling with ethical and methodological issues

My approach to the study as a whole was to 'start with the research issue' (Newby 2014, p. 20) and this was helpful advice in terms of addressing both methodological and ethical concerns in ways which aimed to find a 'coherent and consistent' way to answer the research questions (Mason 2002, p. 32). Social interaction is at the heart of this study and essentially people, along with their 'interpretations, perceptions, meanings and understandings' (Mason 2002, p. 56) provide the source of data here. In social media contexts it can sometimes be easier to forget that online data is 'generated by individuals' (BERA 2018, p. 7) but keeping this fact uppermost was one of my core ethical concerns throughout the study. Reflecting on our own position as researchers should also be key to shaping methodological and ethical choices throughout any study, especially as this position can change at different stages of the study (Ritchie et al. 2009).

My own role as participant observer gave me a distinctly 'insider' perspective on the interactions and interpretations of those participating in the Twitter chat and it was important to address this by being as transparent as possible about my own position. This is discussed more later in the section but included using my Twitter profile and blog posts to highlight my status as a researcher.

From the outset I was keen to complement both individual perspectives and my own insider role with methods which could provide additional insights into the online community under exploration. Ultimately, I was able to bring in more of an 'outside' perspective (Edwards 2010), through using elements of social network analysis as a way to try and understand the structure of the community as a whole. It is important to note that taking this decision was not an attempt at neutrality but an additional lens through which the first research question in particular could be explored. This outside view was one way to consider aspects of the space which I may have taken for granted and one way to demonstrate the 'rich rigor' and 'sincerity' that Tracy includes in her criteria for excellent qualitative research (Tracy 2010). For me, taking on board and reflecting on criteria such as these was an important part of considering how to address ethical issues as a whole.

Which methodological approach was right for this study?

As already noted, I was keen to find a 'coherent and consistent' (Mason 2002, p. 32) approach to exploring my research questions and to ensure that I was considering different perspectives on the online space I was studying. Given that I was examining a specific Twitter chat I knew that this would involve intensive observation and participation in the space over a period of time and this seemed to fit well with an ethnographic approach. A key element of ethnography is studying how people act and what they say within a specific context (Hammersley 2006) with the aim of producing 'accounts of behaviour that provide rich context' (Boellstorff et al. 2012, p. 16) and developing this rich understanding of the online community I was researching was key to the study.

The clear focus of my research on an online space and the significance of ethical issues led me to explore netnography, an approach developed in the 1990s and extended by Robert Kozinets (2015). He defines netnography as the

> name given to a specific set of related data collection, analysis, ethical and representational research practices, where a significant amount of the data collected and participant-observational research conducted originates in and manifests through the data shared freely on the Internet, including mobile applications. (p. 79)

Whilst this definition highlights that internet data is a key element of netnography, Kozinets also stresses the importance of other forms of data collection, including online and face-to-face interviews (Kozinets 2015). The foregrounding of ethical issues was a key factor in choosing the approach, as was its additional description as 'participative, reflective, interactive and active' (p. 97), which aligned to my own thinking but seemed to go hand in hand with a strong ethical focus.

As already discussed, my own position as an insider researcher was significant in shaping my approach but other ethical issues which needed to be considered included whether online interactions were considered private or public, consent and anonymity, and I discuss these further now. Before and during the main observation and data collection period I highlighted my status as researcher and participant observer in my own tweets and in blog posts in order to be as transparent as possible. Using a 'pinned' tweet (one which stays at the top of your posts on Twitter) was one way to highlight my role, as was contributing to the BERA blog series where I discussed the netnographic approach and ethics (Tremayne 2018). Writing in this way was a helpful way to continue to reflect on the issues and to gain feedback from others.

One major issue was how to address questions regarding the anonymity of both the research site (i.e. the Twitter chat) and individuals. In online spaces such as Twitter anonymity is not easy to guarantee (BERA 2018), partly because any quotes made are easily searchable. It was important to make this clear on any information which went to participants and to talk it through explicitly. In terms of whether or not the interactions people shared online were private or public I also took the decision that although I was keen to include some directly quoted tweets in the final thesis that this would only be with the consent of those individuals, drawing on the work of Williams et al. (2017) in considering the most ethically appropriate way to approach this issue.

As I was undertaking research with adults and fellow teachers, I was able to consider more easily how naming the research site and potentially participants might actually benefit those involved (Tilley and Woodthorpe 2011). Although anonymity of site and participants is generally assumed in most research studies, the assumption that it is always the best approach is questioned by some with Walford (2005, p. 83) arguing that it is 'impossible to ensure anonymity' and 'often undesirable to do so'. BERA's most recent ethical guidelines reflect this by stating that participants have a right to be identified if they wish (BERA 2018, p. 21).

The Twitter chat that I was studying was taking place in a space which was already open and visible to anyone and had an aim of sharing experiences and good practice in the further education context. After careful thought and discussion with the main host of the chat and my supervisory team I made the choice to name the site throughout my thesis, following the example of Tilley who felt that identification would be of benefit to the organizations involved and the sector which her research covered (Tilley and Woodthorpe 2011).

How do ethical considerations fit into data collection and analysis?

As already noted, finding ways to include both 'inside' and 'outside' perspectives on the site was important and this was done through three methods of data collection: participant observation of the Twitter chats, interviews and elements of social network analysis to gather and explore data from Twitter. In this section I consider some of the key aspects of data collection and analysis and how they helped to address the ethical considerations raised in the study.

Incorporating social network analysis (SNA) into the study was one way to provide an 'outsider' view of the network, or Twitter chat, which could give an overview of the structure of the chat as a whole rather than focusing on individuals (Scott 2013). This is done by using diagrams or visualizations which represent networks of relations between individuals (or 'actors'). Each point in the diagram highlights an 'actor' and the lines between them indicate the relationship they have to one another (Scott 2013). As a non-specialist I was able to use the web-based tool Netlytic (Gruzd 2016) to gather data, including network visualizations which were particularly helpful in addressing and illustrating the first research question around how teachers participate in a Twitter chat. For me it was important to access a tool which was simple to use, and which provided clear guidance for those less familiar with this method.

Using SNA helped to give valuable insights into the Twitter chat and showed connections and interactions that were not as visible from observation alone and this was important in addressing the desire for an 'outside' perspective. It was also easy to produce visualizations which did not name those participating in the chats as contacting each individual for consent to be named would have proved a huge challenge. However, on its own the social network data provides limited information and does not shed light on the rich experiences of those involved in the network or community. The 'insider' view (Edwards 2010) which was gathered from participant observation and interviews was needed to complement SNA and ensure that the study was genuinely 'participative, reflective, interactive and active' (Kozinets 2015, p. 97).

Observation over an extended period of time is a common feature of ethnographic approaches and was a crucial part of the data collection process. Although I was very much a participant observer the focused observation which took place during the research period also allowed the opportunity to step back more and to observe patterns and routines which may not have been noticed previously (Patton 2002). Conducting research in an online space allowed me to revisit interactions easily and to take time to see how people engaged from more of an outside perspective. This process aided reflection throughout the study and continued in a less formal way during the analysis and writing up phases.

As a regular participant in the weekly chats, I needed to be aware of my roles as both teacher and researcher, and constantly reflect on how I engaged with the chat and with Twitter in general as part of my ethical stance. In my case this was perhaps easier to do because the main focus of the weekly chats was on professional learning and those who participated were interested in and often engaged in practitioner research. However, although there were regular participants in the Twitter chats new people would often join in and this made it important to regularly make my own position clear which I did through tweets and my own blog posts. Sharing my own multiple roles and some of my initial thoughts about the study was an additional way to encourage a more participatory approach and gain feedback from others.

Using interviews

Interviews provided an important opportunity to find out more about some of the participants' experiences and to explore their ideas in greater depth. With my role as participant observer much of the focus of the interviews was on the co-creation of knowledge with those interviewed considered to be 'knowing subjects' (King and Horrocks 2010, p. 136). This fitted very much with the emphasis on a collaborative and participatory approach to the study which aimed to ensure that the research was done 'with' rather than 'to' those involved (Kemmis and Wilkinson 1998).

A major consideration when conducting interviews is when or at what stage in the process to carry them out. From my experience, it was helpful to use the interviews to build on the main observation phase and following this period a request for interview participants was shared on Twitter with the intention of interviewing between six and eight people. Sampling was 'purposeful' (Maxwell 2013) and aimed to ensure that those interviewed covered a range of job roles and types of participation in the weekly chat. Once again, I was very aware of my position as an insider researcher and as a result made sure that I did not only select people who I knew from my own participation in the chat. Eight participants were initially interviewed and afterwards the full transcripts and some of the points I had considered significant were shared with all interviewees as a form of 'member checking' (Creswell 2007) or 'member reflections' (Tracy 2010). This fitted with an ethical position aimed at transparency and at encouraging genuine participation from those involved.

A few months later, a follow-up interview was carried out with seven of the participants which explored the initial themes from the data analysis. This allowed both myself and the participants to reflect on the first interview and their ongoing experience of the Twitter chat. The second interview added depth to some of the points previously made and really developed the sense of knowledge being co-created together. From my own experience, undertaking follow-up interviews was an invaluable part of the data collection and analysis process and I would recommend researchers consider building this into a study.

Ongoing engagement with ethical considerations

As discussed in the section on methodological issues I had already decided that consent would need to be sought for any tweets which were directly quoted in the study. As the data analysis stage continued it was clear that this would involve contacting a number of participants. I built on the doctoral work of Guest (2018) by contacting people via direct message on Twitter and sharing an online consent form with them. This was an effective way of following ethical guidelines but also of engaging more actively with participants who may not have been aware of the study or had not reflected on the question of whether or not their interactions were private or public. As I asked people about the specific tweets I hoped to use this also opened up discussion about some of the key themes within the study and enabled me to share my findings. Although the process of contacting people about quoting tweets was quite time consuming it meant that they moved from becoming sources of data to full participants in the study, with their contributions recognized and appreciated. This participatory approach would not be appropriate in all cases but here ensured that participants did not 'lose ownership' (Grinyer 2002) of their data.

Another way in which the thinking around ethical issues evolved was the way that the follow up interviews provided an opportunity to discuss how people felt about anonymity. I had initially assumed that I would ask interview participants to choose a pseudonym as is standard in most studies but having sought permission for tweets to be quoted this seemed important to revisit. Participants were able to reflect on their feelings about this and as a result seven chose to use their first names rather than pseudonyms, once again ensuring that they retained ownership of their data.

Concluding thoughts

This chapter has provided insights into my doctoral research with a particular focus on how to address some of the ethical issues which arose in this study of an online teacher-learning community. Many of the issues raised are not exclusive to online settings but highlight considerations which are likely to relate to any study. I hope that one of the main points to take away from the chapter is that ethical questions should not be dealt with in a tick box way and need to be revisited throughout any research study. Taking a more participatory approach to the research may have been more time consuming in some ways but provided a richer picture of the community and those who engaged with it and ensured that their voices were foregrounded in the final thesis.

References

Boellstorff, T., Nardi, B., Pearce, C., and Taylor, T. (2012). *Ethnography and virtual worlds: A handbook of method*. Woodstock, Oxfordshire: Princeton University Press.

British Educational Research Association [BERA]. (2018). *Ethical guidelines for educational research*. 4th ed. London: British Educational Research Association.

Carpenter, J., Tani, T., Morrison, S., and Keane, J. (2020). Exploring the landscape of educator professional activity on Twitter: An analysis of 16 education-related Twitter hashtags. *Professional Development in Education*, 48, pp. 1–22.

Cochran-Smith, M. and Lytle, S. (1999). Relationships of knowledge and practice: Teacher learning in communities. *Review of Research in Education*, 24, pp. 249–305.

Colley, H., Hodkinson, P., and Malcolm, J. (2003). *Informality and formality in learning: A report for the learning and skills research centre*. London: Learning and Skills Research Centre.

Creswell, J. (2007). *Qualitative inquiry and research design: Choosing among five approaches*. 2nd ed. London: SAGE Publications.

Education and Training Foundation [ETF]. (2018). *Training needs in the further education sector* [online]. Available: https://www.et-foundation.co.uk/wp-content/uploads/2018/04/1331_Training-Needs-Analysis-Final-.pdf [accessed 30 August 2018].

Edwards, G. (2010). *Mixed-method approaches to social network analysis* [online]. ESRC National Centre for Research Methods, NCRM/015. Available: https://eprints.ncrm.ac.uk/id/eprint/842/ [accessed 30 November 2023].

Eraut, M. (2004). Informal learning in the workplace. *Studies in Continuing Education*, 26(2), pp. 247–73.

Evans, L. (2019). Implicit and informal professional development: what it 'looks like', how it occurs, and why we need to research it. *Professional Development in Education*, 45(1), pp. 3–16.

Grinyer, A. (2002). *The anonymity of research participants, assumptions, ethics and practicalities*. University of Surrey: Social Research Update 36 [online]. Available: http://sru.soc.surrey.ac.uk/SRU36.html [accessed 30 June 2017].

Gruzd, A. (2016). *Netlytic: Software for automated text and social network analysis* [online]. Available: http://Netlytic.org.

Guest, I. (2018). *Exploring teachers' professional development with Twitter: A sociomaterial analysis.* Ph.D. thesis, Sheffield Hallam University.
Hammersley, M. (2006). Ethnography: Problems and prospects. *Ethnography and Education,* 1(1), pp. 3–14.
Kanuha, V. (2000). "Being" native versus "going native": Conducting social work research as an insider. *Social Work,* 45(5), pp. 439–47.
Kemmis, S. and Wilkinson, M. (1998). Participatory action research and the study of practice. In: Atweh, B., Kemmis, S., and Weeks, P. (eds), *Action research in practice.* London: Routledge, pp. 21–36.
Kennedy, A. (2011). Collaborative continuing professional development (CPD) for teachers in Scotland: Aspirations, opportunities, and barriers. *European Journal of Teacher Education,* 34(1), pp. 25–41.
King, N. and Horrocks, C. (2010). *Interviews in qualitative research.* London: SAGE Publications.
Kozinets, R. (2015). *Netnography: Redefined.* London: SAGE Publications.
Lieberman, A. and Pointer Mace, D. (2010). Making practice public: Teacher learning in the 21st century. *Journal of Teacher Education,* 61(1–2), pp. 77–88.
Markham, A. and Buchanan, E. (2012). *Ethical decision-making and internet research: Recommendations from the AoIR ethics working committee (version 2.0)* [online]. Available: https://aoir.org/reports/ethics2.pdf [accessed 30 June 2017].
Mason, J. (2002). *Qualitative researching.* 2nd ed. London: SAGE Publications.
Maxwell, J. (2013). *Qualitative research design: An interactive approach.* 3rd ed. London: SAGE Publications.
Newby, P. (2014). *Research methods for education.* Abingdon: Routledge.
Nochumson, T. (2020). Elementary schoolteachers' use of Twitter: Exploring the implications of learning through online social media. *Professional Development in Education,* 46(2), pp. 306–23.
O'Leary, M., Smith, R., Cui, V., and Dakka, F. (2019). *The role of leadership in prioritising and improving the quality of teaching and learning in further education: Final project report for the further education trust for leadership.* Birmingham: Further Education Trust for Leadership.
Patton M. (2002). *Qualitative research and evaluation methods.* 3rd ed. London: SAGE Publications.
Ritchie, J., Zwi, A., Blignault, I., Bunde-Birouste, A., and Silove, D. (2009). Insider–outsider positions in health-development research: Reflections for practice. *Development in Practice,* 19(1), pp. 106–12.
Scott, J. (2013). *Social network analysis.* 4th ed. London: SAGE Publications.

Solvason, C. and Elliott, G. (2013). Why is research still invisible in further education? *Journal of Learning Development in Higher Education*, 6, pp. 1–17.

Tilley, L. and Woodthorpe, K. (2011). Is it the end for anonymity as we know it? A critical examination of the ethical principle of anonymity in the context of 21st century demands on the qualitative researcher. *Qualitative Research,* 11, pp. 197–212.

Tracy, S. (2010). Qualitative quality: Eight "big-tent" criteria for excellent qualitative research. *Qualitative Inquiry*, 16(10), pp. 837–51.

Tremayne, D. (2018). *Netnography: Exploring 'innovative' approaches to research* [online]. BERA blog. Available: https://www.bera.ac.uk/blog/netnography-exploring-innovative-approaches-to-research [accessed 30 November 2023].

Walford, G. (2005). Research ethical guidelines and anonymity. *International Journal of Research & Method in Education*, 28, pp. 83–93.

Wesely, P. (2013). Investigating the community of practice of world language educators on Twitter. *Journal of Teacher Education*, 64, pp. 305–18.

Williams, M., Burnap, P., and Sloan, L. (2017). Towards an ethical framework for publishing Twitter data in social research: Taking into account users' views, online context and algorithmic estimation. *Sociology,* 51(6), pp. 1149–68.

CHAPTER 16

What Does Ethical Inquiry within a Transformative, Critical Educational Framework Look Like?

Victoria Wasner

This chapter takes the reader through my learning journey of how I came to understand ethical practice in schools as a process of collaborative, student-teacher inquiry. The research project described in this chapter was part of my Doctorate in Education (EdD) at Durham University, UK which I was undertaking long-distance and on a part-time basis whilst teaching full-time at an international school in Switzerland. I begin with an outline of the practice of service learning at the school where I was working as a language teacher and how this practice became the catalyst for my doctoral research and for my interest in ethical education.

Service learning is a 'research-based approach' (IBO 2013, p. 20) to community service activities, intended to connect what is learnt in the classroom with needs of a particular community; it should be 'used in a structured way that connects classroom content, literature and skills to community needs'. In my particular context, it was *international* service learning that was the focus. I draw on personal 'aha – moments' during experiences of international project weeks called 'personal development weeks' (PDWs) where I began to question the ethical nature of these educational opportunities. I also began to wonder to what extent the school could claim that these PDWs were indeed a method of *service learning*, as what I had begun to read and understand about service learning was in conflict with what I had seen and heard from these PDW experiences.

The chapter then illustrates how my immersion in the literature of intercultural communication (Holliday 2011; ; Bhabha 1991), critical multiculturalism (May and Sleeter 2010), transformational learning (Mezirow 1978, 2000, 2009) and critical pedagogy (Freire 1970, 1974; Kincheloe 2012), led me to become interested in *critical* service learning (Andreotti 2006; Porfilio and Hickman 2011) and to question the power relationships that were at play in our international service learning experiences.

I continue by highlighting how these musings led to an exploration of methods of qualitative practitioner inquiry that fit into the kind of critical approach that I had become inspired by (Kincheloe et al. 2011) and how I could find confidence in myself as a *bricoleur* (Kincheloe et al. 2011) in my role as a practitioner-researcher and embrace the 'messiness' or multivocal nature of the research that I intended to undertake. Ultimately, all of these different frameworks enabled me to find justification for student voice as an ethical educational practice (Groundwater-Smith and Mockler 2007; Fielding 2015), which led to my methodology of students as researchers into the school's practice of service learning.

In essence, this chapter depicts how I grappled with the challenge of developing an ethical methodological framework for student voice and practitioner inquiry, in which the concept and practice of service learning would in some way be addressed and challenged. There was no clear linear path to follow at the outset of my research, only that my initial research questions would guide the process:

> Overarching RQ: How does meaningful student and teacher involvement as collaborative inquirers into service learning model a pedagogy for service learning?

Sub-questions:

- What does meaningful teacher and student involvement in inquiry look like?

- How can I model meaningful involvement through my practice?
- How can my practice act as a catalyst for change?

It is therefore not my intention to depict the detailed steps of my methodology over the course of one academic year, but rather to narrate how I got there and ultimately what this process taught me. My analysis of the huge wealth of data that I had gathered over the year did in fact lead me to develop my own framework for ethical collaboration that I named a *Pedagogy of C.A.R.E.*, and I conclude this chapter with an introduction to the principles of this framework in light of what the whole research process taught me and what I learnt about what ethical educational practice can look like.

Nagging questions and an itch to scratch: Service learning

My doctoral research began long before I was aware of it; well, suffice to say that I developed an uncomfortable itch that needed scratching. I remember quite vividly sitting on a beach in Croatia with a group of high school students from an international school in Switzerland, taking part in a week-long personal development week (PDW). I was there as an accompanying teacher; I taught German at that time and was with this particular group of students as their form tutor. As the students swam and enjoyed themselves as if on holiday, I pondered on the educational outcomes of this experience and how they might have matched the school's ideal of young, caring people who 'help to create a better and more peaceful world through intercultural understanding and respect' (IBO 2013). How exactly *were* we changing the world? Were we perhaps engaging in unethical practice?

On the plastic pedestal

The next time that I found myself with a similar itch that needed to be scratched was whilst in India with a different group of students from the same high school as my first PDW trip. I was the main teacher leader and had established the trip through some connections with an NGO in India. Since having been in Croatia, the underlying nature and aim of the PDWs had in fact shifted to fall under a new programme of 'service learning' for the high school, and I had also taken on an additional role as Service Learning Coordinator. During the time in India, and despite the efforts to make this trip service learning, my aforementioned discomfort reared its ugly head once more. My students and I found ourselves sitting on specially bought plastic chairs in the middle of a slum, drinking specially bought water from a plastic bottle, watching children from local tribes performing dances for us. Some of my students had baked cakes and cookies in school over the previous months in order to raise money for the founding of a small school in this slum, as fundraising was part of the school's requirement for participation in a trip such as this. Hence, there we were, as the 'sponsors', being treated like royalty, quite literally being put onto a plastic pedestal. If there ever was a time to feel uncomfortable, to feel like an imposter, an outsider, looking into the lives of others (Andreotti 2006) then this was it. I wondered: Did my students feel this as well? Were they aware of the underlying power relations at play? Was their own privilege itching away at them, and if so, how did it make them feel?

Critical service learning

This was the moment that I began to feel dissonance not only with the so-called 'personal developmen' but also with our potentially unethical practice of service learning. This moment also prompted me to discover *critical* service learning; an approach to service learning with the ultimate goal of being able to 'deconstruct systems of power so the need for service and the inequalities that create and sustain them are dismantled' (Mitchell 2007, p. 50). Critical service learning, as a *pedagogy*, focuses on 'the root causes of inequality by addressing power, privilege, and oppression through a social justice – based approach' (Mitchell 2007). In practice, this means that curricular learning in subject areas within school should enable students to consider their own positionalities in relation to the community 'other' and to analyse historical, social, political and economic factors. I knew that my students had not had the opportunity to address these issues at all before going to India, and I was aware that their curricular subjects were also not explicitly connected to this experience. The fundraising bake sale was simply not enough. I felt that what we were doing was in some way unethical, and our 'good intentions' (Illich 1968) were simply not enough. My internal voice was therefore telling me to pursue critical service learning and to analyse and hopefully improve the school practice of service learning.

My faithful friend

I knew from this moment on that I wanted to engage in research that would help me to pursue these nagging questions and to scratch the itch that I could not shake off. I searched therefore for a route into research that would allow me to develop my ideas in conjunction with others, whilst at the same time being able to continue working in my full-time teaching role in Switzerland. The part-time, 'long-distance' EdD route at Durham University allowed me to spend two summers working on different modules in a classroom setting, engaging with literature, refreshing and updating my understanding of research methods, and collaborating with other like-minded working professionals within education. It was good to know that I was not alone, and that I could share my itch and scratch at it with others.

As I developed my ideas in this setting, my leather-bound research journal was always faithfully at my side. This journal was used to jot down key thoughts, questions, theories, quotes and any other diagrams or concepts that came to my mind, and to make potential connections between them. Using the journal enabled the emergence of a much deeper and interconnected research topic and methodology than if I had tried to only make digital notes. Not only was I able to identify service learning as my research topic, but I could see it taking shape as a research methodology in itself; a collaborative learning process that would reflect the ethical principles of service learning.

As I drafted and re-drafted research questions, I became further acquainted with postcolonial approaches to service learning and global citizenship (Andreotti 2006, 2010). I was learning more about the often 'essentializing' nature of intercultural communication (Holliday 2011), I discovered hybrid spaces (Bhabha 1991) and I engaged with frameworks of transformational learning (Mezirow 1978, 2000, 2009). This literature helped me to develop research questions that would enable the research process and the practical methods with my student researchers to reflect the theories behind it. If I was convinced for example that education should in some way be transformational, then the research process itself should pave the way for transformation in its participants. Further, if I felt that we should not be essentializing our Indian partners and reducing them to our stereotyped imaginings of their lives and identities, then I needed to develop research methods with the students that would allow them to interrogate and challenge their own prejudices and biases.

My (not-so-secret) secret

The moment I read Freire's 'Pedagogy of the Oppressed' (1970), something changed for me in an irreversible way. I must mention this moment as I wish to convey the important message that finding ideas, theories, concepts or particular texts that speak to you is a vital part of understanding what it really is that will keep that fire burning within you throughout a research journey that may last several years! I carried this book around with me everywhere, highlighted something on every page, and felt as if I was guarding a secret that I only I knew about. I read with fascination about an education that allows young people to critically engage with the world whilst at the same time transforming it, in a process that allows knowledge to emerge

> only through the invention and reinvention, through the restless, impatient, continuing, hopeful inquiry men pursue in the world, with the world, and with each other. (Freire, 1974, p. 58)

So, inspired as I was by Freire's (not-so-secret as it turned out) secret of raising consciousness (conscientização), I delved into the literature of critical pedagogy (Giroux 1988, 2014; Kincheloe 2008, 2012) and felt motivated by my discovery that there was a connection between critical pedagogy and qualitative research

(Kincheloe et al. 2011). Furthermore, in my simultaneous reading on service learning, the field of *critical* service learning emerged strongly (Butin 2007). Therefore, in line with critical service learning, critical pedagogy and qualitative research, and my inquiry-based teaching practice within the context of the IBDP (International Baccalaureate Diploma Programme), I knew that learning 'with' and 'from' others as an active collaborator in a process of practice-based research was what I wanted to do. As a teacher-practitioner, I liked the idea of being a co-researcher with students, and problematizing and challenging power relations whilst doing so. My understanding of ethical practitioner inquiry therefore centred on student voice.

Learning *with*

The next step for me in my journey was to engage with student voice literature and to try to make decisions about the research methods that I would employ. Who would be my student researchers? How would I design my research so that I could at once learn alongside the students whilst also helping them to develop their own understandings of what being an ethical researcher looked like? I was ultimately a teacher at the school the inherent power relationships between teacher-student were apparent and unavoidable; how could these hierarchies be acknowledged in a research process that was intended to be ethical? I was aware that in line with a constructivist tradition (Schwandt 2001) and a participatory approach (Kemmis and Wilkinson 1998) to inquiry in my classroom, I felt that as a teacher it was my role to learn 'with' my students as an active collaborator in a process. I saw knowledge, therefore, as something that is 'a process, not a product' (Bruner 1966, p. 72). It was and still is this process of 'being immersed in existing knowledge' and being 'open and capable of producing something that does not yet exist' (Freire 1974, p. 35) that defines for me what it means to be a learner and, subsequently, what it means to be a teacher. With such convictions of knowledge creation being a deeply personal and individual process, I was therefore certain that qualitative research methods that provided a 'thick description' (Geertz 1993) were suitable for my research. I felt that I was bound to my research through my practice, and the two domains were not separate, distinct entities. I identified with

Stenhouse's claim that 'The basic argument for placing teachers at the heart of the educational research process may be simply stated. Teachers are in charge of classrooms' (Stenhouse 1981, p. 109). I knew and understood my setting and my reasons for conducting the research more than anyone else, and because of this, I felt that I did not want to be made to feel that my research had to fit into one particular research 'paradigm'. I knew that there may well have been criticism about the 'validity' of this methodology, as one could have argued that this intimacy could lead to a danger of losing critical perspective, but, my belief was that through interacting with humans in a social setting, it is impossible for practitioners to be separated from their reality; this reality is a 'dynamic part of the picture' and it is their 'notions of reality that ultimately shape practice' (Cook-Sather 2016, p. 13).

In the name of transformation

With the design of my research beginning to take shape, I continued to develop and reflect on the research framework within which I felt I would be working. Being able to understand and articulate this framework was an important underpinning of my research design and a way to help me keep my ethical research intentions in mind. I wanted to ensure that my design clearly emerged from my framework and that my methods would reflect this in turn.

Thus, I drew on my own teaching experiences and motivations for being a teacher, combining them with my developing understanding of my own relationship with the nature of knowledge. I realized that one thing that I had come to know and stand for was that learning should be a transformative process. This transformation was not only applicable to young people sitting in a classroom, but also to teachers, the school and the wider world. In my role as a teacher-researcher in this project, I therefore saw myself as an 'ethical or activist professional'(Groundwater-Smith and Mockler 2007, p. 205); a teacher who was concerned about the wider social and political agenda, and one who was convinced that inquiry has the potential to contribute not only to personal transformation, but also to social transformation. Therefore, one of the places in which my inquiry was located was within a *transformative, critical* framework, as I was very much aware that 'knowledge is not neutral' and that it reflects the 'power and social relationships within society' (Creswell 2013, p. 25). As 'action-oriented critique' (Kinsler 2010, p. 175), such inquiry is emancipatory in the sense that it advances social justice by bringing about unwelcome and uncomfortable news). Whilst I was keen on the terms 'emancipatory' and 'empowering' for my research on student voice, my reading also taught me to be critical and wary of them, to use these terms with caution and not allow myself to fall into the essentialist trap of romantic, utopian ideas about 'authentic' voice and 'empowering' research, which can mask the fact that individual experiences are fluid, dynamic and shifting. Power and empowerment therefore became important underlying aspects of my transformational research framework, and they would inform decisions about my research methods and my guidance of my student researchers going forward.

Students as research partners: Team change makers

So, what would my student voice research project look like? My research was envisioned and ultimately carried out as a process of research phases over the course of one academic year, involving a group of high school students who acted as my co-researchers. The research methods were developed in cycles of inquiry as the year progressed, beginning with my overarching research questions as starting points, but with room for the co-creation of research questions with the students and trying out different mechanisms for generating data. I felt that it was important to develop research questions in conjunction with the students, in order to stay true to the intended ethical nature of the student voice approach. In line with my theoretical framework as described above, the concepts of transformation and enabling student voice were at the heart of my beliefs and intentions, and my continued reflection on and awareness of how we worked together helped me to try to stay true to these convictions. As mentioned in the Introduction, the focus of this chapter is not to include a lengthy discussion of my mechanisms for generating data, rather it is more about how I got there, the reasons for taking such an approach and what I learnt from the process; this learning is ultimately what should guide the reader in their own journey.

The table below offers a brief overview of the mechanisms for generating data that were employed throughout, including an individual semi-structured interview with each of the student researchers at the beginning and end of the year, group discussions, an online platform for sharing resources and reflections (google classroom), observations and visual methods.

In order that I could keep track of the different types of data that I had gathered with my students over the course of the academic year, I created codes (e.g. L1GD) that stood for the 'levels' of data; L1 for example was level 1 data involving the teacher-researcher and the student research team, either as a group or individually, and level 2 (L2) data was that which the student research team carried out with other students in their peer group. Every item of data was stored electronically in a folder headed with these codes, so that when it came to data analysis, I would have an exact and organized overview of everything that had been done with the students. I did not plan all of the methods of generating data in advance, but rather responded to the research process as it developed over time. This 'methodological bricolage' (Kincheloe et al. 2011, p. 168) of choosing methods that were appropriate in the practical context underpinned what I understood to be an ethical research process.

Acknowledging and resisting omnipresent forces!

As I was immersed in the research process, I used my teacher instinct and the insights and ideas from the student researchers to keep the process moving and to make decisions on how to move forward, but once the collaboration came to an end as did the academic year, I was faced with a year's worth of data that needed to reveal itself to me. So how did I allow this huge wealth of data to speak to me? How could I allow my data to tell me a story of its own, without allowing my own biases to influence what emerged? I felt that I wanted to engage with my data on a personal level, and to challenge myself to find the emerging themes without the help of a data analysis software programme such as NVivo. I decided therefore that I would undertake a manual thematic analysis and data coding that involved moving around pieces of paper and post-it notes, drawing connecting lines, brainstorming on flipcharts, sorting data into columns and groups on the floor and digitally, and playing with words. I felt that the use of a software

Code for tool	Description	Phases used
LORJWN	Research journal written notes	1–6
LOA	Reflective audio recording	1–6
L1GD	TCM group discussion	1–6
L1GC	Google classroom	1–6
L1IV	Individual visuals	2
L1PLC1/2	PLC teacher'student meetings	3
L1ICCM	Ice Cream Cone Model	3
L1INT1	Individual interview 1	end of 2
L1INT2	Individual interview 2	beginning of 6
L1GVFL	TCM group visual fortune line	6
L1PDW	PDW forum	6
L1O	Observation	6
L1EM	Email	post 'data collection'
L2FG	TCM focus groups student-student	4
L2FG	TCM individual interviews student-student	4
L2RJ	TCM student research journals	1–6

FIGURE 16.1 *Mechanisms for generating data.*

programme would have somewhat disengaged me from the process of analysis. As a researcher, I was aware that I was 'the person who (was) challenged to apprehend the meaning of things and to give these meanings ongoing life' (Moustakas 1990, p. 12) and that the interpretation and analysis of my data was something that emerged from my own researcher positionality. With ethical practice in mind, during my data analysis I made several concerted efforts to ensure that I was conscious of not forcing the direction in which I might have wanted the data to go. I knew that subjectivity was an omnipresent force, but the fact that I was aware of it and was trying to control it and let the data do the talking is something that I felt justified my methodology and was in line with the intended ethical nature of my research.

Framework of C.A.R.E.: My learnings about ethical practice

As my themes were emerging, the concepts of voice and ethical practice were continuously lurking in the corners of my mind, and a significant struggle was how to present the findings of my data and answer my initial research questions. Unexpectedly, after weeks of journaling and re-drafting thoughts, I had a ground-breaking aha-moment. In a sudden moment of clarity about my research having been about the process, purpose and stance of *caring*, I was able to weave certain key themes into ethical principles for educational practice in an acronym of C.A.R.E. (Consciousness, Action, Responsibility, Experimentation). This framework, conceptualized as a pyramid in order to show how the principles interact with each other in a non-hierarchical way (Figure 16.2), became my own understanding of what ethical collaborative inquiry between teachers and students looked like. Such a research process can be transformative for those involved, be it for an experienced teacher, a novice researcher or a high school pupil. Ultimately, these principles of C.A.R.E. helped me to understand and articulate that *voice* is essential to ethical practice, and that as practitioner-researchers, we can help to make that happen by listening to and involving our students and community partners in the research process.

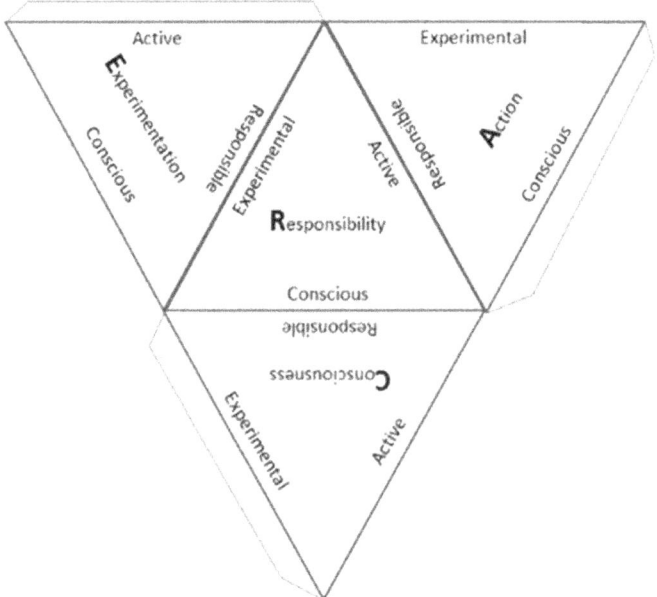

FIGURE 16.2 *Pyramid model for pedagogy of C.A.R.E. (Wasner 2019).*

The ethical principles that belong to this framework became my response to my research questions and were my way of linking the initial topic of service learning to student voice. They have remained with me to this day as convincing principles for ethical collaboration that go beyond these two areas and they can be applied to several different relationships and contexts within educational settings. The first principle of *Consciousness* is about being critically aware of our place in the world, whilst uncovering, questioning and challenging the power structures that hold us there. *Responsibility* is centred on reciprocal, relational learning, listening, dialogue and empathy. *Action* describes exercising personal and collective agency to bring about positive change. Finally, *Experimentation* involves taking risks, being resilient and stepping out of one's comfort zone. All of these principles are understood as cognitive competencies as well as collaborative skills, and they take place within the intersection of a facilitated space that is at once safe and brave (Cook-Sather 2016). For me as an educational practitioner-researcher, this is what ethical inquiry looks like. With the articulation of this framework, one researcher journey may have been over for me, but there are certainly plenty of other itches to be scratched!

References

Andreotti, V.d.O. (2006). Soft versus critical global citizenship education. *Development Education: Policy and Practice*, 3 (Autumn), pp. 83–98.
Andreotti, V.d.O. (2010). Postcolonial and postcritical global citizenship education. In: Elliott, G., Fourali, C., and Issler, S. (eds), *Education for Social Change*. New York: Continuum International, pp. 223–45.
Bhabha, H. (1991). *The location of culture*. London, Routledge.
Bruner, J. S. (1966).Towards a Theory for Instruction The Belknap Press of Harvard University Press. *Cambridge Mass.*
Butin, D.W. (2007). Justice learning: Service-learning as justice-oriented education. *Equity & Excellence in Education*, 40(2), pp. 177–83.
Cook-Sather, A. (2016). Creating brave spaces within and through student-faculty pedagogical partnerships. *Teaching and Learning Together in Higher Education*, Spring (18).
Creswell, J. W. (2013).Steps in conducting a scholarly mixed methods study. Copyright © John Creswell.
Freire, P. (1970). *Pedagogy of the oppressed*. New York: Seabury.

Freire, P. (1974). *Education for critical consciousness*. London: Sheed & Ward Ltd.
Geertz, A. W. (1993).Archaic ontology and white shamanism. *Religion*, 23(4), 369-372.
Giroux, H. (1988). *Teachers as intellectuals: Toward a critical pedagogy of learning*. Westport, CT: Bergin & Garvey.
Giroux, H. (2014). *Neoliberalism's war on higher education*. Chicago: Haymarket Books.
Groundwater-Smith, S. and Mockler, N. (2007). Ethics in practitioner research: An issue of quality. *Research Papers in Education*, 22(2), pp. 199–211.
Holliday, A. (2011). *Intercultural communication and ideology*. London: SAGE Publications.
IBO. (2013). *What is an IB education?* Cardiff: International Baccalaureate Organisation.
Illich, I. (1968). *To hell with good intentions*. Cuernavaca, Mexico.
Kemmis, S., & Wilkinson,M. (1998). Participatory Action Research and the Study of Practice in Atweh, B et al,(1998). *Action Research in Practice. Oxford, UK: Routledge*, 10, 9780203268629.
Kincheloe, J. L. (ed.) (2008). *Knowledge and critical pedagogy: An introduction*. Dordrecht: Springer Netherlands.
Kincheloe, J. L. (2012). Critical pedagogy in the twenty-first century: Evolution for survival. *Counterpoints*, 422, CRITICAL PEDAGOGY in the new dark ages: challenges and possibilities, pp. 147–83.
Kincheloe, J. L., McClaren, P., and Steinberg, S. R. (2011). Critical pedagogy and qualitative research: Moving to the bricolage. In: Denzin, N. K. and Lincoln, Y.S. (eds), *The SAGE handbook of qualitative research*. 4th ed. Thousand Oaks, CA: SAGE Publications, pp. 163–77.
Kinsler, K. (2010). The utility of educational action research for emancipatory change. *Action research*, 8(2), 171-189.
May, S., & Sleeter, C.E. (Eds.). (2010). *Critical multiculturalism: Theory and praxis*. Routledge.
Mezirow, J. (1978). Perspective transformation. *Adult Learning*, 28, pp. 100–10.
Mezirow, J. (ed.) (2000). *Learning as transformation: Critical perspectives on a theory in progress*. San Francisco: Jossey-Bass.
Mezirow, J. (2009). An overview on transformative learning. In: Ileris, K. (ed.), *Contemporary theories of learning*. Abingdon: Routledge, pp. 90–105.
Mitchell, T. D. (2007). Critical service-learning as social justice education: A case study of the citizen scholars program. *Equity & Excellence in Education*, 40(2), pp. 101–12.

Moustakas, C. (1990). *Heuristic research: Design, methodology, and applications.* Sage Publications.

Porfilio, B. J., &Hickman, H. (Eds.). (2011). *Critical service-learning as a revolutionary pedagogy: An international project of student agency in action.* IAP.

Schwandt, T.A. (2001). *Dictionary of qualitative inquiry.* 2nd ed. Thousand Oaks, CA: SAGE Publications.

Stenhouse, L. (1981). Using case study in library research. *Social Science Information Studies*, 1(4), 221-230.

Wasner, V. (2019). Collaborative inquiry into service learning: Ethical practice through a Pedagogy of CARE. Doctoral thesis, Durham University.

Conclusion

What Can We Learn from the Insights of Other Teacher-Researchers?

Maria Campbell, Deirdre Harvey and Mary Shanahan

As stated in the Introduction, each person's research journey is individual to them, influenced by various factors including their beliefs or worldview, personal and professional contexts, motivation for undertaking research and factors associated with accreditation. While we have presented key themes and organized the chapters in a particular sequence, this account and its running order may not reflect the order in which you address the various themes underpinning your research journey. What the various chapters provide are key insights into specific considerations, lessons learned from engaging with each of the themes and, most importantly, the interconnected nature of the various themes and their relatedness to and influence upon the other. Consequently, you are presented with a variety of approaches, perspectives and outcomes. In this final chapter, we look back at some of the key learning that emerged from the experiences outlined in the chapters and signal some considerations for you going forward on your unique research journey.

Theme 1: Refining a research topic and/or formulating research question/s

In the majority of instances, endeavouring at the onset of your research journey that you continue to refine and sharpen the focus of your research through extensive reading and reflection enables you to craft a research question, clearly indicating what your research hopes to discover and implying how you intend to achieve this. Reaching out for support from peers, a critical friend, your tutor or supervisor (if undertaking an accredited programme) and other professionals who may be able to help you navigate this challenging aspect of the research journey is essential and to be encouraged. Similarly, finding ways that support your processing of ideas and information (such as reflective journals) may offer additional support in this endeavour. In some instances, clarity and focus emerge one or more years into the research process when undertaking large-scale or substantial research as part of a doctoral programme, for example. Undoubtably, extensive and continuous reading and enduring you have a means for organizing and tracking key literature and emerging thoughts is paramount.

Theme 2: Paradigms, ontology and epistemology

Grappling with challenging concepts and unpacking new terminology is daunting for all involved in the research journey, regardless of their level of experience. However, especially for those undertaking research for the first time, coming to terms with concepts such Paradigms can prove off putting, especially when there are varying perspectives and opinions presented in the literature. Discovering your worldview, your beliefs and linking them to a paradigm, ontology and epistemology, although time consuming and challenging, pays dividends when it comes to designing your research, selecting your methodology, tools and participants and addressing key ethical issues. In other words, if your worldview indicates that there is a truth waiting to be discovered, then this will influence your choice of conceptual and/or theoretical framework, your methodology, tools, participants and ethical considerations. Again, extensive reading, reflection and, in particular, consultation with tutors, supervisors or peer support groups can prove invaluable in teasing out the finer details and complexities associated with aligning with a particular paradigm.

Theme 3: Conceptual and theoretical frameworks

Locating your research within a wider context or framework is exciting and at the same time challenging. Grappling with the differences between various interpretations of theoretical and conceptual frameworks can prove daunting. For the beginning researcher, selecting one theory which their research will test or examining a phenomenon through the lens of a single concept, is a great starting point. As your confidence and experience grows, you may consider expanding your scope to encapsulate more complex theories and concepts or even combining both to examine your topic. Without identifying a conceptual and/or theoretical framework, there is a risk that your research can be viewed as 'lost at sea' or adrift without an anchor. Selecting a conceptual and/or theoretical framework demonstrates the relevance of what you are researching to wider societal, political, economic and/or ethical issues.

Theme 4: Ethical issues

Axiological or value laden, ethical issues are key considerations at all stages in the research journey. At all times, the well-being of the participants is central to the research process. If undertaking research for the first time, then you may not have considered how your role as a researcher and your other or professional role may bring about a conflict of interest, pressurize participants or deny you automatic access to participants. It is essential to consult and familiarize yourself with ethical guidelines as a starting point, and to continue to read extensively on ethical issues, in particular to those pertaining to your research context and topic and in keeping with your chosen paradigm or worldview. Similarly, ethical issues which you did not anticipate at the outset may arise during the research process and consultation with tutors, supervisors and supportive peers, alongside extensive reading, can help provide solutions to these issues should they emerge.

Theme 5: Methodology

Your methodology or the blueprint for your research links your philosophical assumptions or worldview/paradigm with the research design and action plan. Having a clear vision of what your research intends to achieve enables you to select the most appropriate methodology such as case study, action research, experimental research, for example. Again, aligned with your paradigm, deciding if you will adopt qualitative and/or quantitative methodologies is a key consideration.

Theme 6: Data-gathering and analysing tools

Having identified your methodology, the next step is to select the most appropriate tool or tools to gather and analyse data. The list of tools available to you is extensive, ranging from surveys/questionnaires to vignettes, observation, focus groups, interviews, discourse analysis, thematic analysis to name but a few. Identifying the advantages and disadvantages of each tool, the ways in which each tool can be modified to align with your paradigm are considerations for you in advance of selecting one or more. Extensive reading and consultation with tutors, supervisors and peer support groups is an excellent way of helping you to arrive at a decision.

Theme 7: Participants or sample

Deciding who is best positioned to provide data to answer your research question is vital. Consideration regarding how many participants you need, which groups (if any) can provide insights into what you are researching, how to gain access to them and what ethical considerations that working with this cohort raises will influence your final decision. Extensive reading on the various sampling techniques available to you, procedures to follow and so on, will inform the decisions you make, including whether your positionality or professional role as opposed to your role as researcher, will have ethical implications for your research.

Finally, we want to wish you well on your research journey, to encourage you to stay focused, on task, inspired and to learn with and from the experiences of others. The potential to enhance your own understanding, to stimulate debate and discourse, to design changes to policy and/or practices and to continue to want to do better or see improvement in education policy and practice is to be admired and encouraged. May your research journey be an enjoyable and rewarding experience.

INDEX

accountability 10, 73, 91, 114, 223–4
Additional Support Needs (ASN), *see also* Special Educational Needs; Special Educational Needs and Disability
attachment disorder 42, 45
autism spectrum disorder (ASD) 5, 41–2, 160, 209, 211
  restrictive repetitive behaviours (RRBs) 18, 209, 211–13, 215
agency 232, 240–2, 264
  teacher agency 240–2
analysis 3, 17–19, 34, 44, 61, 69–70, 74, 77–8, 93–6, 99, 107, 113–15, 117, 119–21, 137–8, 140, 155, 166, 169–70, 182–3, 187, 203, 205–6, 216, 230, 233, 239, 241, 244, 246–8, 255, 262–3, 270
  discourse analysis 18, 74, 270 (*see also* discourse)
  inductive analysis 137–8
  narrative analysis 117, 205, 227
  rhythmanalysis 107
  thematic analysis 18, 117, 170, 187, 203, 205–6, 233, 262, 270
anonymity 47, 170, 214, 242, 244–5, 249
  anonymized 213

answerability 19, 119–24
Attribution Theory 211
Australian 6, 99–101, 114
  Australian Curriculum and Assessment Reporting Authority (ACARA) 100–1
  Australian schools 99–100
axiology 7, 9, 148, *see also* ethics, ethical considerations
  axiological 13, 148, 269

Bakhtin 102, 105, 117–18, 123
Bandura 178, 180, 211
beliefs 3–4, 7–9, 11–13, 20, 35, 55–6, 58–62, 64, 70, 87, 89, 119, 134, 140, 149, 152, 160, 164–5, 176, 178, 180, 182, 187, 189, 226, 261, 267–8, *see also* values
  self-efficacy beliefs 176, 178, 180, 182, 187
bias 116, 132, 164, 169–70, 214
  biased 32, 169
  biases 63, 72, 77, 147, 258, 262
  unbiased 32
Bourdieu, P. 102
British 28, 47
  British government 28

capability 48, 100–1, 104–5
case study 4, 14, 69, 139, 140, 162, 182–3, 196, 199, 270
Catholic Church 5, 28

children 4–5, 9, 11, 15, 17–18,
    20, 28, 30–1, 36, 41–2,
    48–9, 56, 62–3, 129–30,
    132, 135–7, 139, 145–55,
    161, 200, 214, 256
  child 10–11, 41, 48, 140,
    151, 153
  child-centred 151
  U.N. Convention on the Rights
    of the Child 160
classroom 58, 61, 70, 88, 104,
    107, 123, 129, 131–4,
    140, 145, 176, 178–81,
    188, 199, 210, 253, 257,
    259–60, 262
coaching 196, 229–30, 232–5,
    239
Cognitive Load Theory 180, 184
collaboration 138, 223–4, 241,
    255, 262, 264
  collaborative 5, 91, 202,
    225–6, 247, 253–4, 257,
    263–4
  collaborative inquiry 263
  collaborative research 202
colonial 101
Comte, Auguste 8
concepts 3, 7, 10–12, 57, 72–5,
    100–2, 105, 109, 113, 119,
    122, 148, 160, 166, 177–8,
    257–8, 261, 263, 268–9, see
    also conceptual framework;
    conceptual tools;
    interpretive repertoires;
    theoretical framework
  conceptualisation 11, 73, 83,
    104, 224
  conceptualise 72, 95, 103,
    107, 198
  conceptual framework 2,
    11–12, 47–8, 69, 72–5,
    84, 89–90, 92, 99–100,
    102–5, 107, 109, 130, 175,
    178, 222–4, 235, see also

  concepts; conceptual tools;
    interpretive repertoires;
    theoretical framework
  conceptual tools 104–5
conclusions 8, 28, 43, 179–80,
    183, 187, 205, 216
consent 47, 154, 169, 186, 204,
    214, 216, 228, 241, 244–5,
    248
constructivism 9, 17, 71, 227
  constructivist 8–9, 35, 61,
    227, 236, 259
  constructivist grounded
    theory 9
  social constructivist 9, 61
Covid-19 19, 84, 175–7, 183,
    188, 222, see also pandemic
Creswell, J. W. 12–14, 34, 88,
    90, 181, 213, 215, 248, 261
Cultural Historical Activity
    Theory (CHAT) 11, 83,
    85–6, 91–4
culture 11, 64, 85, 93, 100–4,
    229
  cultural 11, 78, 83, 85–6,
    91–5, 99–104, 106–8, 145,
    147, 149, 226
  cultural groups 104, 108
  cultural studies 103
  culturally diverse 108
  cultures 28, 93, 240
  intercultural 11, 99–101,
    103–6, 108, 254–5, 257
  multicultural 99
  multiculturalism 254
curriculum 100–1, 104, 106–7,
    121–2, 161

data 3, 9, 14, 16–20, 34, 43–8,
    64, 71, 75–8, 85, 89, 91–2,
    96, 103–7, 113, 116–23,
    134–7, 139, 149–52, 155,
    159, 161–2, 164–6, 169–70,
    181–3, 186–9, 200–6, 217,

226, 231, 233, 241–6, 249, 255, 261–3, 271
analysis   17–18, 34, 70, 77, 96, 107, 113, 115, 117, 121, 170, 183, 205–6, 248, 262–3
collection   15, 34, 43, 45–6, 51, 62–3, 70, 88, 90, 96, 116–17, 129, 134–8, 141, 150, 155, 169, 180, 200, 214–16, 222, 229, 231–2, 239, 244, 246–8
gathering   3, 6, 10, 13, 16, 18, 44, 47, 76–7, 90, 159, 163–4, 170, 177–8, 180, 182, 202, 215, 270
NVivo   262
Deleuze   102
Department of Education   30
Department of Education and Skills   175
Derrida   102
diagnosis   84, 209
  diagnosed   5, 41
  misdiagnosed   5, 42, 49
digital leadership   85, 95
disability   10, 47, 56, 58–9
  disabilities   41
discourse   18, 73–4, 78, 225, 270–1, *see also* discourse analysis
distributed leadership   91
drawing   34, 106, 149, 151–2, 245, 262
  drawings   17, 150–1

education   11, 14, 28–33, 36, 55, 57, 63, 70, 83–4, 91, 99, 101, 103–5, 108, 113–14, 116, 118–20, 130, 133, 137, 147, 160–1, 167, 175, 177, 195–6, 198, 200–1, 205, 209, 215, 221–3, 226, 229, 239–40, 245, 253, 257–8, 271
  educational   1, 6–7, 10, 29–30, 34, 41, 44–5, 47, 56, 101–2, 108, 133, 178, 181, 186, 209, 222, 253–5, 260, 263–4
  educational policy   1
  Initial Teacher Education (ITE)   14, 69–70, 196, 205
intercultural education   11, 99, 104–5, 108
education (Admission to Schools) Act   29, 33
educator   92, 116, 148, 195, 210
  educators   116, 178, 240
empirical   10, 12, 60, 162
Engeström, Y.   86, 93–4
England   32, 56–8, 69, 130, 132, 239
  English   41, 47, 50, 56, 70, 72, 92, 102, 113–17, 119, 129, 239
  English for Speakers of Other Languages (ESOL)   239
  English government   70
  English primary schools   41, 47, 50, 129
  English schools   56
  English Teacher Standards   72
  English teachers   102, 113–17, 119
epistemology   3, 7, 9–11, 35, 69–78, 87, 102, 105–7, 124, 148, 150, 166, 268
  epistemological   8–10, 15, 55–65, 69–72, 75, 105, 118–19, 148, 166, 226–9
ethics   3, 7, 9, 13, 19, 113–14, 118–19, 121–2, 124, 204, 245, *see also* axiology; moral
  ethical concerns   14, 152–3, 186, 241–3

ethical considerations 13, 42, 62, 113–14, 117–18, 121, 123, 154, 159, 169, 204, 214, 239–40, 242, 246, 248, 269, 271 (*see also* axiology)
ethical dilemmas 2, 169
ethical guidelines 13, 169, 245, 248, 269
ethical issues 3, 13, 19–20, 147, 154–5, 169, 186, 189, 204, 239–40, 242–4, 249, 268–70
ethical practice 253, 263
ethical practitioner 259
regulatory ethics 118, 124
ethnography 14, 99, 106, 113, 116, 118–20, 122, 203–4, 244
ethnography-in-education 113
ethos 87, 229

feminist theory 11, 103
focus group 106, 135, 153
focus groups 106, 117, 153, 270
fortune lines 17, 195–6, 200–6
Forum on Patronage and Pluralism 28
Freire, P. 254, 258–9
Pedagogy of the Oppressed 258

Hawthorne Effect 164, 213
Headship 221, 223–5, 227–8, 231, 233–5
GTCS Professional Standard for Headship 223–4, 231
Into Headship programme 221, 223–5, 235
hierarchies 259
hypothesis 44

hypotheses 8, 14
hypotheses, test 14

inclusion 18, 32, 47, 58–9, 91, 101, 160–1, 164–7, 171, 212–13, 217
inclusive 63, 161, 167, 229–30
Information and Communications Technology (ICT) 84–6, 88–96, *see also* technology
inquiry 12, 48, 61, 78, 87–8, 162, 181, 198, 210, 217–18, 242, 253–4, 258–61, 263–4
ethical collaborative inquiry 263
ethical practitioner inquiry 259
Inquiry and Professional Knowledge Model 12, 198
interpretive repertoires 74–5, *see also* concepts; conceptual framework; conceptual tools; theoretical framework
interview 35, 44, 62, 76, 106, 153–4, 159, 162–70, 202–3, 205–6, 230, 247–9, 262
interviews 17, 44, 46, 56, 62–3, 75–7, 96, 106, 117, 150, 152–3, 159, 162–70, 195–6, 200, 202–3, 205–6, 215, 227, 229–30, 242, 244, 246–9, 270
semi-structured interviews 17, 62–3, 76, 117, 152–3, 165, 167, 175, 183–4, 188, 195–6, 202–3, 206, 262
small group interviews 17, 150, 152–3, 235
stimulated recall interview 62
investigation 11, 43, 72, 107, 132, 134, 137, 147, 236
investigate 41, 45–6, 60, 74, 136, 176–7, 179–81, 183, 188, 196, 225, 227

276 INDEX

Ireland 11, 28–33, 159–60, 175, 177
 Government of Ireland 29, 32, 160
 Irish 5, 28–33, 35, 84, 95, 151, 160, 175–7
 Irish Constitution (Bunreacht na hÉireann) 28, 35
 Irish schools 5, 28, 84, 95
 Irish teachers 175
 Northern Ireland (NI) 11
 Republic of Ireland (ROI) 11, 28, 33

knowledge 3, 10, 12, 14, 16, 30–1, 35, 43, 45–7, 49, 51, 56–8, 60–1, 63–4, 70–1, 79, 83, 87–8, 90–2, 96, 101–3, 105, 108, 119, 132–3, 135, 139, 146–9, 151, 155, 163, 166–7, 169, 175, 178, 181, 195, 198, 210–13, 217–18, 226–7, 234, 236, 247–8, 258–60
 new knowledge 30, 88, 90, 234
Kuhn, T. 61

learning 2–3, 5, 14, 36, 43–4, 49, 57, 59, 63, 73, 85, 88, 92–4, 102, 114, 129–32, 134, 137–9, 146, 148, 175–83, 185, 187–8, 195, 197–8, 200, 205, 209–11, 221–3, 228, 235, 239–42, 247, 249, 253–60, 262, 264, 267
 asynchronous 175–82, 187–8
 children's learning 4–5, 9, 11, 15, 17–18, 20, 28, 30–1, 36, 41–2, 48–9, 56, 62–3, 129–30, 132, 135–7, 139, 145–55, 161, 200, 214, 256

critical service learning 14, 254, 256–9
 professional 197, 200, 221, 223, 228, 235, 239–42, 247
 service learning 5, 14, 253–9, 264
 synchronous 175–7
Lefebvre, H. 104, 107
legislation 29, 32–3, 35–6, 160
 legislative 223
lens 2, 11–12, 35, 58, 61, 65, 73–4, 83–4, 92, 154, 159, 181–2, 221, 224, 243, 269
 lenses 72–3, 202
Leont'ev, A. N. 86
literacy 151, 200, 215
literature review 95, 146–7, 149, 177, 189, 197, 199, 203, 205, 224, 232

Maslow, A. H. 178
 Maslow's Hierarchy of Needs 178
media 6, 31–2, 77, 240, 243
 social media 77, 240, 243
 Twitter ('X') 240–8
mentoring 14, 72, 195–9, 205, 229, 235, 239, *see also* teacher mentors
metacognition 129, 131–2, 134–6, 138–9, 141
 metacognitive 132, 135–6, 138–9
 metacognitive behaviours 135
 metacognitive knowledge 135, 139
methodology 3, 5, 7, 9, 11, 13–19, 34–6, 41, 43, 45, 50, 60, 62, 75, 86–9, 99, 105, 113–18, 124, 145, 147–9, 154–5, 159, 161–2, 175, 177–8, 180–3, 189, 197–200, 204, 222, 226–7, 229, 231, 236,

254, 257, 260, 263, 268–70, see also action research; case study; ethnography; phenomenology; research methods
methods 9, 14, 16–17, 35, 62, 65, 69–70, 75, 86–9, 107, 116–17, 132, 135, 141, 147–50, 154, 177, 181, 200–1, 206, 214–16, 230, 243, 246, 254, 257–62, see also methodology; research
moral 36, 70, 118, 169, see also axiology; ethics

narrative 31, 36, 71, 117, 139–40, 160, 167, 203–5, 212, 217, 227, 230
narrative analysis 117, 205, 227
netnography 14, 244
numeracy 147

objectivity 13, 15, 29, 31, 60, 113, 134, 164, 167, 169–70, see also openness
ontology 3, 7, 9, 11, 35, 69–70, 72–8, 87, 102, 105–7, 148, 150, 166, 268
ontological 2, 8–9, 15, 69–72, 75, 78, 105, 148, 166, 226–8
ontological stance 2, 9
openness 13, 109, 232, see also objectivity

pandemic 84, 175–7, 222, 231, 235, see also Covid-19
paradigm 3, 7–11, 14, 16–19, 48, 61, 77, 147–9, 152, 159, 181, 227, 260, 268–70
critical paradigm 8
interpretivist paradigm 8, 77

philosophical paradigm 7 (see also philosophical)
positivist paradigm 8
pragmatist paradigm 11, 17
research paradigm 181
parents 5, 19–20, 31, 33, 41–2, 49, 145–6, 186, 214
participants 3, 6, 10, 13, 17–20, 35, 46, 62–4, 75–8, 86, 89–90, 93–4, 96, 99, 104–6, 116–22, 124, 133, 141, 154, 162–5, 167–70, 183–6, 190, 196, 204, 209–18, 221–3, 225, 227–33, 235, 241, 245, 247–9, 258, 268–9, 271, see also sample
participant 9, 17, 19, 62, 89, 106, 116, 118, 122, 165, 168, 170, 185, 201, 203, 212, 214, 217, 224, 231, 240, 242–4, 246–7
participant selection 19, 212, 217
participatory approach 199, 247, 249, 259
pedagogy 92, 161, 202, 254–6, 258–9, 264
pedagogical 4, 11, 58, 85, 91–2, 180, 202
phenomenology 61, see also methodology
Heideggerian phenomenology 61
phenomenological 60, 62
phenomenon 11, 72, 117, 145, 148, 269
philosophy 60–1, 69, 79, 88, 102, 105, see also philosophical paradigm; research philosophy
Heideggerian philosophy 61
philosophical 7, 13–14, 62, 69, 83, 86–8, 97, 148, 270

positionality 13, 18–19, 222–8, 231–2, 235, 263, 271
positioning 9, 56, 78, 105, 108, 185, 221
power 10, 13, 18–19, 74, 104–5, 108, 130, 151, 153, 204, 221–2, 225, 228, 231, 235–6, 254, 256, 259, 261, 264
   imbalance 18, 221, 225, 231, 235–6
   relations 256, 259
professional 1, 12–13, 44, 56, 70–1, 84–5, 87, 91, 93, 114–15, 117, 160, 175, 189, 195, 197, 198, 200, 210, 221–6, 228–9, 231, 235–6, 239–42, 247, 260, 267, 269, 271
   development 56, 70, 91, 223, 229, 239
   experience 85, 115
Professional Graduate Diploma in Education (PGCE) 195
   professional identity 224–5
   professional knowledge 12, 70, 198
   professional learning 197, 200, 221, 223, 228, 235, 239–42, 247
   professional practice 210
   professionalism 70, 114, 224–6
psychology 74
   psychological 211
   psychologist (educational) 44–5
pupil 17, 48, 129, 132–3, 135–6, 263, *see also* student
   pupil views templates 129, 135, 139
   pupils 17, 33, 42, 45, 48–50, 55–7, 129–39, 141, 197

qualification 1, 42, 175, 176
   teaching qualification 175
questionnaire 2, 16–17, 35, 46–8, 76–7, 151, 175, 184–90, 201, 203, 213–14, 216

race 6, 34, 100–1
   race relations 6, 101
racism 100–1
rationale 4–5, 28, 34–6, 44, 56, 69, 76, 113, 129, 139, 145, 159, 231, 239
reading 5–6, 8, 12, 18–19, 32, 34–5, 37, 42–3, 45, 48–51, 62, 88, 90–1, 102–3, 105, 116, 130, 159, 161, 163, 167, 170, 177, 183, 196–7, 206, 217, 233, 258, 261, 268–71
recommendations 187
reflection 5, 12, 16–17, 19, 43, 45, 83, 87–8, 93, 115, 119–20, 133, 137, 159, 161, 188, 199–200, 204, 211, 223, 226–7, 230, 235–6, 242, 247, 261, 268–9
   reflective journal 5, 42, 44, 48–9, 51, 268
   reflexivity 19, 60, 119, 122, 124, 225–6
religion 29, 31
research 1–20, 27, 29, 31–7, 41–51, 56–64, 69–79, 83–92, 94–7, 99–100, 102, 104–9, 113–20, 122, 124, 129–35, 137–9, 141, 145–52, 154–5, 159–66, 168–71, 175–89, 195–206, 209–18, 221–3, 225–33, 235–6, 239–47, 249, 253–5, 257–64
   action research 14, 42–3, 45–50, 182, 270

INDEX

exploratory research 12
insider researcher 13, 159, 168–9, 240, 244, 248
mixed methods approach 17, 88–9, 149, 181
mosaic approach 154
online research 13, 239–40
participatory research 199, 239, 247, 249, 259
practitioner research 129, 132, 137, 141, 247
qualitative research 15, 17–18, 34, 61, 85, 90, 99, 102, 115, 149–50, 152, 162, 170, 181–3, 187, 200–1, 243, 254, 258–9, 270
quantitative research 9, 12, 15–18, 34, 85, 149–50, 152, 162, 170, 181–3, 185, 187, 201, 270
research methods 16, 35, 69, 75, 200, 257–9, 261
research paradigm 181
research philosophy 79 (*see also* philosophy)
research project 3, 7, 9–10, 13–14, 43, 45, 50, 57, 105, 113, 116, 124, 186, 196, 253, 261
research question 2–5, 7, 9, 16–18, 27, 32, 34, 36, 41–3, 45–6, 48–51, 59, 104, 138, 159, 161, 166, 170, 188, 196–8, 203, 210–12, 217, 222, 228, 232–3, 243, 246, 268, 271
research tool 151–2, 164, 175, 183, 189
research topic 4, 76, 84–5, 87, 100, 239, 257, 268
results 7–8, 30, 164, 170, 187–8, 213, 216–17

review 29, 33, 95, 146–7, 149–52, 154, 177, 189, 197–9, 203, 205, 224, 232–3
rights 10–11, 28, 30, 35–6, 58, 140, 160, 218
 disability rights movement 58 (*see also* disability)
 human rights 160
 rights of the child 10–11, 140

sample 18, 34, 47, 50, 56, 85, 168, 182, 188, 231, 271, *see also* participants
scepticism 56, 58
school/s 4–6, 11, 13, 17, 18, 28–33, 35–6, 41–5, 47–51, 56–8, 62–4, 69, 70, 83–6, 88, 91, 93–5, 99–104, 106–8, 114–17, 120, 121, 123, 130, 132–3, 141, 145–7, 150, 152–3, 155, 159–60, 168, 175, 176, 195–6, 201, 203, 205, 209–14, 221–2, 224–5, 233, 253, 255–7, 259–61, 263
 admission policies 29, 31
 Catholic schools 28–9, 31–2, 35
 denominational 28, 30–1
 elementary school 28
 leaders 4, 121, 222, 224
 leadership 93, 224
 management 32–3, 35–6
 multi-denominational 28, 30
 placement 17, 195–6, 201, 203
 primary schools 30, 33, 36, 84, 95
 schooling 100–1, 123, 152
 system 28, 30
Scotland 19, 209, 221–3, 225, 229
Scottish 195–6, 235

Scottish education 222–3, 229
Scottish government 223–4
Scottish Initial Teacher Education (ITE) 196
Scottish schools 223
social 8–9, 29, 32, 34–5, 42, 47–8, 58–9, 61, 70, 73–4, 77–8, 88, 93, 101, 104–7, 114, 117–18, 148–9, 154, 162–3, 166–7, 169–70, 179–80, 188, 199, 204, 240, 242–3, 246, 256, 260–1
justice 256, 261
research 78, 154
sciences 162, 170
social network analysis (SNA) 246
Social Cognitive Theory 180
sociology 102–3, 105
sociology of education 103
Special Educational Needs (SEN) 10, 41, 51, 56–60, 62, 64, *see also* Additional Support Needs; Special Educational Needs and Disability
Special Educational Needs and Disability (SEND) 10, 41, 56, 209, 211–13, *see also* Additional Support Needs; Special Educational Needs
Special Educational Needs Coordinator (SENCO) 41, 44
specialist 64, 212, 221, 246
statistics 10, 18, 41, 166, 225
Statistical Package for Social Sciences (SPSS) 170
student 17, 28–9, 56–7, 59, 71, 100, 102, 120, 122–3, 175–6, 178–9, 181–3, 187–8, 195–7, 199, 202–4, 221, 231, 253–4, 258–9, 261–2, 264, *see also* pupil
student voice 254, 259, 261, 264
subjectivity 70–1, 77–8, 225, 263
subjective 17, 61, 71, 124, 136, 152, 167
subjects 18, 56, 63, 133, 139, 154, 212, 217, 222, 247, 256

teacher learning communities 240–2
online learning communities 240–2
teachers 4, 11, 17–18, 43, 55–60, 62–4, 70–2, 76, 85, 91, 99–101, 104–6, 108, 113–17, 119, 123, 130, 133–5, 160–1, 165, 167–8, 171, 175–7, 195, 197, 225, 239–42, 245–6, 259–60, 263
early career teachers (ECTs) 69, 72, 113–15, 117, 119
newly qualified teachers 76
teacher mentors 73
teacher-researchers 1–3, 20, 64, 222, 267
teachers' beliefs 58
Technological Pedagogical Content Knowledge (TPACK) 91
technology 57, 62, 84, 86, 92–3, 216, *see also* Information and Communications Technology
technological 91, 215
theme 2–4, 6–7, 9–10, 13–14, 16, 18–19, 47, 160, 187, 262–71

INDEX

thematic analysis 18, 117, 170, 187, 203, 205–6, 233, 262, 270
themes 1–4, 11, 14, 20, 44, 48, 76, 90, 95, 117, 138, 146, 170, 177–8, 180, 187, 205, 233, 248–9, 262–3, 267
theoretical framework 3, 11–12, 14, 16, 59, 83, 86, 89, 91, 93, 95, 261, 268–9, *see also* concepts; conceptual framework; conceptual tools; interpretive repertoires
theory 9–12, 19, 44, 72–3, 83, 85–7, 89–94, 96, 103–4, 108, 179–80, 182, 187–8, 211–12, 225, 269, *see also* conceptual framework; theoretical framework
ecological systems theory 73
organisational theory 73, 85, 241
theories 7, 10–12, 56, 61, 72–3, 75, 86–7, 91, 118, 121, 150, 175, 179–80, 257–8, 269

Timperley, H. 197–8
truth 9, 61, 77, 118, 133, 227, 268

United Kingdom (UK) 223, 240, 253
UK government 223
United Nations (UN) 140, 160
U.N. Convention on the Rights of the Child 160

values 4, 13–14, 61, 77, 86–7, 93, 119, 148, 226–9, 236, *see also* beliefs
Van Manen, M. 61
vignettes 17, 150, 152, 215–16, 270
Vygotsky, L. 86, 93, 178

write 30, 34, 73, 100, 146, 152, 175, 189
writing 36, 43, 48–50, 65, 78, 100, 103, 109, 115, 120, 152, 177–8, 184, 189, 242, 245
writing up 115, 242, 247